WHERE DO

ST JOHN'S COLLEGE c.1880

WHERE DO YOU KEEP?

Lodging the Cambridge Undergraduate

Margot Holbrook

Cappella Archive

Cappella Archive : 2006

British Library Cataloguing-in-Publication Data
A catalogue record for this book is
available from the British Library

ISBN–10: 1–902918–36–3
ISBN–13: 978–1–902918–36–5

Cappella Archive : Great Malvern : England
Printed and bound by Aspect Design, Great Malvern

Contents

Illustrations

Acknowledgements

I want to put on record my warm thanks to those who have helped me with this book. Dr Elisabeth Leedham-Green, Deputy Keeper of the University Archives, led me sweetly by the nose round the University Library and pointed me in the direction of seminal sources. She has nobly read and corrected the proofs and has tried her best to give me some historical validity. I wish I did her more credit.

The frontispiece engraving of St John's College and the drawing of the Spinning House are reproduced by the courtesy of the Cambridge Public Library. Mike Petty, until lately Keeper of the Cambridgeshire Collection, is an unfailing repository of information on all things to do with Cambridge. He cheerfully answered every query and led me unerringly to the document or illustration I sought.

All these pages were typed and put on disc by my friend and ex-secretary Jan Pearson, with her typical good nature and accuracy. Thank you, Jan. I am also particularly grateful for the kind advice of John Hopkins of Downing College in his reading of the text.

My appreciation goes to the Fitzwilliam Museum for permission to reproduce *Winter* by George Dance, R.A, to the *Daily Telegraph* for the obituary of 'Sadie' Barnet, and to the editor of the *Cambridge Evening News* for a copy of a landladies' article of 7 May, 1982.

Finally, my warmest thanks go to all those correspondents who provided such engaging and detailed memories of their time in university lodgings. Their names are acknowledged in the list of Contributors at the end of the book.

Dedication

With my love to David
in thanks for all his encouragement.

1

History

Where to lodge the student is nowadays held to be the least prestigious of concerns in university circles — a task for a veritable chamber-maid (if you will forgive the pun) in the scale of academic posts. Let the new Junior Fellow be given the job of Rooms' Tutor, with all the tedious complaints and reshufflings and antagonisms that will inevitably ensue. Let the Lodgings Office find somewhere for those who can't be housed in college — or even harder, for those thrown out of college for being a nuisance: the academic mind is bent on higher things. It was not ever so.

A very little thought will convince anyone that the housing of the student is a matter of absolutely primary importance — how can he start to study till he has a roof over his head? And this has been recognised from those first and shadowy beginnings of this, our University of Cambridge. We have only to look into the pages of Rashdall's *Universities of Europe in the Middle Ages*,[1] and Damian Leader's admirable Volume I of the *History of the University of Cambridge*[2] to realise that when those first frightened scholars ran away in 1209 from the riots and threats at Oxford to find sanctuary elsewhere, their immediate concern was to settle themselves in houses here and there throughout the scanty and undistinguished little town that it then was. And what is the first mention on record to prove that Cambridge was recognised in official eyes as a University, a *studium generale*? It is embodied in the decree of Henry III dated 1231, and addressed to both his universities equally, granting them several corporate rights.[3] Chief among these is the power to fix the annual rent of the houses let to scholars for lodgings and classrooms. The King's letters patent admonish the mayor and bailiffs against overcharging:

1. Hastings Rashdall, *The Universities of Europe in the Middle Ages*, (Oxford University Press, 1894; new edition, in 3 vols, ed. F.M. Powicke and A.B. Ernden, Oxford University Press, 1936), iii. pp. 274 ff.
2. Cambridge University Press, 1988.
3. I quote from the version in Fowler & Fowler's *Cambridge Commemorated* (Cambridge University Press 1984), p.4, but for the whole text, consult *Educational Charters & Documents* ed. A.F. Leach (Cambridge, 1911) pp. 148-53.

> We have heard however, that in letting your houses you make
> such heavy charges to the scholars living among you, that un-
> less you conduct yourselves with more restraint and modera-
> tion towards them in this matter, they will be driven by your
> exactions to leave your town and, abandoning their studies,
> leave our country, which we by no means desire.

Henry was not only hungry for the honour and prestige that the
two universities and their scholarship lent his kingdom but also
supported university education because it provided him with a
supply of trained clerks for the use of Church and State. So he
didn't want them tempted to take off to Paris or Bologna. The
letter goes on:

> And therefore we command and firmly enjoin you that in
> letting the aforesaid houses you follow University custom and
> allow the said houses to be valued by two masters and two
> good and lawful men of your town assigned for the purpose,
> and allow them to be let according to their valuation, so con-
> ducting yourselves in this matter that no complaint may reach
> us through your doing otherwise, which compel us to inter-
> fere.

The two townsmen in these transactions were called the burgesses or burghers while the two nominated 'masters', under the
title of 'taxors', were responsible not only for settling rents and
the taxation of halls, but also for the assizes of bread and beer
and of weights and measures, tasks in which they assisted the
Chancellor.

University control over rents was built in right from the earliest days. If a landlord refused to let his property to a scholar at
the rent assessed by the Taxors, the Chancellor had the power to
put the scholar into possession of the house, thereby overruling
the actual owner, provided always that the tenant was in a position to offer sufficient caution-money against the rent.

A sidelight on the quality of such lettable property is shed by
this extract from the 'Plea Rolls for the year 1294-5. The Court
was held on a Monday every three weeks from October 1294 till
September 1295, and had power of life and death.

Thomas le Cuteler of Brockisheved of Cantebrige and Margaret his wife complain of Gilbert Sys that he unfairly discharged a sewer to the hurt of his free tenement in Cantebrige after etc . . . so unjustly because the opening of that sewer lies bare against the walls, by reason of which the filth of that sewer causes the walls to decay so that they cannot hold them up. And also whereas Thomas and Margaret have been accustomed to let their house up to two marks a year, now no one is willing to hire it at more than one mark on account of the foulness of that sewer. And Gilbert came and denied etc. and says that he has discharged no such sewer as they say and seeks that it may be enquired into by a jury.[4]

The form, throughout the thirteenth and fourteenth centuries was for the new student to seek out a Master of Arts and enrol his name on that master's matricula or class-list (hence the ritual of matriculation to this day). His next step was to find himself a lodging in a house or inn of the town. Sometimes the master would himself hire a house and share it with his pupils. Such groups gradually escalated into more permanent establishments, which came to be called hostels or hospitia, the name 'a Parisian usage preserved more faithfully at Cambridge than at Oxford', notes Rashdall. By the fourteenth century, scholars were forbidden to live in unsupervised lodgings, and the University licensed hostels for their accommodation.

They were subject by statute to an annual visitation by the V.C., doctors, heads of colleges and proctors. There is no evidence that the equivalent halls at Oxford were liable to any visitation of this kind.[5]

By 1280 there were 34 hostels and several inns housing undergraduates. H.P. Stokes in his book the *Mediaeval Hostels of the University of Cambridge* actually lists 136 of these hostels,[6] though there is some overlapping where the same property goes under different names at different stages of its history. They started off as

4. *Cambridge Borough Documents*, Vol. 1, ed. W.M. Palmer (Bowes & Bowes, 1931.)
5. Rashdall, *op. cit*, p.292.
6. Cambridge Antiquarian Society, Octavo Publications, 1924.

singularly democratic communities, even electing their own 'Principal'. Some might be domestic-style houses lodging four or six men, others were buildings of consequence with gardens and orchards.

We must always keep in mind how small the English universities were: Leader estimates that '. . . in 1377 (Cambridge) had perhaps between 400 and 700 members while Oxford had about 1500. Of the Cantabs about a third to a half were Friars.'[7] A far cry from the ten thousand students flooding into the university of Bologna and needing to be lodged.

Damian Leader says, of hostels like Physick Hostel or St Bernard's that they had their own halls, chapels, libraries and galleries. Each acquired its own characteristic flavour, and many survived for several centuries:

> St Nicholas Hostel . . . with the public name of the Brazen George. The scholars hereof, as eminent for hard studying so infamous for their brawlings by night. Ovings' Inn, the buildings under which the kennel betwixt Caitis and Trinity College emptieth itself. St Thomas Hostel, where now the orchard of the Master of Pembroke Hall, and where the neighbouring leas retain their name; formerly the Campus Martius of the scholars here exercising themselves, sometimes too violently; lately disused, either because young scholars now have less valour, or more civility.[8]

Some hostels chose their residents according to the subject they studied, this property by long custom housing the *Artistae et Theologi*, that one excluding all but the *Juristae*. Borden's Hostel stretched from a frontage in Trinity Street back towards the Franciscan Priory in Sidney Street (now Sidney Sussex). Its residents were all students of Canon Law, an academic discipline discontinued after 1535. It was owned by Clare Hall till the middle of the fourteenth century, then bought by Henry VI in exchange for Clare property to enable land clearance for his chapel and college of King's, but returned to Clare in 1448. Rowland Taylor was Prin-

---

7. Leader, *op. cit*, p.35.
8. Quoted by the Fowlers (*op. cit*) p.9, from Thomas Fuller's list of hostels, made in 1630.

cipal of this hostel between 1533 and 1540, became Chaplain to Archbishop Cranmer for a time and was martyred as rector of Hadleigh in February 1555. Next door, between Rose Crescent and the west end of Green Street, where Hobb's now stands, was the Archdeacon's House which belonged to Peterhouse from 1290 to 1540 for the use of 'Clerks of Ely'. Another Peterhouse property was Rudd's Hostel, originally given to the Hospital of St John by Hugh de Balsham in 1284. The Castle Inn in St Andrew's Street stands on its site, and further into town, the Post Office has replaced the Brazen George.

With the death of Hugh of Balsham in 1288 came the bequest of money to found the first of the Colleges, Peterhouse. Their subsequent growth is beyond the scope of the present study and is plentifully documented elsewhere. By the end of the sixteenth century there were sixteen established colleges. But the reader should be aware that the early colleges were set up for the advancement of knowledge, for prayers to be read and vigils kept for the souls of benefactors, and as a residence and foundation for a master and several senior members, those who were already masters of arts. They were not originally places for students to live, though as they grew and attracted toward themselves more wealth and grants of land and property, so they became better able to incorporate blocks of rooms for undergraduate occupation.

The King's Hall, founded in 1317 and much later on absorbed into Trinity, 'was unique among early colleges in accepting undergraduates into its fellowship.'[9] At Christ's, founded in the 1430's under the name of Godshouse, which was originally for the training of grammar-school teachers, it was built into the college establishment from the first that the student should live in college. This innovation, copied gradually by later colleges, helped on the gradual disappearance of the hostels. Sometimes a college was founded on the site of what had previously been a hostel, as Queens' first building was, superceding St Bernard's Hostel opposite St Botolph's Church. But probably the main reason for the decline of the hostels was their evident inability to maintain discipline.

9. Leader, *op. cit*, p.255
10. The first two of a series of volumes recording the official decisions of the University.

Grace Books A and B[10] are full of records of fines for disturbance of the peace at one hostel or another. The mediaeval student was notoriously riotous, much given to prowling about late at night on nefarious errands and looking for a fight, either with other students or against the townspeople.

Certain hostels would be reserved for one or other of the two *Nations* to which all scholars belonged, depending on their place of origin: you were either a Northerner or a Southerner. (And some historians think that this is the reason for the appointing of two proctors, one to represent and protect the interest of each nation.) At all events, there were plenty of grounds for taking sides and the partisans were forever at one another's throats. In 1521 there was a really serious riot between Northern and Southern factions. Gerard's Hostel, mostly Northerners, made an organised attack on Gonville Hall, largely a community of Southerners, the Gerard's men being actually led by their principal, William Tayte, previously himself a Proctor. 'They burnt the West gate, burst into the college and poured out all the liquor they found in the buttery.'[11]

Again and again measures were passed by the University, forbidding students to keep hawking birds, or against the practice of 'night-jetting', forbidding tournaments and tilting within 5 miles, prohibiting plays and bear-baiting. 'Night-jetting' needs some explaining. We hear of it first in a decree of 23 February 1606 forbidding the practice (and also the keeping of greyhounds).[12] It involved gangs of men prowling at night and terrorising the inhabitants of the town. They would bang at doors, demanding money or valuables from the householder, and if he refused they would threaten to set fire to his house — which at the time would be usually built of wood. The gangs were not necessarily made up of scholars of the University, but some would undoubtedly join in; their identification was complicated by the fact that townsmen sometimes disguised themselves in academic dress in order to implicate the University. As late as December 1751 an order went out that students should refrain from walking the streets carrying lighted torches or links, nor be preceded by others carrying the same,

11. According to Leader (*op. cit*) after Dr Caius. The reader interested in such confrontations should consult Rowland Parker's *Town and Gown*, 1983.
12 University Archives, *CUR* 44. 1, item 144.

'this occasioning great Terror and Apprehension that some parts of the Colleges or Town may be fired thereby'. And in March 1780:

> Whereas of late, in the night-time frequent and violent outrages have been committed in the streets of Cambridge to the great terror of the inhabitants in general and also to the considerable Damage of individuals; we the Vice-Chancellor and Heads of Colleges, conceiving the highest Displeasure at such illiberal and illegal Practices, do hereby declare that it is our determined resolution to punish with the utmost severity in our Power all Persons who shall be convicted of offending against the Peace, good Order and Discipline of the University by any riotous or unwarrantable Act whatever.[13]

The lack of discipline so prevalent in these halls no doubt led to a climate of opinion that preferred to see men living in college, stone-built, permanent and with a resident hierarchy of dons capable of maintaining order.

Even those in nominal charge of a hostel were occasionally at fault: in 1502 the Master, or Keeper, of Clement Hostel was 'presented' — i.e. made to appear before the Vice-Chancellor's Court — for polluting the King's Ditch, which ran along our present-day Park Street to the east of the hostel.

Another consideration was that all hostel-members paid their room and board since there were no foundations to support them. On the subject of costs:

> At the Garrett Hostel in August 1571 Laurence Gordon, son of Anthony, Bishop of Galloway, boarded with Anthony Chevallier, a teacher of Hebrew in the University, paying 3 French crowns monthly for his board, chamber, candle, and the washing of his clothes.[14]

By 1511, members of colleges comprised 90% of the University and even the largest and best-equipped of the hostels had been incorporated into one or another college by the end of the sixteenth century, as gifts and benefactions and bequests permitted. The last to go was Clement's Hostel in Bridge Street. The hostels left few rec-

---

13. University Archives, *CUR* 44. 1, items 137 on.
14. Quoted from Stokes, *op. cit*, p.77, footnote.

ords behind them and we must look to the better-documented colleges to shed some light on how the student lived.

Corpus Christi had the first closed quadrangle and Old Court today gives us a good idea of how these first collegiate buildings appeared. The walls inside were not plastered, the floor was of stone or clay covered with rushes, no ceilings to the upper storey, small windows of oiled parchment with wooden shutters. The rooms would have been unheated.[15]

John Venn's interesting book tells us much about Caius at the beginning of the sixteenth century,[16] and has followed up the careers of sixty four men: three became bishops, two the foremost physicians of their time, sixteen were monks. Of secular clergy many held high church posts; eight were parish priests, and only two were country gentry. 'Most of them would have been called on to part to one side or the other in the great division of the Reformation.' None became a martyr but eight or nine ran risks that caused them grievous suffering, only short of death. Bishop Nix of Norwich commented, 'There is a college in Cambridge called Gunwell Haule. I hear no clerk that hath comen out lately of that college but saverith of the frying panne, tho he spake never so holely.'

But to speak of their physical state, rather than their religious persuasion: Venn describes how Shaxton and Dr Bisbey provided the first means of warming students — a large brazier was obtained in 1565 and set up in the centre of the hall, the fumes being led off through a lantern in the roof, and land was bought, the rent from which should supply fuel, in the form of charcoal, for burning in it during the three coldest months of the year, from All Saints Day to the second of February.

The gift of Shaxton's brazier was to be nightly celebrated by a psalm of thanksgiving. those not present to take part in the singing were not entitled to a place at the fire. This same kind Shaxton also bequeathed 'hangings', presumably of tapestry, and money 'to solace the company at Christmas'. The library was dimly lighted and unwarmed. Benefactors donated money for commemorative windows of stained glass that gave some protection from the weather, both in chapel and in the library where the bulk of the

---

15 See F.A. Reeve, *Cambridge*, (Batsford 1976), p.20.
16 *Early Collegiate Life*, (1913), pp.24-7 and 28-9.

books were in manuscript and were chained to the shelves.[17] In the dining-hall, the walls were bare and the floor of stone covered with rushes.

I am greatly indebted to Professor Christopher Brooke who drew my attention to an article of his in the *Caian* for November 1987 on the allocation of rooms at Caius in the sixteenth century. It confirms what I have written here, with regard to the Magdalene room (*v.* p.12). Caius has the first Matriculation Register which also records to which chamber each newcomer was assigned. Professor Brooke writes:

> Early college buildings varied greatly in layout and arrangement; but there was a remarkable uniformity in the basic unit of student accommodation, the chamber. Between the early fourteenth century — and perhaps even the thirteenth — and the mid-seventeenth century the chambers of every college in Oxford and Cambridge and of many halls besides were intended to be the living and sleeping rooms of two or three, or sometimes perhaps four, fellows and scholars or other students. As numbers fell off and living standards rose in the seventeenth and eighteenth centuries, the chambers became the more ample quarters of one or at most two sometimes with separate bedrooms; and the old chambers were wainscotted and refurnished to suit their novel destiny.
>
> The old arrangements were all but forgotten. But by a happy chance one of the greatest of architectural historians, Robert Willis, while a student or fellow at Caius in the 1820s and 1830s, was able to explore, measure and draw, unaltered chambers of the early seventeenth century in the old Perse and Legge buildings, before they were swept away; and in the 1850s the young John Venn lodged in a room in the Perse building, with a bedroom in the attic.[18]

---

17 And benefactions to the College actually had to mean a felt loss to the giver (Venn, *op. cit*, p.33).

18. R, Willis and J.W. Clark, *Architectural History of the University of Cambridge* (4 vols., Cambridge, 1886), III, 298, 304–11, esp. engraving on 308; J. Venn et al., *Biographical History of Gonville and Caius College* (7 vols., 1897-1978), III, 83n. and *ibid.* for what follows. In preparing this paper I owe much kind help to the College archivist, Mrs Catherine Hall.

A 'queer thing about my bedroom was, that though its size was by no means great, nearly one quarter of it was occupied by what seemed an enormous cupboard'. These cupboards, as Willis had observed, were cubicles or studies: the chamber was divided so that two or three students had individual studies in the corners; the central space was for the common life of the chamber; and after dusk truckle beds were laid out in their midst for sleeping It was already becoming common for college buildings to contain three storeys, and as numbers soared in Elizabethan and Jacobean Oxford and Cambridge, there came even to be occasionally four, as at Clare in the new buildings of the late 1630s. But Caius Court still contains chambers on two floors, with a third floor added to provide cocklofts. These could have been (as in the Perse building) attic chambers for the less privileged; but as each is only lit by a single window it is much more likely that they were always sleeping quarters: that the first-floor chambers were grander rooms in which a tutor worked with his pupils (or some of them) by day, but had to himself at night.

There is indeed a marked difference between the three floors. The chambers on the ground floor are ample in area but relatively low; those on the upper floor are loftier, and the cocklofts are approached by stairs within the chamber on the first floor; thus the cocklofts are appendages to the first floor chambers. The differences are emphasised by the different elevations within the court itself and on the rear of the buildings. In the court we see plain, unadorned, traditional two-storey blocks of chambers; on the other sides, in Tree Court, as it now is, and the Master's garden, we see the third storey with charmingly arranged gables.[19]

To return to Venn: a letter is extant from a seventeenth-century Caius undergraduate who writes home for half a dozen napkins to use in hall: he had been chided for using the tablecloth as a substitute to wipe his fingers on.[20] These are the days before forks had been invented and all scholars carried a clasp-knife as

19 The *Caian*, November 1987, pp. 56-9.
20 At Oxford, an undergraduate who washed his hands in a bucket of well-water, provided in hall for drinking, was fined 1*d.*

a matter of course, to cut up their food. Our correspondent also sends for 'pictures' for his college room but what these were like is unspecified. Fasting in Lent Term was mitigated by hampers of food sent up from home, but all meals until quite recent times were of the plainest, and even in the nineteenth century men were carving rough hunks off joints in the most primitive fashion.[21]

Three or four students might share a room with their tutor. There were few vacations: students would not go home for Christmas and they lived with their tutor by day and night, and hence came much under his influence. By 1637 more rooms had been built in college so there was scope for less crowding, but only a Fellow Commoner, a nobleman, would have a room to himself. A new class system is developing, moving away from the democracy of the mediaeval university. The account book gives a list of men who paid for their board and lodgings under the title 'pensionarii': rich and well-connected priests, already ordained, but seeking a university education as a ladder to advancement, came as pensioners, rented good chambers and made themselves comfortable. Latimer wrote: 'There be none now but great men's sons in Colleges and their fathers look not to have them preachers.'[22] Waiting at table would be done by poor students who finished up the remains of their betters' dinners. A system of 'sizarships' was established to enable poor men to obtain a college education. Their servitude was temporary and many became Fellows and Masters in the course of time. In 1745 sizars were forbidden to wear the same gown as pensioners, and in 1767 they struck against serving at table. Winstanley sums up the class structure in the following passage:

> Noblemen and fellow-commoners were never more than a fraction of the junior population of the University. The majority of the undergraduates were admitted as pensioners . . . they were commonly not wealthy . . . but the poorest of the pensioners were not as financially hard-pressed as the sizars who must often have had a very hard struggle for existence.[23]

---

21 Venn records of his own undergraduate era (1850s): 'Sweets and cheese had to be specially ordered: soup, fish and game were absolutely unknown.'
22 F.A. Reeve, *Cambridge*, (Batsford 1976).
23 D.A. Winstanley, *Unreformed Cambridge*, (Cambridge University Press, 1935) pp. 200 ff.

With the exception of noblemen and wealthy young men, a student could expect very little privacy, and not much space to himself. At the founding of King's College statutes laid down minimum standards of accommodation, for example that each student must have a separate bed (evidently not commonly the case elsewhere.). In 1598 at St John's, before Second Court was built, 70 men lived in 28 rooms: to cap that, Sidney Sussex packed 130 men into 35 rooms when they allocated the living space for the academic year 1623. The Fellows' Building at Christ's, begun in 1640, was designed specifically to house fee-paying pensioners and fellow-commoners and only four Fellows were to reside in the new building. It must have offered the conference standard accommodation of its day, providing noble and well-off students with surroundings worthy of their rank.

In trying to imagine and flesh out the mediaeval student in his setting, I paid a memorable visit to the Senior Tutor's rooms on Staircase E at Magdalene.[24] The Chapel, Hall and First Court of Magdalene date from the time when this was a hostel for Benedictine monks from the important Abbey of Crowland, and so belongs to the middle of the fifteenth century. It was known as Buckingham College after 1483. Dr Clary kindly gave me permission to see this room, as it affords a unique example of the way college accommodation was designed for the mediaeval student.

The entrance is through an open doorway from the path along the south side of First Court. A steep bare wooden staircase leads draughtily upward to two doors, an outer 'oak' now fire-proofed, and the inner an ancient, and surely original, door bolted at will from the inside by a carved wooden shaft. One steps into a large high chamber lit by several windows on either side and extending across the whole width of the building. The windows have stone ribs and architraves and are arched at the top. The ceiling is massively beamed, with several huge oak beams, trimmed with an adze roughly, and interspersed with slighter ones all running in the same direction across the room. The walls too are made of vertical oak studs, separated by unpainted panels of plaster each about a

---

24 The source for my information was Michael Grant's book, *Cambridge* (1966) but since my visit I have discovered a reference by Leader (*op. cit*) to what he calls the Monk's Room.

foot wide, with pargetting patterns of diamonds or cross-hatching or other geometrical designs. This plasterwork is not white-washed and is greyish, with these deep incisions in it.

On the south wall is a handsome stone carved fireplace, very like those of clunch in my old mediaeval house in Ashwell, with an open hearth in which recently used dead coals are lying. In Tudor times, peat and sedge would have been brought as fuel by barge and unloaded at the wharves by Magdalene Bridge. The floor-boards are of old planking, probably oak, wide, unpolished and mostly bare, except for a patterned rug between the three sofas grouped around the fire. Everywhere is darkish, dusty, stark. Two wrought-iron lamp standards provide lighting. The only picture is an oil painting of Pepys on the wall next the door. An under-graduate called for interview by his Senior Tutor might well feel a bit intimidated. But, I notice, a shelf beneath a window at one side holds a reassuring row and variety of some ten sherry bottles and glasses.

This is today a very masculine room; dark claret-coloured stiff curtains hang dustily and a trifle depressingly at the windows and are surely rarely-drawn. The sofas are pleasant but plain, and don't match; they certainly have no sybaritic cushions. The work table is a huge workmanlike piece of furniture, piled with books and pap-ers. I respect the evidently conscious intention to keep this space timeless and austere. Beside the fireplace and recessed in the wall at waist-level is an arched cavity vaguely basin-shaped — contain-ing a large stone ball and having drainage holes in its base. This must surely be a washing place, though when I described it to him, Professor Leonard Forster suggested the words 'aumbry' and 'piscina'. But I don't think it would have been for holy water. I see the young monks kilting up their brown habit as they fetched water from a pump in the court below and brought it up here in jugs or buckets, for washing and perhaps for cooking. Then the waste-water could be flushed away through the holes into some ancient drainage-channel to a ditch running into the river — which itself flows in a parallel line to this side of the court.

The most exciting feature of the room is in the four corners, or rather, three since one has been blocked up. There you find little screened-off ante-rooms, each with its own window to give much-

needed daylight — consider the cost of mediaeval candles, prohib-
itive even though the university had the power to control both
price and supply. These arched cubicles with their wattle and daub
partitions were to give privacy for each man to study. Perhaps four
students would share this total space, or more likely still, a master
and three pupils. And they would each have their private work-
place and use the central area for living, eating and sleeping, the
latter no doubt in their truckle beds that slid beneath each other
and pulled out at night. The cubicles vary in size but that may be
due to later construction work. The one nearest the wall basin and
the fireplace is very small indeed and would admit only the most
basic table and stool. It is used by the Senior Tutor to store his coal
bucket and logs. Was it perhaps allocated to the youngest or poor-
est pupil? The thought even crossed my mind — was it once a
close-stool cupboard for common use?

The two remaining cubicles are on the north wall. One is very
ample, almost another apartment, perhaps ten feet by eight, and is
used now as the Senior Tutor's study. The last is a neat little space
with the stone reveals to the window covered in Perspex, through
which you can still decipher the antique scrawls, doodlings, sig-
natures, initials and quotes of the innumerable students who have
over five centuries sat and scratched their heads for ideas to complete a no-doubt overdue essay. Here too they tried out their new
compasses on the soft clunchy stone. Perhaps the biggest cubicle
was the master's, in which he taught as well as thought, and presumably prayed? It is particularly interesting to observe the
mediaeval sense of priorities — privacy for study but none for
sleeping. As John Venn remarks in *Early Collegiate Life*, 'the *common*, as distinguished from the individual life, was a much more
prominent and permanent characteristic in early times'. And here
it is, illustrated in wood and stone.

Dr Caius laid down in his statutes stringent regulations as to the
amount of food that fellows might have in private, in their own
rooms. There was once a Master of Magdalene who kept his cows
in that court outside to which we now return, and allowed the
chapel and hall to fill up with their dung. Things reached such a
pass that the Fellows complained to the university about his shrew-
ish wife and his unhygienic habits. But that must have been in Mag-

dalene's degenerate period, long after the days when the college was mainly frequented by Benedictine monks, wearing the distinctive garb of their order. You can still hear the swish of their rough gown-hems as you descend that bare wooden staircase and call up an image of one who sat in that gloomy alcove above, praying and debating whether he was strong enough to cling to his faith to the very stake, as kings and queens succeeded one another, exacting each a different religious allegiance.

The dissolution of the monasteries threw the two universities into higher relief as the main centres of learning, and they suffered but withstood, Cambridge surviving the execution of five vice-chancellors, only to meet many more questions of divided loyalty with the Civil War, the Commonwealth and the restoration of the Monarchy. Nor were mind and soul alone in torment. A constant cause of interruption was the plague. All through the Middle Ages there had been sporadic outbursts of plague about every four years; accounting for perhaps ten per cent of student deaths. When it raged most fiercely, the colleges and hostels emptied. In 1625 the whole university was evacuated in terror of the plague, and between 1630 and 1645 came nine more outbreaks of pestilence, due largely to the absence of sanitation and the poor condition of the King's Ditch which was simply an open sewer. The first of these infections alone caused 347 deaths.

Against this perilous and tumultuous background, ministers with their political manipulations and the vanity (or piety) of kings, each served to provide funds, land and backing for new colleges, and most students would, by the late seventeenth century be living within their college precincts. 'Until the closing years of the eighteenth century all undergraduates could be accommodated in the colleges, so it was not necessary to licence lodging-houses.'[25] But the reader will no doubt be aware that discipline was poor and scholarship slack for most of the eighteenth century and the university stagnated. Some statistics will illustrate this: according to Winstanley, 'it was calculated that in 1781 only 3 colleges had more than 50 resident members *in statu pupillari*, and only 7 more than 40'. If anything he considered these figures too favourable.[26] In

25 Winstanley, *Unreformed Cambridge*, p.340, note 32.
26 Winstanley, *op. cit*, P. 186.

1801 the town population reached 9,276 (about 5,500 in 1700) with 632 undergraduates. Contrast this with the 1800 students in residence in 1573, while between 1610 and 1640 there were more undergraduates than at any time in the next 200 years. It is significant that no college was built between Sidney Sussex (1594) and Downing (1807).

The latter part of the eighteenth century is most wittily described in Gunning's two volumes of *Reminiscences of Cambridge* (1854). The university acquired a reputation for horse-play, hard drinking and expensiveness: its young men came up rich and heedless, kept horses and women and idled away their first two years, to rush frantically to private crammers just before the final exams. In 1811 the Vice-Chancellor denounced all such behaviour in a set oration:

> . . . Breaking of lamps and windows, shouting and roaring, blowing of horns, galloping up and down the streets on horseback or in Carriages, fighting and mobbing in the town and neighbouring villages; in the day-time breaking down fences and riding over corn-fields, then eating, drinking and becoming intoxicated at taverns or alehouses, and lastly in the night frequenting houses of ill-fame, resisting the lawful authorities and often putting the peaceable inhabitants of the town in great alarm.[27]

Pitched battles between town and gown frequently broke out, particularly on 5 November when a fair amount of blood was sure to run. Gunning relates how in April 1829 the proctors were grossly insulted when they tried to discipline an unruly mob of students: the punishment given to the culprits was so lenient that the proctors resigned *en bloc*, whereupon the Vice-Chancellor threatened expulsion if such behaviour was repeated.[28] On a more pacific note, it is amusing to read of the undergraduate's increasing interest in the decorating and equipping of his living space. A pamphlet of 1785, *Ten Minutes' Advice to Freshmen* by 'A Questionist', makes, among others, the following recommendation:

> The first thing to be seen after, if it be nor already provided, is the furniture of your room. And here I would advise you, should you be recommended to Mr S. the upholsterer (as probably you

---

27 Winstanley, *op. cit* p.214.   28 H. Gunning, *Reminiscences*, ii, p.367.

will) to be very constant in your application to him — in short — to dun him heartily, or you never will get what you want. He has, in general, so much business upon his hands that, notwithstanding he will make you promises, and with the greatest civility imaginable, of sending your chairs, table etc. immediately, , et from his being obliged to pay an equal degree of attention to so many other customers, it is great odds but you are neglected. Insist upon having what you have purchased instantly sent home; and if you find him still dilatory and yourself unprovided for, tell him, once and for all, that if you do not receive the rest of your things within a reasonable time sufficient for their conveyance to you, that you will return him every stick of what you have already received, and apply somewhere else. This is the only way to succeed with him, and as it is very probable, if your father or guardian be with you, that the bill for your furniture will be discharged immediately, I see not the least reason why you should not be immediately attended to.

After you have, with some trouble, got possession of such articles as are absolutely necessary, I would recommend to you to endeavour according to the length of your purse, to see that every thing be *comfortable* about you. Buy whatever minutiae you may probably want for constant use, at once; and do not defer procuring them till you have suffered as much inconvenience from their deficiency as is equivalent to treble their purchase.

I have known a man more incommoded for 3 years together from the want of a cheese-toaster, than he would almost have been from the want of a bed to lie on.

Let not this be your case . . .

The period is also well documented in works of biography, autobiography and in many fascinating novels, all of which are sources of rich material about the young man's career at Cambridge. I am much indebted to Graham Chainey's *A Literary History of Cambridge* for directing me to a most enjoyable course of reading in the literature of the eighteenth and nineteenth centuries.

We are now entering the era and territory of that section of the present work that details the doing of the Lodging-House Syndicate, and the reader must turn to chapter III to see how the university reacted specifically to reform and revitalisation. Even before the tragedy of Lawrence Dundas, a fly-sheet dated December 6th 1794 and entitled 'A Letter to a Member of the Senate' refers to the dangers attending the accommodation of undergraduates in lodgings, and about 1793 there was a design to bring forward a grace 'to prevent colleges from admitting more young men than can be accommodated with appartments (sic) within the walls of the colleges'.[29]

With the new century and the successful end of the Napoleonic Wars came the spirit of change. Sir Arthur Gray estimates (how correctly I cannot judge) that between 1810 and 1828 numbers grew from 2469 to 5104: he ascribes this increase partly to the fame of teachers such as Porson, but chiefly to the development of the public schools.[30] The question of where they were all to live became suddenly pressing.

But before continuing with my chronological account, I propose to digress into a totally different subject, that of the power of the university in its dealings with the town. The reader of the Spinning House (chapter II) will no doubt be shocked at its revelations, but I trust he will understand its relevance in the general scheme of this book.

---

29 Winstanley, *op. cit*, chapter I, p.340, note 32, citing Christopher Wordsworth *Social Life at the English Universities in the Eighteenth Century* (1874) p.356.
30 *Cambridge University: An Episodical History*, (Cambridge, 1926).

2

The Spinning House

A CURIOUS GROUP OF BUILDINGS IN CAMBRIDGE.

I want to attempt an in-depth study of the Cambridge Spinning-House, both as institution and metaphor, because it so neatly encapsulates the power exercised by the University and the rage, fear and ill-will that it generated in the town. Its history fits into a manageable period of time, belonging to an age when people had learnt to keep reasonably accurate and detailed records and these are well-preserved in City and University archives.

We begin with that celebrated Thomas Hobson, the Carrier. He lived in Trumpington Street and the stables where undergraduates so signally failed to exert their knowledgeable judgement of horse flesh occupied the space where St Catharine's chapel now stands. Looking East from his house across the Leys that were to house the Downing site, he had land and farmhouses, barns and a dove-house, no doubt providing fodder for his horses. If you find it hard to imagine such rusticity in St Andrew's Street, remember that Christ's College itself stood without the Barnwell Gate and that the town of Cambridge still, at this time of the seventeenth century, looked to the River and its wharves and to the close-clustered settlement around the Castle.

Hobson made a deed of gift in 1628. I have seen a nineteenth-century copy densely written in lawyers' Latin and dated July, the fourth year of the reign of Charles I. Under this deed, he left the land, messuage and tenements described above to six citizens and burgesses of Cambridge and six members appointed by the Vice-Chancellor of the University, who were to oversee a charity and erect premises to be used as a workhouse for the destitute and a house of correction for offenders.[1]

A painting of Hobson on horseback hangs on the staircase of the President's Lodge at Queens': he looks rubicund and healthy. He died in 1630 and in due course the Spinning House was set up according to his instructions. It owes its name to the fact that a weaver or wool-comber was usually appointed to act as Master and employ its inhabitants to spin the wool or flax. So it continued as late as 1808 though part of it was already used in the 18th century for the confinement of 'lewd women'.

From early times the Proctors were charged to safeguard the morals of their students and to keep the streets clear of tempting and soliciting women. Rowland Parker describes them swooping in force on Barnwell in 1675 and the following order was made by the Vice-Chancellor and Heads of Colleges . . . 'that hereafter no Scholar whatsoever (except officers of the University performing their duty in searching houses) upon any pretence whatsoever, shall enter into the house of Francis Harvey, or William Butler, or William Larkin, or Edward Davies, or John Clark, or into any other house of bad report in Barnwell; and that if any Scholar shall presume to disobey this Decree he shall for his misdemeanour and contumacy be immediately expelled from the University'.[2]

Barnwell was always notorious for disorders and 'infamous for harbouring lewd women, drawing loose scholars to resort thither'. Hence the ironic name for Maids' Causeway.

The University's terrors about temptations for the young go back a very long way. In 1635 a decree by the Vice-Chancellor and Heads forbidding students to wear their hair long also ruled on the employment of bed-makers — 'no woman under the age of 50 years to make any bedds.[3]

Sometimes, evidently, the Proctors protested against their responsibility for patrolling the streets, which must always have been

---

1. I am indebted to Enid Porter's brief account of the Spinning House, 'For Unruly and Stubborn Rogues', *East Anglian Magazine*, Vol.18 (Nov.1958-Oct.1959), pp. 72-77, CO 5, City Library.
2. Rowland Parker, *Town and Gown*, p.139.

a damp, dangerous and unsavoury way of spending the evening. An order for 7 February 1793 spells out the necessity:

> Wheras several very respectable members of the Senate have complained to the Vice- Chancellor that the public streets have of late been much infested with lewd and disorderly women; and in consequence of their complaint the Vice- Chancellor represented to the proper officers of the University how necessary it was become for them to be vigilant and to exert themselves in removing such a nuisance; and wheras Mr Hunter the junior Proctor declared to the Vice- Chancellor that 'he did not believe it to be his duty to inspect the public streets for the purpose of taking up women suspected of incontinence and of being common streetwalkers, and that he would not do it till he was convinced it was his duty'.

At a meeting of the Vice-Chancellor and the underwritten Heads of Colleges called for the purpose of deliberating the unprecedented declaration of the Proctor, it was unanimously agreed:

> 1st. That the University by virtue of their Charter sanctioned by Act of Parliament, have an undoubted right to cause the Public Street to be inspected, and loose and disorderly women to be taken up and sent to the Spinning House or house of correction;
>
> 2nd. That it appears from antient and immemorial usage that the Proctors for the time being are the officers deputed by the University to make this Inspection and to take up and carry the above-mentioned women before the Vice-Chancellor for examination.
>
> 3rd. That it is therefore the duty of the Proctors to continue to act according to this antient and immemorial usage, and to be diligent in frequently inspecting the streets and in endeavouring to remove such nuisances as are now complained of; [and lastly] that a contumacious and wilful omission of so important a duty is highly culpable in itself, disgraceful to any Proctor who is guilty of it, and injurious to the common morals and discipline of the University.[4]

---

3. MS Orders of Vice-Chancellor and Heads, University Archives, *CUR.* 44.1, items 137 ff., 1574-1688.   4. *CUR* 44.1 (179), 7 February 1793

Poor Mr Hunter no doubt complied. The Charter referred to dates from its grant by Queen Elizabeth, who with the exception of herself, clearly thought all women had a bad influence on places of learning, even the virtuous ones:

> Understanding of late, that within certain Houses as well the chief governors, as the Prebendaries, Students and Members thereof being married do keep particular Households with their wives, Children and Nurses, wherof no small offense groweth to the intent of the founders, and to the quiet and orderly Profession of Study and learning Her Majesty therefore expressly willeth and commandeth that no Manner of Person, being either the Head or Member of any College . . . within this Realm, shall have or be permitted to have within the Precinct of any such College, his Wife or other Woman to abide and dwell in the same.
> 9th August third year of our Reign.[5]

And a further discouragement to marriage and to women in general was published by one of her successors, King Charles, more mindful of the dangers of mixing gentle and base blood, and of the laws of inheritance. From Newmarket in 1629 he issued the following order:

> Wheras we have been informed, that of late years many students of that our University, not regarding their own birth, degree and quality, have made diverse contracts of marriage with women of mean estate and of no good fame in that town, to their great dispertagement, the discontment of their friends and parents, and the dishonour of the government of that our University; we will and command you, that at all times hereafter, if any taverner, innholder or victualler, or any other inhabitant of the town, or within the jurisdiction of the University, shall keep any daughter or other woman in his house, to whom there shall resort any scholers of that University of what condition soever, to mispend their time, or otherwise misbehave themselves, or to engage themselves in marriage without the consent of those that have the guardiancie and tuition of them . . . that you command the said woman or women . . . to remove out of the University and

---

5. Quoted in *Cambridge Commemorated*, Fowler & Fowler (C.U.P. 1984) pp.29-30
6. *ibid*, pp. 65-66   7. Enid Porter, *op. cit*

four miles of the same . . . And if any refuse to . . . that you imprison them till they remove or put in such bonds with sure-
ties.[6]

It was against such a background of contempt for women and insistence on a monastic rule of life that the Spinning-House
became exclusively the University's mode of combatting lust. By
the end of the eighteenth century conditions were highly insanitary and the prison reformer Howard 'found 17 women
working in a room 19 feet square with no fireplace or sewer'.[7]

Not only did the University have power to lock the women up,
it also punished them physically. The Vice-Chancellor could
summon the Town-Crier to whip them, and paid him one shilling per woman for his pains. The mind flies in horror to King
Lear:

> Thou rascal beadle, hold thy bloody hand.
> Why dost thou lash that whore? Strip thine own back;
> Thou hotly lusts to use her in that kind
> For which thou whipp'st her.[8]

Which brings me, by a natural progress of thought, to the Reverend Adam Sedgwick, elected Woodwardian Professor of Geo-
logy in May 1818 and spanning most of the century with his long
life. As Senior Proctor one imagines him a tall black stalking figure scouring the high streets industriously seeking out sin. On 7
January 1828, as an act of exorcism perhaps, in preparation for
the Lent Term, he committed 15 girls to the Spinning House in
one day. The post-Freudian eye may squint a little quizzically at
this Valiant-for-Truth, but as County Records show, the siring of
bastards was common among students. One of those Sedgwick
took was Eliza Wright, a servant in a lodging-house, aged 18.
The Committal-book that records her first apprehension goes
on to list 13 more arrests for each of which she was given 2, 3 or 4
weeks' imprisonment in the Spinning-House.

That December Sedgwick — after intervening apprehensions
of dozens of others — arrested Mary Ann Robinson, aged 21,
giving as her last situation Mrs Brett's lodging-house in Jesus

---

8. *King Lear*, Act IV, sc.vi.

Lane. She was to be taken on 10 more occasions. Another Proctor of great repute, Henslow, arrested Ann Jones also 21, at
Murry's, a lodginghouse in Barnwell, although this address doesn't
sound like a lodging-house for University men.

I take these three examples from among hundreds of others to
illustrate the connection between the Spinning-House documenta-
tion and the rest of the present study.

At Oxford, in evidence to the first Royal Commission on the University, Dr Pusey wrote:

> It has pleased God that I should know very extensively what have
> been the temptations to young men, both here and at Cam-
> bridge: Lodging-houses are the worst form of temptation. Else-
> where, men themselves (if they fall) seek for temptation; in lodg-
> ing-houses temptation besets them . . . The facility of easy and
> familiar intercourse at any hour, day by day; the necessity of
> being *solus cum sola*, when meals are brought and removed; the
> habit of those who keep the lodgings to allow the door to be
> opened by the maid-servant, when they are gone to rest, and too
> frequently the thoughtlessness or lightness of that class of serv-
> ant, who are, I believe, often employed not as regular servants
> but by the term only, and whose wages are eked out by the
> lodger, are perils from which the young should be shielded.[9]

The reader will note that Dr Pusey is only concerned at the peril
confronting the young man. He does not enquire how many innocent young servant-maids were seduced by uncaring under-graduates and their future path to the Spinning-House assured.

Soon after the setting-up of the Lodging House Syndicate in
1854, it received a memorial from the parish clergy about the immorality prevalent in lodging-houses, and pointing out what difficulty the lodging-house keeper met in employing respectable
women servants, as was the custom especially in larger lodging
houses. To meet this, the Syndicate proposed a new stipulation into
the licence granted to lodging-house keepers, and after 1859 each
had to promise not to employ any female servant under 30.[10] Presumably no woman over 30 was capable of arousing sensual desires.

9 W.A. Pantin, *Oxford Life in Oxford Archives*, (O.U.P., 1972), Lodgings.
10. University Archives, *CUR* 124, March 1859.

The University of Cambridge Dr
to Mrs Wright Keeper of the Spinning House
for Woman Committed from November
4 1834 to November 2nd 1835

		£	s	d
Adams Ann	15 days			
food firing Table beer & soap 10½				
day			12	6
Ayton Ann	46 days	1	18	4
Broom Ann	42 "	1	15	–
Bird Sarah	88 "	3	13	4
Bexseley Louisa	7 "		5	10
Bentford Sophia	122 "	5	1	8
Baldwin Frances	9 "	"	7	6
Baldwin Charlotte	39 "	1	4	2
Bitcheno Mary	14 "	"	11	8
Barton Phœby	39 "	1	12	6
Bridge Sarah	14 "	"	11	8
Banyard Rebⁿ	21 "	"	17	6
Baker Mary Ann	42 "	1	15	0
Beavis Sarah	17 "	"	14	2
Cowling Sarah	32 "	1	6	8
Cruise Ann	1 "	"	"	10
Corbett Sarah	64 "	2	13	4
Clarke Ann	1 "	"	"	10

An extract from the Spinning House accounts for 1835

But before plunging into the copious and no doubt psychopatho-
logical documentations of the Victorian regime on the subject of
prostitution, shall we turn, for a little light relief, to one of dear
Henry Gunning's more amusing anecdotes from a less censorious
age?

He tells of a certain Dr Kipling whose daily habit was to ride out
for exercise to 'the Hills' i.e. towards Wandlebury. 'Returning one
day, he picked up an ostrich feather which he saw drop from the
hat of a lady who was proceeding very slowly about fifty yards in
advance'. Very gallantly he rode up and presented it to her and
she, explaining how her groom must have stayed behind drinking
in the servants' hall at Babraham, expressed her dismay at being
alone. So our hero escorts her back. As they meet parties of young
men coming towards them, Dr Kipling becomes more and more
aware of their pointing and guffawing and it dawns on him that the
lady he is accompanying is no lady but notorious in the eyes of the
smirking undergraduates. He claps spurs to his horse but the 'lady'
applies her whip and inexorably keeps up with him. They reach
the town neck and neck with incredulous faces staring and pointing. Luckily the naive doctor's stables are in Emmanuel Lane and
he sharply veers off and eludes her at last, no doubt crimson faced.
She was Jemima Watson, an expensive courtesan, who lived in
fashionable lodgings and entertained the aristocracy. Evidently no-
one thought of clapping Jemima in the Spinning-House.[11]

This charming incident belonged to a time when, on a man being
summoned to his Tutor's room to answer a charge of being found
in a house of ill-repute at Barnwell, the tutor barks at him, 'I do my
whoring in London, Sir.' A case of not morally fouling your own
door-step, I presume.

The University Archives hold three committal books dating from
1823 to 1894.[12] The first is a slimmish, square, leather covered,
rather elegant volume: it lists at least 445 names of women apprehended between 1823 and 1836. When they realised the size of the
problem, they invested in larger record-books and the two other
volumes are vast and cumbersome tomes, four or five inches in
depth. All follow the same format and the pages are printed, ready

---

11. Henry Gunning M.A., *Reminiscences of the University Town and County of Cambridge
from the year 1780.*   12. T. VIII. I-3.

for the manuscript entries. Each double page records two cases, the particulars spreading right across the open volume. The entries are not chronological but refer to the woman apprehended. They list her name, age, parish, the names of her father and mother, and whether dead or living, the address of her last situation, her present address, the date of her apprehension and by whom (i.e. which Proctor) taken, the nature of the charge, the punishment decided upon, and a final column for remarks, so quite a slice of social history is laid bare upon each page. A new entry is begun for each woman on first offence: if she offends again, the turnkey or clerk turns back to her original entry and fills in the subsequent committals.

Some entries might list a woman once, and maybe she would be warned and discharged if she were lucky, whereas others will be filled from top to bottom with multiple arrests: there is room for 12-15 and when the space is full a new entry is made further on in the volume and its number (each entry is numbered) noted on the original record. Some women were arrested once a month on a regular basis and under such names there may be thirty, forty, fifty entries.

A total of 1820 names are listed in these three volumes and it would be a tedious task to count how infinitely many more arrests they record. Considering that for most of the nineteenth century there were only about 1500 students at the University, the scale of service by prostitutes seems inordinately large. There were of course the townspeople themselves who must also have provided a clientele but it is significant that the Spinning-House was unoccupied during the Long Vacation. The University was only concerned to chasten immorality in so far as its own charges were threatened.

Those taken up by the Proctor were defined as 'omnes pronubas meretrices et mulieres incontinentes notabiliter delinquentes'.

The handwriting in the Committal books varies of course as the person employed to keep the record changes. Often he is not very literate and mis-spells the girls' names, blots his copy, fails to enter the year as well as the day and month of arrest. One insists on writing the name of the parish as 'Hitching'. Some parts of the record were usually filled in by the Proctor making the arrest, and occasionally the Vice-Chancellor himself in pronouncing sentence, will write a note.

The form was that the Proctor would confront the girl, she would be escorted by his two Bulldogs to the Spinning-House where the Proctor charged her and she would be confined overnight. Next morning the Vice- Chancellor would attend the House to hear the case as brought by the Proctor, and he would deliver the appropriate sentence. The girl was not allowed counsel or anyone to defend her and had no appeal against the sentence passed. It was a completely private court, totally in the power of the University and the girl was helpless once taken in its toils. The charge against her was almost always 'street walking' and she could be imprisoned for simply loitering around street-corners: it was not necessary to prove that she had been soliciting. Thus the University had rights of arrest far exceeding those of the police. As for the girl, she had no rights at all.

The only loophole offered, and that very occasionally, was when the Vice-Chancellor was ill or out of town and could not attend on the morning after an arrest: in such a case it seems the girl had to be discharged. The same applied if the Proctor were not available. How girls must have prayed for such a lucky deliverance.

Who were all these myriad women who flocked to Cambridge to answer the physical needs of some hundreds of still-growing young men? Let us retrieve what we can of their personal history from the pitiful remnants in the committal books. They were almost all single, and in their teens: they came, if not from the town itself, from surrounding villages, Fulbourn, Wimpole, Trumpington; from towns like Ely, Bury St. Edmunds, Norwich, or even from places at a considerable distance like Birmingham, London, Lincoln.

In town the same address turns up again and again: the Lucern Ground, the Gravel Pits, Gass Lane in the early book; later Barnwell figures prominently, Union Row, Short Street, Fair Street, 'back of New Square'. Sometimes they have a father and mother living — Mary Ann Chapman has both: her father is a labourer on a small farm at Haslingfield, but she was 'seduced from home' at the age of 18. Eliza Callitch is only 14 and lives with her father and mother at Castle End. She acquires eleven convictions but was once 'discharged the next day on application from mother'. She had to serve a whole week in solitary confinement for resisting arrest but it can't have taught her a lesson because on the eleventh committal she was given three weeks' punishment 'further committed one week for disorderly conduct — to go to the Castle (gaol) next time she is disorderly'.

Sarah Tupling, 19, had no father or mother. 'Her father was a shoemaker in Trinity Street who married the sister of the notorious Fanny Wells.' Sarah lived with Mr Balls, a Currier, from the age of 10. The first time she came to the Spinning House of her own accord because she was diseased. But she was arrested on four subsequent occasions and sentenced 'to be sent to the Castle for a fortnight as soon as she was well.'

A sad little story surrounds 18 year old Mary Bitchino who was found in 1831 'walking the streets with a gownsman'. A note says 'never lived with her parents (father and mother in Gass Lane, Barnwell). Brought up by her grandfather who is in good circumstances — never used to work — was treated kindly by her grandfather till the winter of 1829 when she came on a visit to her father and mother in Cambridge, was seduced and returned to her grandfather who on discovering her state withdrew his protection'.

Three young girls must have egged one another on, rather like modern giggling teenagers, one imagines. Eliza Owen 17. Elizabeth Gilder 16, and Elizabeth Rutter 17 were found and charged with 'walking about out of their proper line of way and not able to give any good account of themselves'. Eliza Owen was probably the ringleader as she 'had been previously reported to the Proctors as light in character'. All three were reprimanded and discharged on that occasion, but alas, all three had further apprehensions.

A fourth girl was taken the next month with Gilder and Rutter. Martha Young lived in the Garden of Eden (off Parker's Piece) with her father and mother, Joseph and Mary Young and had lately been servant to Mrs. Sharp in Silver Street. Martha must have given up her bad company because there are no further convictions.

Some girls must have been quite intrepid. On one of many committals, the charge against Frances Wright 'was aggravated by her having disguised herself in man's clothes and introduced herself into a lodging-house'. She did herself no good by using 'abusive language and interrupting the Proctor'.

Rebecca Roberts was another charged with 'attempting to enter Trinity College in disguise'. She was in service in a lodging-house, where she no doubt acquired a taste for young gentlemen.

Sarah Ann Ford (*alias* Papworth) 'got over the wall (of the Spinning-House) the same day as she was arrested; re-taken twelve days later. Riotous'. A year later she was found in the rooms of a student of St Peter's College (as Peterhouse was then known). One unlucky girl was found in bed with a gownsman on Christmas Day at Suttons, Mill Road.

Some girls must have emulated those cows that persistently crash through hedges in pursuit of freedom. Sarah or Susan Norman (whose mother was a bedmaker at Trinity) and Jane Nelson were each sent to the Castle for a month at least twice in their careers for attempting to break out of the Spinning-House, once on the same November day, which tempts one to suppose they had a conspiracy and helped each other to escape.

Others must have been a great trouble to arrest in the first place: 'The Proctor was obliged to bring Mary Ann Roberts in a fly', while as for Mary Ann Horsepool, on her fourth arrest she 'collected a large crowd in the street by crying and moaning insomuch that the Proctors could not bring her to the Spinning-House'. She was sentenced to six weeks for being such a nuisance, but was liberated after three days, 'a young man having offered to marry her and take her away immediately from Cambridge'. Jane Osborne 'was very violent and most abusive and threw pepper into the constables' eyes'.

An odd but cryptic case concerns Eliza Nunn whose father was said to be a surgeon at Royston. The note says 'she was upon the town four years ago, sent to the penitentiary, discharged because pregnant, after received home and returned to the Town'. From 1824 she had 28 convictions, the last sentencing her 'to go to the Magdalen two weeks'.

Another persistent offender was Susan Dean, with at least 40 convictions, one punishment being 'a month or till Mr Okes pronounces her to be well'. Mr Okes was the prison surgeon and we will later discuss his charges to the University for the pills, lotions, draughts and poultices and ointments he used to treat these diseased women. I give two sad sample cases of women continuing to solicit in the streets though far gone in pregnancy.

One from 1831 shows Maria (or Martha) Fuller arrested at the end of February, (note the dates) and 'discharged on account of being near her time', and re-arrested in April but again 'discharged next day in consequence of recent confinement'. Follow carefully the account of Emma Pawley, found street-walking in February 1844 and sent home on account of being pregnant. The next day she is charged with 'laying hold of a gownsman' and kept in the Spinning-House for a week. On 5 March the Proctor forebore to arrest her on account 'of being still close on her confinement'. Arrested on 30 April, 'she was let go on account of her baby', born, poor little wretch, on 11 March.

Sometimes, however, a woman will plead her child as an excuse to get off, like Rhoda Grant, many times apprehended, put in solitary confinement and punished by a month's detention in the County Gaol. In October 1840 'she was discharged in consequence of her having a sucking child and according to her account dangerously ill. Taken again within an hour on Midsummer Common'.

Two women Hannah King and Mary Payne, living Back of New Square, were taken together and put in the Spinning-House, Mary for two weeks, Hannah for three because she resisted the Proctor's man. The authorities were not always harsh and allowed the women each to keep their child with them; they gave orders that they were to be kept apart from the other inmates of the house. Both had one previous conviction. Mary Payne 'has two other children in the workhouse'.

One can only surmise what dreadful need and hunger drove these women to the streets. Occasionally there was pressure from a different quarter: Mary Ann Allen is described as 'a married woman whose husband hawks her about as a prostitute — husband admitted as much at the Spinning-House'. She was discharged but another wretch used to set his wife to show off her wares on the railings in Jesus Lane while he hung about nearby to see if the lure worked.

The reader will naturally suppose from the evidence that these girls were desperately poor or out of work. But in two instances, a woman went street-walking with her servant. Elizabeth Chapman and Lucy Barton 'were admonished and discharged on promise of not giving the Proctors any more trouble. Her servant Elizabeth Chapman was sent home to Haverhill by the Carrier.' And another — possibly less innocent — pair was arrested the following year: Fanny Floy of Wellington Row was sentenced to two weeks in the Spinning-House, probably for leading her young servant into trouble. Eighteen year old Elizabeth Powell was discharged.

The next entry shows a rare note of cynical disenchantment: Emma Kirkupt, only 15 was 'discharged on account of her youth and on promise to give over her present line of life . . . . March 1841 . . not kept'.

Rarely, a woman would challenge the right of the University to take her up for simply being out in the street. We see this when Mary Ann Bolen, a persistent offender, was arrested: 'she was violent when taken and broke window in the street — and declared it to be her intention to do the same thing whenever she was taken, unless in the company of a gownsman.' She was sentenced to one month in the Castle for this outburst.

What a regiment of pathetic womanhood, abandoning their health and talents and expectations of happiness to a short life of skulking in squalid alleys. A feminist-orientated world must view a little oddly this juxtaposition of one lot of men requiring the services of these women and another set of men locking the women up for daring to quench that need. Id and superego in full flood of opposition, and not a pretty sight on either side.

Why did so many dozens, no, hundreds, of women turn to prostitution? To understand rather better, we need to look at the alternatives and at the nature of the times. Most of these women were uneducated and would look for unskilled employment as servants and shop girls; some might be apprenticed to dressmakers and milliners. Sarah Collins was, before her thirteen apprehensions, apprenticed to a dressmaker at Ely from whom she ran away. Dickens has several marvellous chapters in which servant-girls are ill-treated by their mistresses and the life, from early morning till late at night, was dreary toil even in a caring house. Many of the girls would have been employed as servants in a lodging house, where they would of course first come into contact with undergraduates

— sometimes disastrously: others would work in the the many pubs and hotels in Cambridge where the chambermaid or barmaid was no doubt encouraged to behave pertly towards the largely male customers. Mary Ann Webb was an assistant bedmaker at Corpus, in spite of the ban on employing young or attractive women in such a position.

Some were undoubtedly downright 'bad-uns'. Being given a fortnight in solitary confinement in October 1842, Margaret Longman is described as a 'very bad character — frequents all the low fairs in the country, connected with very dangerous characters'.

Occasionally we hear of one who is barely responsible for her actions, like Louisa Newman, daughter of Charles Newman, living in Melbourne Place. She was taken three times in 1882 for accosting and street-walking. Her father said (confirmed by Mr Lucas) that 'she had been in Fulbourn Asylum and was now of weak mind'. When Ann Moore was asked about her last situation, she answered she had 'not any for last 11 years'; as she was then 23, the implication is that she hadn't worked since the age of 12.

There was no great range of jobs and certainly no pleasant ones. And the times were impossibly harsh. There had, for one thing, been a run of hard winters: in February 1799 a woman on her way home to Impington from the market in Cambridge was buried in a snowdrift and survived, being found and dug out on the ninth day.

In the wake of the French Revolution society was full of unrest and public demonstrations and dangerously liberal ideas were alike penalised and savagely suppressed. In the thirties agricultural workers suffered falling wages and starvation: arson attacks in the Midlands and East Anglia spread as near to Cambridge as Coton. A new Poor Law imposed Malthusian principles and beggars and vagrants were beaten and harried from parish to parish. It was a crime to be poor, but worse to complain, as the Tolpuddle Martyrs and the Welsh Chartist leaders found to their cost. The potato crop failed in 1845 and this caused widespread suffering in England and utter starvation in Ireland. Gross import duty on corn forced up the price of flour and helped the rural economy to collapse. The repeal of the Corn Laws meant farm rents were reduced and so the landowners themselves lost money and were helpless to aid the agricultural worker. In Cambridge itself, much dislocation was caused by the coming of the railway which saw practically a cessation of the old water-way traffic.

In the county, the enclosure movement came late and left the labourer without his traditional margins of support: he lost his right to common grazing, to gleaning after harvest and gathering firewood, and the game laws spoilt his chance of the occasional lucky free meal. Instead he was made utterly dependent on paid employment. When this dried up he was forced into the new workhouses where his family was split up, the sexes segregated, and only degrading work offered.[13] If the breadwinner died, his widow and children were left bereft of all resource. A report as late as 1905 found 11,000 paupers in the county, still.

The reader needs to form some idea of where the Spinning-House was and what shape it took. He will remember the Hobson bequest. On the land so cleared a court of buildings was erected. A plain front stood along St Andrew's Street next to the Fountain Inn which is still there, its highly bogus-looking facade bearing the date 'founded 1749'. On the other side was built in 1836 a plain rather classical pilastered building for a Baptist Chapel, with railings in front and a gateway with twin lamps. This has since been replaced by the ridiculously Scotch-baronial mish-mash of St. Andrew's Church. The Spinning-House itself was pulled down in 1901 and a new police station put up: this too has disappeared and the site is presently occupied by Nelson Mandela House and the housing offices of the City Council.

The University gaol, at the time we are mainly concerned with, consisted of a residence for the keeper and his wife and household, probably at the street-side of the building. An arched and heavily gated doorway must have led to some sort of office where the Proctor would deliver his prey. The prison itself had, in 1846, 4 day-rooms with adjacent sleeping cells. According to the Surgeon, Mr Fawcett, appointed in October 1842, a fire was constantly kept in the day rooms, and there was a w.c. to each set of cells.

Ten women could be accommodated in squalid cells 9 foot by 7 foot, with no heating and an iron sheet let into the wall, containing a small glazed square to admit light. There was an iron bedstead in each cell with what Mr. Fawcett described as sufficient covering,

13. Michael J Murphy, *Poverty in Cambridgeshire*, (Oleander Press 1978).

The first and second floor cells in the Spinning House

two blankets and a quilt. In the exercise yard was a common privy, and a separate portion of the House was set aside as the hospital where those with infectious diseases were isolated. There was a dark cell for those committed to solitary confinement, for misconduct in the prison. If you go to the Folk Museum on Castle Hill you can still see windows taken from these cells, and in the yard behind the archway is an iron door, rusting and rotting but still the pitying eye can make out the spy hole through which the keeper surveyed his prisoner and the turn-table to pass through the meagre rations of food.

Mr Fawcett is at pains to point out that, in addition to those apprehended, prostitutes frequently apply for admission when afflicted with disease. He almost makes out a case for regarding the Spinning-House as a social benefit. Maybe this was indeed the case: the women were at least treated free of charge. The dread word 'diseased' crops up frequently among those charged, occurring almost as a matter of course after about their third committal. They were all entered in 'Mr Okes' Book' and were not allowed to leave until Mr Okes had examined them and was satisfied that they were well enough. These women must have been riddled with V.D. and infected half the town. Some, maybe those past curing, were passed on to the Refuge, presumably a workhouse hospital.

We are in possession of these invaluable details about the physical shape of the Spinning-House because of a death and subsequent inquest that caused a furore at the time and brought considerable disrepute on the University.[14] The facts are these: Elizabeth Howe, a girl of 19, was arrested on the night of 6 November 1846 and taken to the House by the Proctor, Mr Kingsley. She was put in a cold cell with another girl committed at the same time, Harriet King, and they both slept in what they alleged to be a damp bed, covered only with two wet blankets. She was discharged the next morning by the Vice-Chancellor already visibly ill and went home to her lodging at 7 Union Row kept by Mary Ann Rose. Here she took to her bed and never left it.

A medical attendant, Mr Newby was called on 16 November and visited her frequently: she could not move her arms and legs, was in some pain and her skin very dry and hot. He gave her purgatives, put a blister on her neck, ordered a foot-bath and prescribed drugs (opiates) to minimise her pain. But in spite of his constant attention, she gradually declined, became insensible and died in the early hours of the first of December, 24 days after her arrest. According to her doctor's post-mortem examination, he found 'her uterus healthy but the ovaria on the left side enlarged; on cutting it open it was found to contain a foetus'. Mr Newby describes an ectopic pregnancy. Might a modern medico associate this with her illness and death?

A public inquest was held at which many people were called to give witness on oath: a hairdresser who was one of the jurymen, Lionel Branton of Fitzroy Street, had visited the Spinning-House the previous day and had found two beds very damp. The bed had two blankets and a quilt or rug and the blankets were damp. The beds were shorter than the matresses by two feet. The walls were damp, and glass broken in the windows of three cells. (No doubt smashed by earlier disorderly occupants). The girl's mother, also called Elizabeth Howe, signed her statement with her mark, testifying that her daughter had been healthy enough in the past. The

---

14. University Archives, Endow.I.3-23.

Keeper of the House employed a maidservant, Eliza Patten, who had greeted the girl on committal 'Betsey, don't you know me?' She made a loud defence of her own careful housekeeping: she always aired the beds when they were not occupied, warming the bedclothes with hot coals; she insisted she had served a breakfast to Elizabeth Howe the next morning, consisting of tea and sugar and bread and butter.

Harriet King's evidence is particularly interesting and is signed with her mark at the end of the submission. She was taken at the same time as Elizabeth (they were both said to be 'entering the house in Hobson Street') — do they mean a brothel? — and they shared a bed and a cell.

> 'There was a night convenience in the room: the bed had three blankets and a rug. I did not take my clothes off but deceased did. The window was open but we could not fasten it, . . . there was glass in the window; Deceased had no breakfast I am positive of that.'

Harriet was ill all the time she was confined in the House. She served two weeks' punishment on account of having resisted arrest.

In the committal book she is described as a tall girl, who had lived as Elizabeth did at 7 Union Row, Mrs Rose's house, in 1845, but gave her address as 11 Union Row at the date of the inquest. Union Row must have been a real red light district as different houses in the street crop up frequently in the records. Emma Osborne also lived at no. 7 and was one of the witnesses. She had no chamber pot the first night she was confined and got very ill through the cold conditions, having a swollen eye so bad that she 'thought she might lose it'. She complained that 'the food at the SpinningHouse is bad and dear: the Keeper gets it from what shop he thinks proper.' She must have been a kind girl because once she was freed she went to fetch medicine for Elizabeth and was going on to tell Mr Newby that his patient was worse when she fell foul of the Proctor once more and he not believing her errand, sent her straight home

Five other girls, all in the Spinning-House on that November night were called to testify: Eliza Wright (of 3 Union Row) and Eliza Green (two of the four Elizas on oath) shared half a quartern loaf (4*d*) for breakfast with 2d of butter. Their blankets were also very damp. Eliza Cook, another lodger at 7 Union Row, swore that her bed too was very damp. Two must have been difficult customers: Martha Walker *alias* Alice Walsh had been sentenced to a month on 20 October 1846 with the remarks 'most violent and abusive, . . . had to be brought (to the Spinning-House) in a fly'. Her occupation is given as 'doing for her sister Mrs Collis who is in the Hospital'. This woman Collis keeps a brothel in Union Row' (*v.* entry 670, Committal Book 1836-1850). As a witness, she had seen Elizabeth Howe in the prison on the evening she had been arrested. She had been taken ill in the street: ('I am liable to fits') and water had been thrown over her, so that her clothes were wet and nothing dry given her. Her bed had been very damp and two other females slept in the room with her.

The last witness, Emma Burcham, slept in Elizabeth's bed the next night (7 Nov.) with Harriet King. That night she called for water for two hours but got none though she was sure the Keeper heard her: he allegedly said if she had been dying he would not have brought her any. Emma stayed and put up with it for ten days and then broke out and got away. The Committal Book records her arrest on 30 October when she was given a week but 'made her escape', taken again on November 6 and escaped again on Sunday November 15.

As far as I can see, there were another five women in the house that night who were not called as witnesses. Perhaps they occupied the set of cells on the opposite side of the building? But no wonder conditions were so crowded that the women had to double up. Compared with some of these Elizabeth is said to be a quiet sober girl. 'I never saw her drunk', said one acquaintance. But she is no innocent, and the Howe surname occurs on several entries, Maria, Sarah, Elizabeth, Ann.

Her own (no. 558) gives her parish as Foulburn (sic). She has a father and mother there, and a sister Emma apprenticed to Miss Canham, milliner. Elizabeth's last situation was with Miss Milner of North Terrace as a servant. Before the fatal arrest on 6 Novemer, she had been apprehended four times,12 May 1844, 31 October (?), 12 March 1846, and 9 May 1846. The first time she had been admonished and discharged on giving a promise to go home to Fulbourn, but she served a week in the House each for her second and fourth offences. which is why Eliza Patten recognised her. So Mr Kingsley, the Proctor, was perfectly justified in arresting her on the word of his Bulldogs that she was a known prostitute.

The jury brought in a verdict that Elizabeth Howe died of rheumatic fever caused by a violent cold caught at the Spinning-House and by being confined in a cold and damp cell. They were so convinced they went much further.

> 'The Jury cannot separate without expressing their abhorrence
> of a system which sanctions the apprehension of females when
> not offending against the general law of the land and confining
> them in a gaol unfit for the worst of felons.'

The Coroner entirely concurs, and obeys the jury's direction that the papers in the case should be sent to the Secretary of State for the Home Department. This was not to be hushed up as a local matter; the town was scandalised. He wrote to Sir George Grey, Bart., on 7 December 1846, adding that he entertained 'considerable doubt as to the power claimed by the Proctors to apprehend without warrant prostitutes who are not guilty of disorderly or indecent conduct'. The Coroner also observed that the Keeper of the Spinning House, Edward Wilson, was allowed to sell provisions to the persons under his charge.

Ministers in those days attended to their own correspondence by hand and Sir George was sufficiently struck by the case to write as soon as the 12 December to the Vice-Chancellor, rather avoiding the question of the University's right to imprison but insisting in no uncertain terms that 'these glaring defects' be remedied without delay. He protested at there being a male keeper of a house wholly for the detention of females and at the practice of selling food to the inmates, which lent itself to short measures and extortionate prices. (A witness on oath complained bitterly at paying 2d for a bit of butter that would only be 1d outside in the market.) The letter goes on to refer to previous complaints about the Spinning-House from the Inspectors of the Prison Service who were by no means satisfied that it was properly conducted. He even suggests that it should be closed down until the necessary improvements had been effected.

The Vice-Chancellor of the time was Dr Philpott, Master of St Catharine's, who replied without loss of time, also in his own — extremely elegant — handwriting and on beautiful blue foolscap-sized notepaper that unfolds as crisply today as if no-one but Sir George had ever opened the envelope. Vital evidence, he says in the first letter, had not been put before the inquest, but in fact none is adduced. Then in seven closely written pages he attempts a defence, claiming — as a reason for the unreformed state of the House — a long-standing suit in the Court of Chancery with regard to Hobson's Trust in which the property of the house is vested. Until a judgement is given in this suit, it has not been possible to appoint trustees and apportion a sum of money to carry out the improvements undoubtedly called for.

Dr Philpott counters the argument about a male keeper with the mention of the Keeper's wife who, since 1834, has acted as Matron. It would be impractical, he goes on, to run the House with a Matron alone in charge. 'The females confined in the House are chiefly of the most profligate and abandoned character and cases of insubordination and violence are of frequent occurrence, when the presence of a male officer is absolutely necessary'. As to the selling of provisions, he quotes the fixed sum allowed daily for each woman's maintenance (7*d* a day) plus an allowance of all the coals and candles and soap required and a pint of beer daily to each prisoner. The University is contemplating a better deal and the letter explains the intention of the authorities to establish a dietary: he promises the daily attendance of a chaplain to attempt the moral education and redemption of these women.

Indeed committees must have met, and experts given their advice because by March 1847 the Vice-Chancellor is in a position to send Sir George his proposed regulations for the management of the Spinning-House and a dietary. Sir George must have been largely satisfied because the only amendment he prescribes is that when a prisoner is sentenced to solitary confinement and a 'low diet', i.e. bread and water, the punishment should not exceed three days. Reform did arrive and the box of papers quoted (*v.* note 14) holds a dirty, much-handled linen-backed plan of 1852 showing how space in the Spinning-House is to be re-arranged, taking in some land from the Fountain pub next door. Under the revised management, manuals of regulations lay down how the matron, the chaplain, the surgeon and the inmates are to conduct themselves.

For the last named, the rules were printed on card and hung up on the walls of each cell. The prisoner is to bathe and put on the dress prepared for her; to occupy a separate cell, to follow such employment or devote herself to such means of instruction as the prison offers; to keep her cell clean. The cells are to be locked from 8 at night till 8 next morning in winter and till 7 in summer; meals are as laid down in the dietary (*v.* below) and food and drink are not to be brought in; the prisoner is not to see friends or family except by written order of the Vice-Chancellor or his deputed officer, and then only for a quarter of an hour in the presence of the matron. The punishment for bad behaviour or neglect of these rules is solitary confinement and for bread and water, for a period not more than three days.

DIETARY	
for persons confined in the Spinning House Cambridge for periods not exceeding one month	
Breakfast	6*oz.* bread — daily
	2*oz.* Tea — weekly
	7*oz.* sugar — weekly
	1½ pints milk — weekly
Dinner	5*oz.* cooked meat
for 4 days	6*oz.* bread
in the week	½*lb.* potatoes
for 3 days	6*oz.* bread — if more than 3 inmates
in the week	1½ pints soup — ditto
	12*oz.* suet pudding — if less than 4 inmates
Supper	6*oz.* bread or 1 pint of oatmeal gruel daily

And here is the dietary, signally deficient in vegetables and fruit, but enough to keep body and soul together and maybe, far more than a starving girl might find to live on if thrown out in the street from her home or place of employment. It too, was printed and hung up so that no-one should be in doubt as to

what they were entitled. But the University has had a fright and
word must have gone out that the Proctors should moderate their
vigilance. We have seen the numbers arrested part of the century
— let us compare the record for a few years now.

A report in May 1849 shows 87 committals between 30 June 1847
and 30 June 1848. The women were confined for a total of 665 days,
among them Sarah U. who was committed 8 times and served 81
days of that year in the prison. 11 women came at their own request, for medical treatment, and stayed 101 days between them.

The Chaplain's report for the year ending 29 September 1855
shows 32 committals; 10 for 1 week, 11 for 2, 3 for 3, 7 for 4 and 1
poor prisoner for 5 weeks. 14 persons have been committed once, 4
twice, 2 three times, and 1 four times. The chaplain's name is F.W.
Whitehead and he has tried hard, he says, to bring about a change
of heart by prayer, the reading of the scriptures and personal ex-
hortation. But he sees very little hope of amendment — the prisoners are, he says, 'of the most degraded and hopeless character'.
Only three among them could not read at all, eighteen could read
and ten could write, but only one or two with ease. The same long-
suffering Chaplain gave the figures for the year ending 29 September 1886 and he has only two committals to report, one for 4 days
imprisonment and one for 14. They were both first offenders.

However, this is chasing ahead too fast. Two other scandals over
the Spinning-House were to hit the University before the end of
the century, and both are dealt with in exhaustive detail by Winstanley in his books *Early Victorian Cambridge* and *Later Victorian
Cambridge*.

The first case is the celebrated one of the seven so-called 'milliners'. The story goes that some undergraduates projected a ball at a
public house in Great Shelford (the de Freville Arms conveniently
beyond the precincts) and had invited some girls of the town to be
their partners. Apparently breakfast had been ordered for the following morning so it was to be quite a swinging party. On the evening of 30 January 1860, seven girls and two undergraduates were
sitting in a horse-drawn omnibus, in full evening costume, going
quietly along St Andrew's Street. But a 'jealous rival' had sent word
to the authorities. Let us hear the tale as it appeared in the *Daily
Telegraph* for Thursday 2 February:

THE PROCTORIAL SYSTEM AT CAMBRIDGE

On Monday last a very characteristic illustration of the liberty of the English subject was exhibited at Cambridge. About seven o'clock in the evening, an omnibus freighted with seven females dressed in evening costume, and two males, was quietly making its way past the town gaol when the driver was suddenly pounced upon by three or four men, who compelled him to draw reins, while a preconcerted signal summoned from the inner side of the gaol door the guardians of University morality who, it appears, had received an anonymous communication that a vehicle laden in the way found would travel that road about the time mentioned.

Anyone acquainted with the summary way in which the University officers execute the powers with which a Royal Charter has entrusted them will easily follow the brief remainder of the story. The driver was ordered to conduct his cargo of suspected goods to the 'Spinning House', and in the upshot five of the females were condemned by the Vice-Chancellor to a fortnight's imprisonment and two were acquitted. The two males found in the conveyance will probably meet with another kind of punishment.

These females were what is popularly understood as 'gay women' although the circumstances would not warrant anyone in taking them for Dianas in Chastity. According to report they were suspicious milliners, who had arranged with a number of University men to have a private ball at some distance from the town, but were intercepted by the anonymous communication of a jealous rival. To those persons who are uninitiated in the mystery of University authority, the following extract from the report written by the special commissioner of the *Morning Chronicle*, in its palmy days, may be useful as well as edifying, as showing how we noisy Britons can tolerate a little Perugia at home while we are so indignant about the bloody one abroad:

The form of trial (speaking of the Spinning House) if it be not an abuse of words to apply such a term to the process which the prisoner undergoes previous to her final committal, is as repugnant to every principle of justice, as it is opposed to the notions of

every person who boasts of English customs and of English liber-
ties. The Vice-Chancellor attends at a private room in the
establishment every morning during term, to sit in judgement
upon the presumed offenders. The public are not admitted;
no friends of the prisoner are allowed to be present; all legal
assistance and advice are denied, and the accused can call no
witnesses. The Proctor, or one of his men who arrested her,
the gaoler or the *multum in parvo* who acts as snob, and the
Vice-Chancellor who sentences her, are the only persons
privileged to attend this extraordinary court of justice during
the trial of the unfortunate culprit. The prisoner is brought in
by the gaoler; her name, age and address are entered in the
minute-book by the Vice-Chancellor. The proctor, or one of
his men, states that he saw her in such a street or place and
'suspecting her of incontinence' arrested her. The gaoler is
asked if he knows her, or if she has ever been under is charge
before; if he replies in the affirmative, the warrant of committal for such period as the Vice-Chancellor may direct is made
out and the prisoner is ordered to be removed.

The warrant, though I was not able to obtain a copy of it,
sets forth that the person therein named was brought before
the Vice-Chancellor upon such a day, she 'being suspected of
incontinence', and that as he is 'satisfied of the accuracy of
such a charge' the governor is thereby directed to keep the
said person in safe custody for 'the period therein' mentioned.
The whole, therefore, that is necessary to obtain a conviction
in this court is to be suspected by the proctor or his men and
to be known by the gaoler.

No evidence is required to prove any overt act on the part
of the prisoner; it is not necessary that she should accost any
man in the streets or be seen in his company. Although proceeding upon the most legitimate business through the streets,
any female whom the proctor may chance to suspect of incontinence is liable to be dragged off to this sink of iniquity.

It is amusing to note that this reporter, just like his successors
nowadays, got several of his facts wrong. If we consult the Committal Book for the day in question, we find the names of the
seven girls 'taken by the Proctors and Pro-proctors' and charged

with being 'in company with members of the University'. They were Sarah Ebbon, 20; Charlotte Fuller, 18; and Emma Coxall, 19; and each was given a sentence of three days' imprisonment. Rosetta Aves, 17 and Louisa Kemp, only 14, her occupation given as a dressmaker, were admonished and discharged. Harriet Bell, 22 was given a week in prison, and Emily Kemp 22, another dressmaker, and the sister of Louisa, received the sternest sentence of a fortnight's imprisonment. All of course spent that night in the Spinning-House and were called before the Vice-Chancellor, Latimer Neville, Master of Magdalene, next morning. Emily Kemp was no doubt given a heavier sentence because she was thought to be leading her young sister into corruption; in the event she was released after five days. The outcry was formidable. The Town seized upon the case and letters in the *Telegraph* thundered with righteous indignation.

> Ought this state of things to continue? [asks 'Caustic', writing with great prolixity and restating all the facts from the beginning.] Has not the time arrived when public opinion ought to be brought to bear upon the question, in order to procure the abolition of this iniquitous power, doubly hateful because exercised in the person of priests, and directed against a class which, God knows, stand far more in need of loving exhortation and advice than of harsh treatment and imprisonment?
>
> It cannot even be urged in favour of the system that it aims to suppress the vice against which it is professedly directed. Prostitution flourishes at Cambridge in greater degree than in most towns of the same size. In spite of the proctors or 'bulldogs' St Andrew's Street and Trumpington Street exhibit, night after night, a spectacle which may well remind the beholder of the Haymarket or the Arcades.

Letter-writers to the Editor chose to conceal their identity under pseudonyms. The next example comes from Paterfamilias who exclaims plaintively

> . . . I have known ladies belonging to the most respectable families in this town, daughters and wives of prefessional men, men of position and of family (not tradesmen or college servants) stopped, and insulted in the most gross and offensive manner,

purely and simply because they were walking unaccompanied in
the street, and did not happen to be personally known to the
Proctors for the time being; and I think that in the cause of
justice and common decency, you ought to ventilate this subject and assist the inhabitants of Cambridge in overthrowing
this system, by which clergymen of the Church of England are
compelled so to disgrace their cloth, and bring odium upon
her ministers. I may add that the police of this borough (one
of the most efficient bodies in the kingdom) if instructed to act
in a sensible manner, would be perfectly competent to keep
the streets in much more decent order than they are under
proctorial supervision.

And an incredibly wordy, almost incoherent, letter signed by
Lex ends up with this stirring cry:

> . . . But whatever may be the opinion of the public concerning
> the cause of University immorality or the panacea adopted for
> its cure, there is one principle upon which it is the duty of
> every free man to insist, viz. that no person or corporation of
> persons shall have the power to arbitrarily seize upon, try in
> secret, and condemn to imprisonment any individual whom
> the common law of the land theoretically declares to be the
> equal of all others of the Queen's subjects. Until this principle
> be enforced, we have little room to denounce the Virginian
> slave-holders; and I trust that your advocacy will cause some
> Members of Parliament to stand boldly forward and claim for
> females who are too weak to keep themselves, as large a share
> of the law's benefits as is accorded to thieves and murderers.

Emma Kempe brought an action against the Vice-Chancellor
the following November in the Court of Common Pleas. The
jury found the Vice-Chancellor culpable in that 'he did not
make due enquiry into the plaintiff's character' but the judge
ruled that he was not legally bound to do so and entered a verdict for the defendant, a costly victory for the University.

Put on its guard, it sought legal advice and the process of arrest and charging was tightened up. Witnesses were to be examined on oath but the suggestion that the prisoner was entitled to
legal representation was carefully refused. For the next few dec-

ades proctors were careful only to arrest women known to be of immoral character, and the wholesale confining of girls in the Spinning-House largely stopped.

The Town, alerted to the threat to civil rights, prowled about and looked for trouble, the more disreputable element seeing an opening for scraps and alarums, as it always had. Harriet Herring did her best to attract some sympathy from the by-standers when. she was arrested:

> October '48: behaved ill along the road to the Spinning-House.
> October '49: walked very slowly and a mob gathered but did not resist.
> November'49: the same complaint as above.
> Caroline Morton arrested in 1857 'was brought with some difficulty and attracted a great crowd by her outeries'.
> Mary Ann Bird: 'a rescue was attempted'.
> 1891 Annie Clark: 'very violent and abusive. Crowd collected and one man was arrested and taken to Police Court'.

But in the early 1890's, at least two Heads of Houses commented on the social scandal of the streets and the Proctors were commanded to be more vigilant. Winstanley dramatically sets the scene: 'The hour was striking and the woman appeared'.[16] Enter, stage left, Jane Elsden of Dullingham aged 17 but already known to the Proctors, with two committals for street walking in January and February 1891. She was given sentences of 14 and 21 days for each offence, and on the second occasion 'was very violent when apprehended and used bad language. When sentenced, said 'it won't alter me. I'll continue to be a prostitute'.'

That same afternoon she escaped while the assistant matron wasn't looking and fled to her father, Walter, at Dullingham. Foolishly perhaps, the Vice-Chancellor issued a warrant for her arrest, and this time, having committed a criminal offence, she appeared before the Borough Magistrates, who were bound to commit her to the Assizes.

Not only the *Daily Telegraph* but the *Pall Mall Gazette* trumpeted the affair with talk of an 'Academic Star Chamber', and questions

15 D.A. Winstanley, *Later Victorian Cambridge* (C.U.P, 1947) chapter IV: The Cambridge University and Corporation Act.

were asked in the House of Commons. The furore was such that
the Home Secretary gave the order for Jane's release. The
Borough and the University were forced to confer and the whole
question of University privilege seemed ultimately at stake. A substantial element on the Borough Council were in favour of 'pro-
moting a bill in Parliament to abolish all university jurisdiction over
all residents not members of the University'.

Throughout 1891 the acrimonious discussions, reports, referrals
and counter-referrals continued, covering not only the present
Spinning-House issue but also the Vice-Chancellor's powers of dis-
communing, issuing wine-licences and permitting theatrical perfor-
mances. The university's main contention was that if Proctorial
powers were curtailed the police did not have sufficient authority
to keep the streets clear of prostitutes. It was so far conceded that
Spinning-House cases should be heard in public and that the prisoner should be defended by Counsel.

In such a delicate situation, the Proctors agreed to exercise the
utmost caution, and hoped to avoid making an arrest, with the eye
of the world upon them. They hoped in vain.

A pro-proctor, Frederick Wallis, had no real option but to arrest
Daisy Hopkins on the night of 2 December. Let us look at entry 525
in the last of the Committal Books (1849-1894). Here she appears as
Daisy Hopkin [sic] aged 17 and living at 36 Gold Street. She gave
her last situation as being with Mrs. Lowson at 10 Brunswick Walk.
The charge was 'walking with a member of the University'. Daisy
(with a sister) was already known to the Proctors, had been warned
more than once and her name appeared on the police register of
suspected women.

She was brought next day before Vice-Chancellor, Dr Peile, Master of Christ's; the case was heard in public and she was represented by a lawyer, A.J. Lyon. The undergraduate in whose company
she was arrested very reluctantly gave evidence on oath that he had
asked her whether she could take him to a room and that she had
replied that she could. The facts were undeniable and there can be
no question of her guilt. She was sentenced to 14 days' imprisonment and the charge book notes 'behaved violently on being sentenced', no doubt rather spoiling the impression created by her
navy blue outfit.

The rest of the story made legal history and is a compulsory part of every aspiring young lawyer's study of precedents. For all the Vice-Chancellor's careful handling, he made one fatal mistake and this was pounced upon by the lawyer in the case. 'Walking with a member of the University' is not a criminal charge; the words 'for an immoral purpose' had not been used, and Daisy Hopkins was released from custody and the proceedings against her quashed. She sued for damages on the grounds of false imprisonment and the case was heard at Ipswich in March 1892. It failed but the University never recovered from its public humiliation and the taint of tyranny.

Dr Harry Porter and Mr Peter Tranchell wrote an operetta based loosely on a telescoped history of Jane Elsden and Daisy Hopkins. It is called *Daisy Simpkins or the Spinning House* and was first performed in May Week 1954 at Gonville and Caius. Dr Porter describes it as 'a light-hearted exercise in the Gilbert & Sullivan mode' and I am grateful to him for letting me see it. The chorus of Cambridge working-girls had a good verse:

> The Spinning-House is grey and old
> The Spinning-House is damp and cold
> With a Matron who's been sent
> In order to prevent
> Any kindness being expressed
> Any decent food or rest.
> The Spinning-House is dread and drear
> The Spinning-House is our great fear.

One views a little cynically the love-duets of Daisy and her admirer Cayley:

> If love were new,
> There could be virtue in abstaining.
> But love we know,
> An old friend always true.
> And sin can be pure,
> And to goodness passion strives to fly.
> The clerics may deny it,
> But sin cannot be all of darkest dye.

Daisy's real-life partner was a married man whose career was ruined by this incident and its exposure in Court. He left the university and had his name removed from the Boards of his College. I don't think 'love' had much to do with the squalid temporary alleviation he sought and was prepared to pay for.

The Cambridge University and Corporation Act finally went through in 1894: it did not deprive the Vice-Chancellor of his right to issue wine licences nor the Proctors of their right to arrest any common prostitute but the Spinning-House court was wound up and the charged person in future was taken to the police station and, if to be tried, before the Borough Magistrates Bench. The Vice-Chancellor's consent for a licence for the performance of stage-plays (and casual entertainment) in any theatre or other place in the Borough was no longer to be sought, and the consent of the Mayor was alone sufficient. The University's power to discommune had long been queried by the Borough Council, but it dropped the matter on receiving a memorial from forty or more leading Cambridge tradesmen who all vociferously pleaded for its retention since it effectively prevented undergraduates from running up bad debts, at least locally. In 1901 the Spinning-House was pulled down and a new police station built.

Cambridge was not of course alone in setting up a prison for loose women. I am indebted to the late Leonard Forster who drew my attention to an equivalent in Amsterdam, the Oude Zijds Achterburgwal Spinhuis, described by Simon Schama in the *Embarrassment of Riches* (Collins, 1987), a review of the Dutch Golden Age.

From 1597 'fallen women', vagrants, whores and thieves were sent to these houses of correction lodged on sites of the dissolved religious orders, for stiff doses of improvement at loom and wheel. For a copper coin, the general public were admitted to watch the inmates at their labours in both the Tugthuis (for men) and the female Spinhuis: they were obligatory stops on a tourist itinerary. (Male prisoners who refused to work were put in the 'drowning cell' where water rose steadily to the ceiling unless they pumped furiously to avoid a ghastly death.)

By 1737 this display of the imprisoned whores was an opportunity for unabashed prurient pleasure in which the prison authorities shamefully colluded. They permitted access through a barred partition 'on which occasion it is customary for them (the whores) to entertain their visitors with such abominable discourses and indecent actions as are shocking to any men of sense or morality'.

One such traveller, Joseph Shaw, saw over 100 in the Spinhuis in 1709 'clothed in the gay habiliaments of love, adorned with plumes of feathers on their heads, patched and painted and just as they used to charm and coax the fond, admiring and deluded gulls who know not the fatal Arts of women'.

Schama says, 'Those who survived the years of hard whoring between 18 and 30 did so at the price of disfigurement from repeated doses of venereal disease, spells in the Spinhuis, repeated banishments and clandestine returns'.

Here is the career of one such case, Jannetje Hendriex *alias* Jeanne dans le Coin, born 1630, arrested at 13 for petty theft and sent to the Spinhuis for 3 years (they had vastly longer sentences than in Cambridge). Banned a year later for malicious slander. Back in the Spinhuis in 1648. At 18, she was condemned to be flogged on the public pillory but spared because of her pregnancy. Banished for 4 years after having stood in the pillory with a sign on her breast proclaiming her infamy. More banishments, five more floggings, then a six-year stretch in the Spinhuis. Freed in 1672, she was banished but stole a basket from a woman, for which she was sentenced to another flogging and three more years in the Spinhuis.

More than a thousand prostitutes plied their trade in the busy dock-area of the later seventeenth-century Amsterdam. Some details strike a familiar note: 'Five prostitutes arrested in 1696 mostly in their teens and early twenties, were all identified as seamstresses as well as whores.' Laying such suffering on as a tourist spectacle must have outraged some of the burghers, and perhaps they were moved to reform. Here we have a Montpellier doctor, Guillaume Daignon describing the Amsterdam sights in 1777

'La Speenhuys est une Maison de Force, pour les filles de mauvaise vie; on les y occupe spécialement du filage . . . elles sont diviseés par chambres; dans chaque chambre il n'y a qu'une ving-

---

16. Guillaume Daignon, *Réflexions sur la Hollande*, quoted in *La Hollande et les Hollondais*, ed. R Murriss, 1925.

taine de filles, surveilleés par une maîtresse . . . la chambre est un
enclos où une espèce de laboratoire fermé par des barreaux à
travers desquels on les voit. Ces filles sans avoir un air bien
contrit, ont un maintien fort honnête et fort décent; elles sont
mises simplement mais très proprement; elles sont en géneral
très fraiches et très agréable à voir . . .'[17]

Fraiches. A very different picture.

Committal to a Spinning-House cell was not the only peril that
beset the prostitute; then as today she provoked the hostility and
violence of her customer and became at times the target of his
accumulated guilt. Such a poor girl was Emma Rolfe who, perhaps after a typical teenage row with her father, left home at 16
to go 'on the town' (as they themselves described it) with her
friend Ann Pepper. She went to live in 'Mrs Crispin's house' the
better to ply her trade, and three weeks lay dead on Midsummer
Common with her head almost severed from her body.

The *Cambridge Chronicle* for August 1876 describes the murder
in detail and the town must have been petrified by the horrific
accounts. It happened near the railings by Brunswick Walk.
Emma went with a man — who had already been drinking — on
to the common and asked for a pint of beer. He got annoyed, refused to humour her, produced a razor from his pocket and
slashed her neck. He went back to the Garrick pub and was seen
with his jaw shaking. On coming out, he met a policeman who,
attracted by the screaming, had discovered Emma's body. The
killer, Robert Browning, his hands blood-covered and still holding the razor, gave himself up. In court next morning he
claimed the girl had stolen a shilling from him and that had provoked the attack, but no coin was found on the body. Two thousand people attended Emma's funeral.

The case of Regina *v.* Browning on a charge of murder was
heard in the Magistrates' Court on 25 August 1876 before the
Mayor, J. Death, D. Adams Esq. Dr. Okes (Provost of King's)
and C.F. Foster Esq. He was remanded in custody till the following Tuesday and the case was sent to the Assizes at Norwich.
Robert Browning was hanged at the Castle on 14 December 1876
'in a contrite and god-fearing frame of mind'.

3

The Lodging—House Syndicate

Cartoon from *Granta*, 2nd December, 1927

You might say it was poor Lawrence Dundas who started it all.
Lawrence was a nineteen-year old Trinity man who (unfortunately) got asked to dinner with six other undergraduates by a Fel-
low-Commoner of St John's, K.A. Jackson. So, on 5th February
1818 they all assembled about seven at Jackson's lodgings, kept by
Dyball in Bridge Street. The evening proved very bucolic and
celebratory and by eleven when it came to an end, the diners were
considerably drunk. Lawrence Dundas was so drunk he could not
put on his gown unaided and had to be helped into it by Mrs
Dyball, she no doubt pleased to see the party at last breaking up.
Dundas and a fellow-diner, Wigram, had a vague plan to go on to
Barnwell, the haunt of purchasable women, and indeed Wigram
ran off in that direction, leaving his friend Lawrence to stumble
after him as best he might.

He got as far as Parker's Piece and there fell into a muddy ditch.
Stripping off most of his clothes he almost strangled himself with

his own socks and pantaloons and was quite unable to get out. They found the boy dead next morning, sitting in eighteen inches of slimy water with his head and shoulders along the bank so that the water was almost to his mouth. The Coroner's Court delivered the verdict that he died, not of drowning, but of exposure, due to the icy night on top of having been heavily intoxicated.

We owe these facts to the Rev. F.H. Maberley, M.A. who published at London a little pamphlet entitled *The Melancholy and Awful End of Lawrence Dundas* as soon as possible after the verdict, preaching an impassioned sermon on the temptations of drink and fornication. This Maberley was something of a fire-raiser, one who in this century would have marched with CND. In his own time he led risings of labourers in Cambridgeshire against an iniquitous Poor Law and was on one occasion rescued from gaol and carried in triumph on the shoulders of his supporters to address a meeting on Parker's Piece.

But to concentrate on the present case: the point of the pamphlet was to appeal to the University to correct the laxity of its discipline and the prevalent licentiousness. 'Scarce any control is exercised over the students even in college, and less over the lodgings in the town'. He quotes innumerable texts from the Scriptures in denouncing the demon drink and the dangers attending 'looking on the wine when it is red'. In his opinion a drunkard is one who is not habitually drunk but has on one occasion been drunk, just as a thief or murderer for one crime is so branded for the rest of his life.

'Again, with regard to women of the town', although he is not often in Cambridge in the evenings, he says 'I have seen them parading the streets in the most impudent manner, accosting many that they met and in some cases walking and talking with men of the University in a drunken state'. He calls vehemently on the University 'to arise from its slumber'. What he recommends are more frequent examinations and more to be required of a man in taking a degree. 'Let their studies be classical and biblical as well as mathematical' — so, he thinks, they will have less time for mischief. He advocates the appointment for life to the office of Censor. feeling that the Proctors are inefficient thanks to their annual appointment. By the time they become proficient or useful in their work, their spell is up and they are replaced.

Maberley is urgent and adamant: 'the blood of poor Dundas lies upon the University'. He calls on the Vice-Chancellor to remove the causes of licentiousness: first he must clear the streets of prostitutes. The next step is to put an end to lodgings in the town with the dangers they pose of drinking and the facility for students of being out all night. He imagines young women sitting up for the undergraduate's late return and the direful consequences latent in their meeting when he does at last amble home. He demands that the University authorities should reprehend the employment of young women to wait upon the men, even in college. If private sources of funding are not adequate, Parliament, he says, should advance the money for colleges to build themselves adequate accommodation for all their members.

Then the argument becomes risible. 'Next, let the disgraceful and licentious pictures, exhibited in the Fitzwilliam Museum be removed: for this is another cause of licentiousness'. He means of course the paintings of naked or near-naked women. We learn for the first time that an undergraduate must be accompanied by an M.A. of the University to view these works of art. Maberley exhorts the authorities to make an example of those implicated in the present case and others like it. He wants punishment inflicted and the pain made known to prevent a reoccurrence. A final plea is to parents of undergraduates who are encouraged to pray.

Mark how soon the University reacted. Prompted, maybe even catapulted by complaints like this, in March 1818 an actual system emerges, showing concerted action on the part of the Vice-Chancellor and the Proctors. One wonders whether the end of the Napoleonic Wars played a part in such a focusing of attention? Did men come thronging back to the University, as happened so noticeably after subsequent wars? Does Peace itself perhaps inspire a mood and an optimism conducive to study? It is certainly recorded in Volume 11 of Gunning's *Reminiscences of Cambridge* that in April 1818 a Grace was passed for the annual appointment of two Pro-Proctors on account of the great increase in the number of students and the necessity of their finding lodgings in the town. Sir Arthur Gray claims that between 1810 and 1828, numbers grew from 2469 to 5104[1]: this he ascribes chiefly to the development of the Public Schools.

Whatever the cause, the first regulations for lodging houses were laid down and printed:

1. All houses to be annually licensed by the Vice- Chancellor and Proctors;

2. The licence to be signed by the Vice- Chancellor and a Proctor upon application from the Master and Tutor for the college of the student in question and a certificate from them stating that the occupier was of good character;

3. The lodging-house-keeper must live in the house;

4. He must lock the door at 10 p.m. and list any lodger entering or leaving after that time;

5. If a lodger were out at night, the lodging-house-keeper to report the fact to his Tutor;

6. No lodger to have a key;

7. The lodging-house-keeper is not to supply or receive in his house any dinner for a lodger, unless his Tutor's written permission is obtained first;

8. All applicants for a licence are to sign a promise to comply with these regulations;

9. Any false return or evasion of regulations to result in suspension or revokation of the licence;

10. Tutors are to make occasional visits to all houses to see that these Regulations are observed, and particularly to enquire about servants employed in lodging-houses.[2]

From this time forward, undergraduates lodging in houses not so licensed were deemed not to be resident nor keeping terms: in other words they could not qualify for a degree, no matter what the quality of their work. So the young had to mark carefully what they did before reserving rooms in the town.

In the Rare Books Room in the University Library, you are allowed to consult a little yellow pamphlet, unbound, that has survived since these days. It is prefixed with the regulations, as set out above, and then follows a list 'of persons licensed by the Vice-Chancellor and the Proctors to receive students as lodgers in their respective houses. Two hundred and fourteen names follow, show-

1 Cambridge University: *An Episodical History* (Cambridge, 1926)
2. Cambridge University Archives: *CUR* 124, March 1818.

ing the streets in which the houses are situated, listed under parishes, but giving no street numbers (presumably these had not as yet been invented) and noting the college to which each house is attached, or by whose Master they were recommended to the Vice-Chancellor.

In this first list, there is no indication of what occupation the lodging-house-keeper followed when he wasn't attending to his lodgers.[3] It has a charming archaic air: Peterhouse is called St Peter's College, Pembroke is Pembroke Hall, Corpus Christi is Bene't College, St Catharine's is Catharine Hall, Sidney Sussex is Sidney College and Queens' is printed as Queen's College.

St John's, Trinity and Queens' were the largest users of lodgings, not having then built the vast amount of accommodation we associate with them nowadays. Next came Christ's and Jesus; then the others with one or two houses each, St Catharine's, Bene't, Pembroke, King's, St Peter's, Sidney and three houses for Trinity Hall. All the lodgings listed were very close to college indeed, only the most central area being regarded as suitable.

Idly turning the pamphlet over, I made the most endearing discovery: scrawled in faint pencil on the back was a gardening memorandum — 'gooseberry stems, take up cabbages — sow flower seeds — spread double daisies' etc. What proctor's or librarian's hand had jotted down those instructions for his leisure time, almost 200 years ago?

When Charles Darwin gave up reading medicine at Edinburgh and came up to Christ's as a 'pensioner' (i.e. full fee-paying undergraduate) in the Lent Term 1828, he took lodgings over Bacon the Tobacconist who at that time had a shop in Sidney Street.[4] There is a blue plaque at first floor level on Boots, to mark the site. Checking this, in July 1993, in the shop-window directly below, a huge poster proclaiming 'any three condoms for 99p'. What would Darwin have thought of that? Some of us still remember a later Bacon's on Market Hill. While there he took up beetling, a hobby that was to have eventful consequences, and in emulation of his cousin took to keeping a dog. Later on, animals were forbidden in lodgings but evidently Mr Bacon was amenable.

---

3. Cam.c.818.1 1.

4. Adrian Desmond & James Moore, *Darwin*, Michael Joseph, 1991.

In the following year, Parliament passed a bill allowing dissenters and Roman Catholics to hold public office. But the University certainly did not practise thorough-going religious toleration; when a pair of troublemakers came to Cambridge preaching atheism, and lodged in the vacation with William Smith at 7 Rose Crescent, his licence was revoked on the grounds that he had been housing infidels.

TRINITY LODGE, *Nov. 9,* 1842.

———

ANNE CHALLIS, Lodging-House Keeper, of Jesus Lane, having been convicted before us of having her house in such a condition that her Lodgers could go out and come in during the night without her knowledge, and also of making inaccurate returns, Agreed that her Licence be revoked, and that notice thereof be sent to the Tutors of the several Colleges.

W. WHEWELL, *Vice-Chancellor.*

H. W. COOKSON, *Senior Proctor.*

J. H. HOWLETT, *Junior Proctor.*

Two or three more little printed notices survive, the lettering most handsomely done. Two are headed St Peter's Lodge, the Master of that college being the Vice-Chancellor of the day, and both dated February 1839.

AGREED, That the Lodging-House License of Wm. SHELDON of Magdalene Street, in the Parish of St Peter, be revoked and that notice thereof be sent to the Tutors of the several Colleges.

W. HODGSON, *Vice Chancellor.*

J. BURDAKIN, *Senr. Proctor.*

HENRY ARLETT, *Junr. Proctor.*

The second goes:

> AGREED,That the Lodging-House license of C Nurrish of Jesus
> Lane in the Parish of All Saints be revoked, in consequence of
> her having made a false return, and that notice thereof . . . etc.

The authorities were adamant from the first about doors being
locked and proper returns being made to College of the times at
which an undergraduate lodger entered the house after ten. Many
lodging-house-keepers must have felt sympathetic about one of
their men coming in late or being innocently delayed. Some could
no doubt be bribed or begged not to announce the irregular
behaviour. But there were serious consequences. Benjamin Lang-
ton living at 22 Jesus Lane in the Parish of All Saints was convicted
of making a false return and his licence was revoked for the Lent
Term 1853, a notice being sent to the tutors of all colleges. This
would effectively mean that he earned no rent for that whole term,
since no University member could lodge with him.

Evidently the University became convinced that a more formal-
ised structure was required for the proper control of lodging
houses, and in February 1854 a Syndicate was set up to advise. It
recommended that a Syndicate be permanently established, consisting of the Vice-Chancellor, the Proctors, the Proctors of the preceding year, and four other members of the Senate elected by
Grace, whose term of office and replacement were to be gradually
spaced-out so as to give a yearly infusion of new blood. And thus
was born the Lodging House Syndicate destined to live for 138
years, until its demise in September 1992.

The Syndicate acted immediately to define the limits within which
licences may be granted:

> No licence to houses situated on the north side of the Town
> beyond the road leading to Chesterton, and to none on that road
> beyond Wentworth House.[5]
> On the east and north east sides, to no house beyond Belmont
> Place in Newmarket Road, Emmanuel Road, Parker Street, Park
> Terrace and Regent Terrace.
> On the south to none beyond St Andrew's Terrace, Downing
> Terrace and Benet Place.

---

5. In this century the home of the literary critic I.A. Richards.

To the west and north west to no house beyond the river up-
wards from Magdalene Bridge.
(Wider limits will be allowed for houses licensed for married
lodgers only.)

Lodging-house keepers were soon required to make additional
promises to those already exacted under the form of licence.
Now they had to swear 'not to supply or receive for any student
provision for any entertainment whatever on Sunday without an
express permission signed by the lodger's Tutor', and on top of
that, 'not to receive as lodger any person who is not a member of
the University, without permission'. A little later, under the
Vice-Chancellorship of William Whewell, lodging-house keepers
were required to note in their returns the hour and minute at
which their lodgers came in after 10 at night.

The first list of persons licensed to let lodgings under the new
dispensation appeared on 29 May 1854, with the addresses listed
under the parish to which the house belonged. It was to appear
in this fashion until 1877 when the format changed and put the
streets in alphabetical order, with an index of streets showing
the page on which an address was given.

What is more intriguing from the point of view of social history is that the 1854 list specifies the occupation of the lodging-
house-keeper. Let us take a quick survey of the trades they
mostly pursued: this being Cambridge there was a high proportion of people producing clothes: shoemaker, tailor, bootmaker,
robe-maker, draper, staymaker, hatter, haberdasher, watch-
maker, they all served to make glorious the young gownsman.
Others attended to his studious side as bookseller, compositor,
printer, chapel clerk, stationer, university marshall, book-
binder, print-seller, engraver. And then there were the construction trades as upholsterer, carpenter, plasterer, plumber,
cabinet-maker, slater, whitesmith, brazier, paper-hanger. Where
eating played so large a part you naturally have baker, college
servant, fruiterer, confectioner, druggist (to attend after Feasts
called the Lesser Exceeding?)

But occupations like innkeeper or wine-merchant or brewer
are significantly absent from the list because no licence would be

granted to anyone dealing with intoxicating liquor, for obvious reasons. And in an economy where the horse was still the main mode of transport, here are the saddler, parcel-carrier, leather-cutter or livery-stable keeper. Toyshop-keeper, gardener and laundress don't quite fit into any of those categories. But what a catalogue of skills it makes. It is clear that the lodging-house keeper typically belongs to the artisan class and is a practitioner of a trade to which he was probably apprenticed, or that it took at least an appreciable time and practice to learn.

How would a modern street-survey compare, especially in terms of sheer practical usefulness?

The other deduction one can make is that it was the presence of the University with all its divergent needs that gave employment to most of these people and profited from the skills they had to offer. Town was indeed immensely on the payroll of Gown. Kelly's *Directory* for 1876 gives the main form of employment for the town as serving the needs of the University.

Before leaving the subject of occupations, one man made a queer combination of being a chiropodist and an upholsterer. Mr Green Kempton of 25 Jesus Lane was an osier-grower, presumably for making baskets; and James Addison of 18 Pembroke Street is described as a naturalist.

It is striking how the names survived and the profession of lodging-house keeping was handed down in families. Henry Vinsen who built coaches at 7 Downing Place in the parish of St Andrew's the Great must be the grandfather or great-grandfather of the Mary Vinsen who kept a genteel lodging house in my own time until a great age.

From early days it became one of the Syndicate's tasks to authorise the residence of those undergraduates who, for one reason or another, lodged in exceptional circumstances. It was recommended in December 1856 (and confirmed by the Council of the Senate in the following February) that the Syndicate be empowered to grant permission to students (on application from the Head of their College) to reside in their own or hired houses or with their relations, under special circumstances to be approved by the Syndicate. Two cases of men living in houses inadvertently not included in the licensed list were referred to the Senate and passed by Grace for the undergraduates concerned to be allowed to have kept term for the period in question. It was established that the Syndicate did not have the power to grant a licence retrospectively.

In February 1857, permission was given to 26 people to reside with their parents, uncles or aunts, or in their marital homes (some students were married). Pratt of Jesus was, in May of the same year, given permission to live in his hired house at 11 Trumpington Street and thereafter such permissions became more frequent. By the following year, Syndics had assimilated the new Council Statutes and considered their permission was no longer necessary for men to keep terms by residence in their parents' homes.

Throughout its life, the granting of permissions was a major Syndicate role, and in the first decades a record of each permission was printed formally and deposited with the Registrary.

It was rare for the Syndicate to be approached from outside the University and I have found no subsequent appeal to the memorial that the Cambridge clergy suddenly addressed to it in 1859. It is long-winded, but beautifully written out on blue paper and signed by fourteen signatories, the incumbents of the 14 Town Churches. I give it in full, both because of its interesting matter and because it so captures the flavour, caring but moralistic, of the mid nineteenth century.

A Memorial from the undersigned clergy of Cambridge to the Lodging Houses Syndicate.

Gentlemen. Recent investigation into the state of the Lodging Houses of Cambridge has brought to light facts, which must fill the Authorities of the University as well as those charged with spiritual oversight of the parishes of the Town, with alarm and anxiety.

In the first place, with regard to the servants employed in these houses, it is found that cases of the different kinds enumerated below, are not very uncommon.

1. Cases of girls being employed as servants in lodging houses, who are already prostitutes, though their real character is unknown to their employers.

2. Cases of servant girls in Lodging Houses being seduced by the lodgers, and being dismissed when their delinquency is found out.

3. Cases of servant girls in such houses being solicited by the friends of lodgers, and also of such attempts on their virtue being made, even when the lodgers themselves are steady men.

In the next place, with regard to the Keepers of Lodging Houses; altho' it is fully and thankfully acknowledged that a large number of them are respectable persons, and that they use laudable endeavours to prevent the occurrence of evil in their houses; still, there appears reason to fear, that not a few Lodging House Keepers do not take sufficient care to ascertain the good character of the servants whom they engage, or to protect the virtue of these girls whilst in their service; and further that there are some who actually connive at licentious practices, carried on in their houses and with their knowledge.

That the circumstances stated above are in some degree notorious in the class of society from which servants are obtained, will appear from the fact that Keepers of Lodging Houses in general and indeed even those of them who are most respectable, find great difficulty in obtaining really good servants. Young women who are careful of their own character have a great objection to becoming servants in Lodging Houses and respectable careful mothers are strongly averse to their daughters entering into such service.

It also appears that the discipline, which University authorities require to be observed, with respect to the time at which the students return home at night, and other such matters, is in many cases not sufficiently enforced. In some of the houses, the absence of the lodgers at a late hour is not reported so that facilities are afforded for irregularity and vice, which prove very detrimental to the morals of the students and also to those of the young women living in our parishes. The fact that there are not a few houses in which this laxity of discipline prevails, has a very injurious effect on those Lodging House Keepers who desire to act conscientiously. The competition among Lodging House Keepers is great, and the importance of letting their rooms as a means of supporting their families is so strongly felt by them, that those who are most anxious to act rightly are tempted to connive at conduct which in their consciences they condemn, and at irregularities which by the term of their licences they are bound to report.

We earnestly beg you, before granting Lodging House licences for another year, to consider whether some steps cannot be taken to stop, or at any rate, to mitigate these evils; and we venture to offer for your consideration the following suggestions for this end. The various plans here proposed might be employed either singly or in combination.

I. It might be ascertained how many students require accommodation outside college walls in ordinary years, and a limited number of licences might be issued according to the want of lodgings thus ascertained. The houses so licensed should be filled before any other licences were granted, and when they were full an additional number of houses might be licensed, if more were wanted, sufficient to supply the further demand. It is our opinion that in any scheme for the better regulation of Lodging Houses, the principle of limitation is very important.

II. The keepers of certain of these lodging houses whose respectability was thoroughly ascertained, might receive a guarantee that their houses should always be full, and in return for this guarantee they might be required either to wait upon the lodgers themselves, or to engage no servant who had not been approved by the Lodging House Syndicate. The least deviation from this rule should subject the housekeeper to the loss of his licence. We have reason to believe that they would gladly submit to this restriction on condition of the above named guarantee.

III. Houses might be hired by the various colleges and a system of out-college Porters and Bedmakers established. In each house there might be a man who should act as a College Porter, and a woman, his wife or sister, who should perform the duties of a College Bed-maker. These servants would be found by the college which hired the house; and the college would receive the rent of the rooms let as lodgings.

IV. The University might appoint a special Lodging House Inspector with proctorial authority, and might make it his duty to take care that the Regulations of the University with regard to Lodging Houses were duly observed and to report any infraction of them to the Lodging House Syndicate. His recommendation might be made a necessary condition for the granting of any Lodging House licence.

V. Lastly, Hostels might be erected and no student allowed to reside outside the walls of a college or hostel, except under special circumstances, and with special permission from the authorities of his college.

14 signatories from all the Town Churches

14 May 1859

After solemn conferrals in response to this thunderbolt, the Syndicate agreed the following statement:

1. That it (the Syndicate) shall meet for granting licences on the Tuesday after the division of the Michaelmas Term;

2. All applications for licences to be sent to the Vice-Chancellor a fortnight before, accompanied by a certificate signed by a Master and Tutor that the applicant is a person of good character and that the lodgings offered are healthy and clean and to be let at a reasonable sum;

3. Provisional licences may in special cases be issued during the course of the year;

4. Registers to be kept of all those licences granted, of all those refused, and of all suspended or revoked;

5. The lodging house keeper is to fasten the shutters as well as the doors, keep keys in his own possession, and the doors not to be opened after 10 except by the master or mistress in person.[6]

To our eyes, this doesn't answer the complaint of the clergy at all. Evidently some Syndics were in favour of including a further clause, to the effect that landlords should not employ a female servant under 30 but this paragraph is marked 'withdrawn' and never seems to have applied.

Another reason for describing this exchange in detail is because it ties up so neatly with the chapter on the Spinning-

---

6 Its confirmation signed by 'Jos. Romilly, Registrary' who wrote the splendid diary that sheds such light on the period, and who put in order the University archives.

House. As set forth there, many of the servant-girls employed in lodging houses were later to be clients of the House of Correction, and quite possibly the practice of terminating their employment at the end of terms played a part in turning their attention to another source of income.

The Syndics took their duties very seriously; the Vice-Chancellor himself attended in the Chair, and meetings were held every month, in some cases twice a month as at the beginning of the Michaelmas Term when they met in the Arts School to consider applicants for licences. Written objections had to go to the Vice-Chancellor beforehand, or the objectors could attend and confer with the Syndics in person. The flavour is that of a small community in which people knew their neighbours personally and could make valid estimations of their worth, honesty and reliability. Above all, the opinion of the Proctors was respected.

A licence to two people in Portugal Place was issued for the remainder of the term (Michaelmas 1858) only, 'there being an improper house in the neighbourhood'. But happily the following term the licence was extended, 'the Proctors having stated to the Syndicate that they are no longer dissatisfied with the condition of the neighbourhood'. The reader is shocked to find Frederick Mortlock, of the banking family, losing his licence for employing several servants found to be women of bad character. Worse still when Elizabeth Stevenson of 32 Green Street had her licence revoked for allowing a lodger 'to introduce a female and live with her there for a fortnight'.

Other heads were to roll: Mrs Cotchell of 10 Tennis Court Road lost her licence 'having contracted a habit of intoxication'; Pilson in Malcolm Street lost his for dishonest practices (unspecified), and Lazarus Cohen was not granted a licence because he 'was discommuned last term for lending money'.

Most shocking of all, we read that in May 1866 the Syndics agreed 'to revoke the licence of Mary Symonds of 11 Brunswick Place, who had been committed to the Spinning House on Wednesday last'. On consulting the Committal Book, the plot thickens considerably. Mary Symonds (or Simonds) turns out to be a woman of 40, judicially separated from her husband. The charge against her is not merely soliciting or street-walking: 'she was found with an undergraduate for an immoral purpose', and to show how seriously they regarded the incident she was imprisoned for 14 days. Her name never appears again. Was it, one can't help speculating, one of 'her boys'?

By the mid-sixties, it must have become evident that more lodgings were needed and would have to be sought in areas beyond the very centre of the town. So the radius within which licences could be granted was expanded to include Clarendon Street, Victoria Street, Earl Street and New Square. Park Side and Maids Causeway as far as Fair Street. The railway station at Cambridge opened on 30 July 1845 and heralded an unprecedented era of house-building and town expansion. A comparison of the Baker Map of 1830 with the Rowe Map of 1858 shows how the new streets fill up the fens, brickfields and open spaces. The cholera epidemics of 1848-9 alerted public attention to sanitation and the water supply, and led to the closing down of pestilent and overcrowded yards in the middle of the town.

The case of William Bruce shows how scrupulous the Syndicate was in observing the regulations; he was a '10 year man' of St Peter's College, 40 years of age and in Holy Orders, but unmarried. So he needed, and was granted special permission to reside in the house of Isaac Barber in Station Road, a house which had been licensed only for the use of married men.

An undergraduate had to be covered with special permission to keep the term at 23 Maids Causeway (past Fair Street and therefore beyond the formal limits) because he was forced to move out of his licensed lodging at 7 Park Street suddenly when a fellow lodger was seized with typhoid.

What noisy incident prompted the Syndicate to demand this extra promise from all landlords: 'not to admit hired musicians into my house at the instance of any student lodging with me, without an express permission signed by his College Tutor'? A note in the minutes of the Proctorial Syndicate gives us the clue: they had received a letter from the Rev. Charles Gray of Trinity making a complaint about 'the practice of bands of four to six musicians going into the Lodging Houses to play and sing in a noisy and sometimes

---

7. 25 November 1865. University Archives: Min.VI.6.

improper manner for the amusement of undergraduates; so making disturbances which must affect many neighbouring houses'.[7]

Syndics were empowered now to grant permission for residence retrospectively in cases where it was clear that the Tutor had been inadvertent in applying at the proper time, but they still had to recommend a Grace in order to do so, and this would have to go through the normal Council of the Senate procedure.

The Minutes suddenly reveal where the Syndicate met; evidently they had no fixed home and wandered from the Museums and Lecture Rooms to the Fitzwilliam Museum, to Christ's College Lodge when the Master invited them there, to the Syndicate Room at the University Library, the Senate House and the Divinity Schools.

A Trinity tutor complains that the rule about not requiring a student to take a room for more than one term was systematically violated; and that landlords generally raised the price of lodgings above that given in the printed lists. With possible reference to this, Syndics spelt out that licences were granted on the understanding that the prices named shall include all ordinary attendance.

In 1869 comes the first mention of a new animal, the non-collegiate student, and permission was granted to several people the following year 'on the recommendation of the Board for the Superintendence of non-collegiate students'. This foreshadows the setting-up of Fitzwilliam House. Such students were often older and had already been in employment. They sought university education perhaps in order to staff the schools set up now that the government had made elementary schooling compulsory. Certainly they came from a wider strata of society than previously, and brought with them a wealth of experience. Often they were already married. So the question of their residence was regarded more leniently from the first. Sarah Barker lost her licence at 32 Green Street for leaving the door open, but was allowed to keep non-collegiate students as lodgers.

In October 1873 it was agreed to grant licences for married men and noncollegiate students only to those persons who on 2 October 1873 had obtained licences for married men while non-collegiate students were increasingly given special permission to keep terms by residence with an M.A. of the university. They could evidently be trusted to work. But conventional undergraduates still had to be restrained from nipping in and out of windows at improper times, and poor Henry Cox at 68 Bridge Street was caught out with his shutters unsecured twice by the Senior Proctor. His licence was suspended 'so far as regards his ground-floor rooms until the end of the Midsummer Term'. But he must have ignored this because in May a policeman reported to the Watch Committee that Cox's shutters were unfastened again at 1.45 a.m. This time he was seriously admonished.

Sometimes the landlord stood up for the students. Mr Carpenter refused to give the name of the undergraduate from whose rooms on All Saints Passage a great noise of trumpet and other musical instruments proceeded, and to crown all, was insolent to the Senior Proctor. He had his licence revoked for the next Michaelmas Term and perhaps thereby lost all chance of letting.

A notice was sent round to all Tutors requesting them to make sure shutters could be fastened by means of a key kept by the landlord, before recommending ground floor rooms for licensing.

A landlord of Sidney Street lost his licence for leaving the door unlocked after 10 p.m. and 'that he took under his protection a notorious prostitute and walked with her past one of the pro-proctors'. And when the Junior Proctor was walking by Mrs Surrey's house at 27 Malcolin Street, he saw her niece throw a gown out of an upper window to enable a student outside to enter the house in his academical dress and so to deceive his Tutor (presumably waiting for him within).

The limits for licensing were extended yet again to include Hills Road as far as Station Road and the Causeway (Maids Causeway) as far as Brunswick Walk; and a year later (1875) Newmarket Road as far as Church Street, Panton Street, Norwich Street and Bateman Street, the three latter all in New Town. If applications for licences were not made to the University Marshall by the date publicly announced, a fee of two shillings and sixpence instead of one shilling was to be charged, if a licence was granted.

House physicians and house surgeons, needing to work in the wards overnight at Addenbrooke's, were given permission to keep terms while residing at the hospital.

At Michaelmas 1875 Mr. Cunningham, the Medical Officer of

Health, applied for a list of licensed lodging-houses and clearly interested himself in the level of sanitation offered. The Public Health Act had been passed in 1848 but it was not till the seventies that the laws were enforced. Did this public attention precipitate a momentous decision of the Syndicate? At the February meeting in 1876, they agreed 'that it is desirable that the Syndicate be empowered to appoint with the approval of the Senate, an Inspector of Lodging Houses, with stipend not exceeding £50 *per annum*', and that such an officer should be a member of the Senate. For over a year, sub-committees were formed and reports passed to and fro until the appointment of a secretary was confirmed by Grace of April 19 1877. Mr F.G. Howard of Trinity was chosen from the candidates in May, to hold office for a year in the first instance.[8]

In connexion with the residence of non-collegiate students, we hear now the first mention of Cavendish College, set up in 1876 as a fruition of the County Colleges Association's aim to spread higher education, particularly to would-be teachers. Its students came up at an earlier age than undergraduates and most expected to get degrees and become full members of the university. It closed in 1892 and its buildings in Hills Road were taken over and became the basis for Homerton College.

One of Mr Howard's first duties would have been to enquire into the case of Ellen Masterson and the conduct of her house. And here the chronological account is interrupted in order to look in depth at the effects of Syndicate intervention in the lives and conditions of lodging-house keepers.

---

8. It would be tedious to keep mentioning the appointment and reappointment of Secretaries. For a complete list, see Appendix I.

4

Crime and Punishment

Ever since the first secretary was appointed in May 1877, it has been one of his major duties to inspect the houses licensed under Syndicate rules. News of an impending visit would no doubt travel fast. I myself, in the relaxed and egalitarian nineteen eighties, remember a landlady whom I hadn't yet visited saying, 'O yes, I heard as Mrs Holbrook was in the Lane'. The tom-toms had been at work, and the Lane was of course Jesus Lane. But my calls were of a social and pastoral nature and coercion amounted to little more than a gentle suggestion that 'possibly these pillows could do with replacing' at sight of the stained and yellowed ticking on a bed stripped for the 'vac'.

Imagine instead a visit in the 1880s and 90s from the Revd F.G. Howard or the Revd W.W. Buckland, dark-suited (would he have worn his gown, this being an official visit?), a clerical collar, a high black hat or mortar board, gloved hand peremptory on bell or knocker. Surely poor Mrs Blagg's heart must have quivered with apprehension as she ushered him into her private parlour? For her livelihood was at stake. If she lost her licence there were no other students in the city to take her rooms, no factories and offices to supply alternative work that she could do, no unemployment pay to make up for lost income: and on top to bear the contumely of neighbours and the pain of lost reputation.

To revoke a licence was the final sanction, used quite frequently by the full Syndicate but only in extreme cases after cautioning and much consideration. There were many intermediate steps and they all involved a measure of interference in the lodging house-keeper's private life. To hold a licence meant the end of a private life indeed. The well-being, virtue and liberty to study of the undergraduate were paramount. The lodging house keeper was only on the scene to make his residence possible and to minister to his needs. The undergraduate was *in statu pupillari* and for the most part a minor. Towards him the university adopted a highly paternal role. So, to secure the right environment, in what ways did the Syndicate exercise its powers and how was the life of the lodging house-keeper affected? What did the Secretary's visit portend?

First, the Syndicate could part husband and wife. Let us return
to that Ellen Masterson who lived at 10 King's Parade, the most
central and desirable a place for a lodging house. She is in trouble.
The Syndicate has laid down that she is to have a provisional
licence in force only during the absence of her husband from Cambridge. Not only that but her wine licence is not to be renewed: she
can't have both wine and undergraduates on the same premises,
nor husband either. A year later she and another lodging house-
keeper, Eliza Mutimer of 2 Quayside, are each licensed on condition that their husbands do not enter the premises.

The following June (1879) Joseph Masterson, husband of Ellen,
appears in the minutes and is given permission to be at 10 King's
Parade during the daytime on condition he does not sleep there at
night. One wonders precisely what method of checking was in
force. But how is the marriage to survive such division? Rebecca
Moss's licence for 1887-8 will not be renewed if her husband remains in Cambridge. John Moss, a gyp, was proved guilty of
dishonesty, dismissed and must be turned out of his pretty house at
9 Little St Mary's Lane. Eleanor Constable would lose her licence
unless a distinct undertaking is given that her husband will not
have any access to the house at 19 Portugal Place either in or out of
term-time in 1893.

We are better informed about the domestic tragedy behind doors
at 11 Market Hill because when Edward White made an 'aggravated assault' on his wife one night in 1898 she rushed upstairs to
claim protection from her lodgers. The court case is fully reported
in the local newspaper and Mr White sentenced to a month's imprisonment with hard labour. His licence was revoked as a consequence and the Syndicate resolved not to transfer the licence to
Mrs White because they thought her incapable of managing so
large a house.

She was not altogether an innocent victim of a bullying husband
but culpable of employing as a servant a woman who had recently
had an illegitimate child. The minute goes on in brackets '(since
which the father had married her)'. But if Mrs White were to apply
for a licence for a smaller house, she might yet be successful on condition the husband is not admitted and any attempt on his part to

gain admittance reported to the Secretary. No hope of reconciliation there and poor battered Mrs White now has to find another home and move her children and furniture into it unaided, with a faint hope that maybe she'll be allowed to gain a livelihood one day as long as she stays alone.

What was there about 11 Market Hill that made the man of the house delinquent? A terse note the year previous to the incident above records that Hannah Eagle is to have a licence at that address conditional on her husband's complete exclusion from the house. So the Whites can't have been in possession more than a few months and now have to up sticks again. A later note in the locked black book records that Mrs White suddenly departed to Oxford where she took a licensed lodging-house.

Walter Scott belies his good name and is convicted for embezzlement. His licence is of course revoked but granted to his wife so that she can go on letting, though the occupation is described in January 1901 as having become less profitable lately. The Boer War has started and many sets are left unlet because the young men who would have occupied them have embarked for South Africa. Nevertheless Mrs Scott wants to carry on at 15 Park Parade and the Secretary, the newly appointed Revd. C.A.E. Pollock of Corpus Christi, is instructed to call on her to ascertain whether Mr Scott is to return to the house or not, on his release from gaol. He is to be released in December and the licence granted last October will be cancelled if he goes home. At the end of the Easter Term 1902 the Syndicate brought up Mrs Scott's case again and granted her a licence for the following year, 'in the hope that her husband may obtain regular work during that period'.

Maybe their attention had wandered because at the same meeting they had sat in judgment over the shocking case of a draper, Edward Boyce of Milton House on Christ's Pieces. He, much the worse for drink, had threatened and ill-treated his wife in such a brutal and public scene that the two Emmanuel men lodging there had to be removed to another house. The licence was to be held in future by Mrs Sarah Phoebe Boyce on condition that the lease and furniture of the house were made over to her legally and that Mr Boyce was not to be resident while the undergraduates were present.

There is a happier end to the story of Harriett Emma Farren whose husband had deserted her when they were running a house in Portugal Street. She is to be granted a licence at 23 Regent Street for 1902 if the Secretary can obtain satisfactory evidence of Mr Farren's reputable life since that sad time in 1896. Mr Pollock makes a favourable report in October and we surmise that they are back together in the new establishment.

Even in the twenties of the present century this marital intervention went on, though in this next case, with good reason behind it. Mrs Aves neglected to report to the Syndicate that her husband was affected with T.B. in the Long Vacation and had been removed to Papworth Hospital. She was severely reprimanded and the husband was not to return to the house without a medical certificate of freedom from infection.

Secondly, the Syndicate could and did split up a family. Anne Brazier had as her eldest daughter a girl subject to hysteria and at times unable to control herself. The Secretary was directed to inform Mrs Brazier that her licence could only be continued on condition that this daughter should be excluded from the house in term-time. The Syndicate had misgivings about another daughter whose conduct at 21 Market Hill was disapproved of on moral grounds: Mrs Emmerson was commanded to find somewhere else for her girl to live in term-time.

Miss Noakes, the Proctors said, had unsatisfactory associates at 19 St John's Street (just at the very time Rutherford was in lodgings opposite). Her mother was required to ensure she was absent from the house during term. When Mrs Noakes moved to 56 Jesus Lane two years later she was advised not to apply for a licence on account of continued complaints about this daughter's conduct.

William Sell's daughter had some years ago had an illegitimate child: it came to Syndicate ears that they had moved in with her father at 3 Little St Mary's Terrace. They were ordered to leave. A similar case has a happier outcome: the daughter of Sarah Neville of 8 Earl Street had had an illegitimate child away from Cambridge and had now (1897) returned to her mother's house. But since it was said that she was about to marry the father of the child, no steps were taken. As a wife she would not morally infect the young gentlemen lodging there.

The mother of a Caius undergraduate discovered (in his pocket, perhaps) a foolish letter written to her son by the landlord's daughter. Henry Ranner, a postman, was informed that his licence would be revoked if his daughter came to Cambridge while members of the University were in residence at his house in Gifford Place.

In 1906 a landlady's daughter, Miss Tupling, was reported to be suffering from T.B. Though she didn't sleep at Park Parade, she had her meals in the house. The Syndicate was sufficiently agitated to ask Dr Laurence Humphry of Lensfield Road to advise them, and he agreed to act, in matters such as this, as a 'standing referee', provided he had the concurrence of the doctor attending the patient, and the assent of the patient to have the nature of his illness communicated to the Syndicate. Having thus protected his Hippocratic oath, he reported that Miss Tupling was not expected to live long and her mother realised she would be unable to let her rooms for that Michaelmas Term. In the event the poor sufferer died conveniently on the first of October and the house having been disinfected under direction of the Medical Officer of Health, was after all available as lodgings.

Sometimes the premises were simply too full. When Robert Craven asked for a fifth set of rooms to be licensed at 6 Bene't Street, he was refused on the grounds that an additional bedroom was required for the proper accommodation of his own family. Evidently the Secretary had been round to inspect the sleeping arrangements. He must have been shocked when he called at 18 Silver Street, then a lodging-house (office of the Lodging House Syndicate from 1960 to 1992 and presently of the Accommodation Syndicate) to find that Mrs Storey, being short of space allowed sons of 13 and 11 to share a bedroom with her maidservants, several years older. She was severely reprimanded.

Even in 1992 a house in King Street was so overcrowded that the licence was not renewed. Five children slept in the minute kitchen and four in one bedroom, and water was not laid on in the W.C.

Non-family members of the household were also under surveillance. From early days the Syndicate complained about the character of girls employed as maidservants in lodging-houses. As seen in the chapter on the Spinning-House. Mrs Parsley of 12 Trumpington Street and Mrs Ellis of 72 Jesus Lane were called before the

Syndicate and censured for having received into their service without making proper enquiry — and for afterwards retaining — two
girls who had lost their character. A Tutor of King's complained
that an immoral girl had been employed at 12 King's Parade, and
the Syndicate being aware of the fact summoned Mr Stroud to appear before them at a meeting six days hence. He was questioned
but did not satisfy the Syndicate that he properly appreciated the
responsibilities and duties of a lodging house-keeper and was told
he must apply at the end of term with fresh testimonials if his
licence was to be renewed.

When the Proctors found and reported a front door unfastened
in Park Parade the owners excused themselves to the Syndicate by
saying they had gone out and their young servant had left the door
open. Unfortunately she lied to the Proctors, claiming that an older
woman was present in the house. She was dismissed on Syndicate
orders.

On occasion, it was the premises themselves that were unsatisfactory, perhaps because a moneylender carried on his business in a
room of the house on certain days of the week, or where the landlord was also licensed to sell beer on the premises like Alfred Bar-
ratt in Bridge Street, or wine and spirits as did Edmund Graves in
Bene't Street. Paget of 22 Bridge Street was refused a licence
because he was a pawnbroker.

For some reason in 1892 whole streets were declared undesirable, and no licences were granted to houses in North Terrace,
Willow Walk and Coe Fen Terrace. The clue to this is that all three
streets border commonland, Coe Fen and Midsummer Common.
And there are contemporary accounts of how respectable women
could not walk in these areas (certainly not after dark) because they
were so notoriously the haunt of prostitutes and their customers.
Frequently these outdoor couplings would be accompanied by violence, oaths and drunkenness — not a pretty sight for the innocent
undergraduate. (*v*. ch. 2 for the account of an appalling murder
near Brunswick Walk.)

A letter was sent in January 1893 by Mr Musgrave Francis, a solicitor, on behalf of his client Mrs Burbush asking the Syndicate to
reconsider their proposed action about the subletting of part of her
premises in Bridge Street as a tobacconist's shop. The danger was

that a young woman had been placed in sole charge of this shop. The Syndicate did not like the arrangement and desired a change but allowed the arrangement to continue for the present, without fear of a withdrawal of the licence.

They went to extraordinary lengths in 1904 to set out the conditions under which Mr Peck the chemist at 25 Fitzwilliam Street could hold a licence. When any University lodger was in residence, the following steps must be adhered to:

> that the door from the shop parlour be treated as if it were a second front door to the house and locked by Mr Brewster at 10 p.m.;
> that Mr Peck shall only be able to enter the house by this door after 10 p.m. by ringing a bell from the shop parlour;
> that University lodgers shall not use this door at any time and no-one but Mr Peck himself shall use it after 10 p.m.

Mrs Flack was only allowed a licence till the end of the year (1894) because her house at 38 Jesus Lane had unsatisfactory conveniences. When the Bursar of Jesus (who owned the house) wrote to expostulate at this decision, the Syndicate refused to change their mind. It is interesting that the College did not offer to improve the sanitary arrangements.

An application from Eliza Blunson to have a lodging house at 3a St Mary's Passage was refused on the grounds that the School of Cookery was conducted at that address. No doubt the point was that attractive young women would be in and out all day while acquiring the culinary art.

The licences held by Hugh Welford and other tenants in Portugal Place were not to be renewed in 1893 'unless the Syndicate are thoroughly satisfied as to the dryness of the basements'. Present day Welfords live in their basement at Portugal Street so I trust the damp problem has been cured in the interim.

There are signs that the Proctors, the Chief Constable and the Watch Committee all kept on very good terms and exchanged information on crime and offenders and possible trouble-spots to their mutual advantage. In several cases members of the Syndicate were also magistrates and would have personal experience of police court cases. Certainly they read the local weekly newspaper,

The *Cambridge Chronicle* and were aware when the members of the community were arrested and charged. Anyone convicted of a crime was certain to lose his licence.

Robert Alderton had his licence in Rose Crescent revoked and five subsequent applications refused as a result of a court case about fighting with a cab-driver over a fare at the station. W. Pont of 8 Short Street was denied a licence because he 'supplied a prostitute with saddle-horses' according to the Senior Proctor. Thomas John Hobson of 4 Coe Fen Terrace was sentenced to three months' hard labour for embezzling and stealing £12.10.0. from his employer and had his licence revoked in consequence. Emma Kemp was reprimanded for employing Edle Smith, convicted of stealing a registered letter containing £5 from an undergraduate.

Miss Hannah Mills made an application to run a lodging house at 24 Orchard Street but had it rescinded on information that she had two illegitimate children and had been suspected of conniving at the thefts committed by one of these in certain churches. Another cab-driver Arthur Bell lost his temper at the railway station and used obscene language for which he paid in 14 days' hard labour and the loss of his licence in Victoria Street. His more modem equivalent a taxi-driver, Charles Wallman, appeared as a defendant in affiliation proceedings in 1921, and in the course of the case, evidence was given that his taxi was employed for immoral purposes. Wallman lost the licence for both taxi and lodging house.

Daisy Hayward was reported by the police as having been drunk on Coe Fen and quarrelling with a drunken man. Her house was subsequently raided by the Proctors as undergraduates were known to be resorting there for purposes of drinking. The Thurgood daughters were seen consorting with undergraduates and this report by the Proctors was confirmed by the women police. Their mother lost her licence, and so did Mrs Kissner whose daughter lived at home and was reported by the police as *persona de malo suspecta* and figuring on their black list.

A complicated case concerns a publican, Alfred Fletcher, who in 1884 ran a lodging house at 11 Park Place and the Miller's Arms in King Street. He was convicted and fined (and lost his licence) for supplying liquor after hours to a man who was already intoxicated and in the company of two loose women. It must have been a very luckless evening because the women later stole the drunk's watch and money.

The dusty court books in the County Record Office at Shire Hall are full of cases (in the magistrates' court and at petty sessions) of felony, perjury, bastardy, theft, assault, robbery with violence and using obscene language. The magistrates sat every day of the week, dealing out summary justice. Quarrelling neighbours made frequent appearances and sometimes there were lodging house-keepers. Mrs F. Newman of 4 Parker Street was cautioned for uttering scandalous statements against Mrs S. Newman of 5 Parker Street. Were they sisters-in-law? And the licences of Mrs Stubbings and Mrs Barker at 19 and 20 Portugal Place were not renewed, partly because of their quarrels and also on the grounds of the inconvenient arrangements in the construction of the two adjacent houses.

The modern mind finds it hard to excuse the Syndicate for taking away the licence of George Cooper in Trinity Street. His 'crime' was to have encouraged the marriage of his daughter Eva to Mr F. Starkie, lately an undergraduate of Trinity Hall and lodging at this address. But land and money and estates had to be protected and the University in 1884 could only see this as an unfortunate alliance.

Sometimes there is no question of a criminal record, only a vague suspicion that all is not above-board. What are we to make of an application (for a licence) refused to the Rev. S.M. Statham, B.A. of Queens', 'because of questionable past conduct and connection of Mrs Statham, née Clara Bull of Park Street'? Was that another mesalliance? A photographer in Hills Road was deemed unsuitable, 'his examination in bankruptcy having been most unsatisfactory'.

No-one could have been more virtuous than Josiah Chater, first a men's outfitter and tailor and then founder of the accountancy firm that still bears his name.[9] He lived, with two or three servants and nine children at 19 Fitzwilliam Street and applied for a licence in 1880. But his application was refused since he insisted on being allowed to fix his own prices, and the Syndicate of course would not

1. Enid Parker has edited his fascinating diary, 1844-1884, under the title Victorian Cambridge, 1975.

tolerate such a condition. It was just as well in fact because the Chater children were very prone to measles and whooping cough and
diptheria, and at one moment Mrs Chater had eight of them in bed
at the same time.

The Secretary was gifted with the knack of turning up at the
lodging-house at precisely the wrong moment, and several licences
were lost in this manner. In July 1881 he found Sarah Miller in a
state of intoxication at 6 Park Street: she had been a bedmaker at
Caius and they had dismissed her in the Lent Term for the same
weakness. In August 1926 at one p.m. the then Secretary found
Mrs Lawrence completely drunk when he called at 2 Free School
Lane. On several occasions undergraduates were removed from a
house by their Tutor because of their landlady's insobriety.

Other entries in the secret locked book kept by the Secretary are
so cryptic as to leave one breathless with unsatisfied expectation.
John Hunt of 54 Trumpington Street is not to have a licence granted, 'Ruined servant summer 1892'. And what shall we think of
T.R. Hubbard of Prospect House, who 'was severely reprimanded
for allowing Madame Blondin to lodge in his house without permission'? Presumably he offended against the rule that forbade the
landlord to take lodgers other than members of the University
without consulting the Secretary. Was Madame Blondin part of a
theatrical troupe or a circus?

Alfred Brockett was refused a licence because he had his mother
living with him in Thompson's Lane. She had been dismissed from
service at King's, 'having been found with a gyp under disgraceful
circumstances'. In respectable Maid's Causeway, Miss Ransom
could not qualify as a lodging house-keeper because 'Mr Ransom
convict late of Bridge Street proposed to live in the same house
with his children'.

Another cause of offence not so far touched on was betting,
coursing, and frequenting with low characters of the turf and gam-
ing-table. William Arthur Plumb (22 Sleaford Street) was concerned in a case of 'welshing' at Cottenham Races; the son, living at
the house, was convicted and fined — so father lost his licence.

5

Fin de Siècle

The extent to which the Syndicate scrutinised and controlled the private life of its licence-holders was considerable but most lodging house keepers were entirely respectable and law-abiding, getting on with their business without Syndicate intervention. However other concerns occupied that body.

For one thing, they worried about students sharing rooms. Farming out the responsibility, they agreed in 1878 that all applications for licences for the joint use of one sitting-room by two undergraduates be made through the college tutor concerned. But in the case of two non-collegiate students (note again the different standard applying to this species), both called Craster and presumably brothers, the Syndicate itself gave permission for them to occupy one sitting-room and one double-bedded sleeping-room at 26 Hills Road. By 1882 they had unbent on this point so far as to give several pairs of undergraduates permission to keep term while residing at houses where they shared a sitting-room as long as they had separate bedrooms, and this applied even to brothers

Landlords had to pay for the privilege of a licence and the following scale of charges was adopted:

1/- in ordinary cases
2/6 if the application was made within the fortnight before the general licensing day (in November each year)
5/- if the application for the current term was made after the general licensing day

An account of all fees from applicants was to be kept in a book, to be laid on the table at meetings.

But the really important issue of the day was water. 'When, in Victorian times, it was still considered that it was not necessary to provide baths for undergraduates because terms lasted for only eight weeks, a student of Trinity acquired a tin bath and asked the bedmakers to fill it with water from the fountain. These venerable ladies were indignant, but the situation was resolved by the forma-

---

1. Quoted from *The Cambridge Nobody Knows* by F A Reeve.

tion of the Waterworks Company in 1853.[1] Provost Okes and Whewell effectively founded the company, not so much out of concern
for the town's hygiene and convenience. but because King's was
given money to have a fountain.

The Secretary was directed (May 1878) to draw up a circular,
warning landlords about the dangerous state of well-water in the
town. The Syndicate considered it highly important that water
from the Cambridge University and Town Waterworks should be
laid on to all houses, and to encourage this, account was to be taken
in future in fixing rents. The houses so supplied would have a
distinguishing mark in the printed list of licensed houses, and
rooms in those thus singled out would command a higher rent.
And so the list published that Michaelmas has asterisks indicating
those houses connected to the waterworks: It gives the occupation
of the householder, the number in the street and the price of each
set per week.

In 1879 the list is sixteen pages long, bearing witness to the newly
extended radius within which licences could be granted: 'on the
west and north sides of the Town as far as the River, Magdalene
Street and the Chesterton Road (to Strange Villas).[2] On the east
and south sides of the Town as far as Brunswick Walk, Newmarket
Road (to Christ Church), Fair Street, New Square, Jesus Terrace,
Elm Street, Melbourne Place, Parkside, Park Terrace, Regent Terrace, St Andrew's Terrace, Hills Road (to the Railway Bridge) and
Bateman Street.'

Cambridge was growing, particularly in the area towards the station. The town had been lit by gas from as early as 1834 and electricity was to appear in the 1890s with Peterhouse the first college to
be lighted throughout by this means. Now we hear of proposals for
a new tramway system. The trams are horse-drawn, and 30 horses
are to be employed. The track is laid from the station to a terminus
opposite Christ's with two side-tracks, one to King's Parade and
Market Hill, the other to the tram terminus in East Road on a site
bought from William Eaden Lilley. The first passengers travelled
by tram on 28 October 1880.

---

2. Isaac Strange, the Boat builder, had built two villas and given them his own name,
on some ground going down to the river alongside Magdalene Fellows' Garden, formerly Strange Yard.

The trams ran until 1914 when they were finally ousted by the faster and more efficient omnibus companies. A joke of the time went, 'If you're in a hurry, walk. If not, take a tram'. Josiah Chater was a prime mover in the setting up of the tram service and was employed as the Cambridge Secretary. When their last child was born (the thirteenth) they christened him Bertram and thought that very witty.

But to revert to the subject of water, by 1883 the Secretary (T.F.C. Huddlestone of King's) was in a position to send out a printed notice to all Tutors reporting that 766 lodging-houses were licensed that November, of which 613 or 80% were supplied with water, either from the waterworks or from satisfactorily-tested well water. He went on to recommend Tutors to send their pupils to the better-provided houses, so as eventually to bring about the disuse of well-water where a satisfactory analysis was not forthcoming. The Secretary was authorised, as such, to become a member of the Cambridge Sanitary Association, then in course of formation. Two years later, of 764 licensed houses, 662 were supplied with water from Cambridge Waterworks and 92 with well-water examined and passed by a competent Analyst. These houses provided 1552 sets of rooms of which 1383 were occupied in Michaelmas 1884.

A report from the University Chemical Laboratory stated that the well-water of the house of William Coe at 51 Jesus Lane was bad and contaminated. (There were water and drainage problems in Jesus Lane even in the present writer's day.) He was told that his licence would be revoked unless he got the house connected to the waterworks by the 25th of March, 1885.

A note to the Senate remarked, revealingly, that though the number of matriculating students had increased, new college buildings and changes affecting residence had caused a lessened demand for lodgings: on that score, the Syndicate proposed not to extend the area of licensing any further at that stage and no licence was to be granted if the water supply was not satisfactory.

The Syndicate made known its wish to appoint an Inspector to help the Secretary monitor sanitary conditions, and recommended a salary of £50 a year to be paid to such an officer. The Senate gave its approval, and the duties of the inspector were laid down very specifically:

He shall supply the Secretary with a sketch diagram, when practicable, of the drains and pipes of the house inspected, and
with a written report thereon, which the Inspector shall treat
as confidential and for the information only of the Syndicate.
He shall specify in his report what work is necessary to put the
house into proper condition so as to secure the following ob-
jects, viz:

1. that the sewage shall have free exit from the premises;
2. that no sewage gas shall find its way through the house
drains into the house
3. that the drainage system of the house shall be isolated from
the Public Sewer in such a manner as shall prevent germs of
disease from entering the house through the drainage system;
4. that the water supply to the house shall be
uncontaminated;
5. that the house shall be well ventilated;

He is to distinguish what is primary and what secondary in recommending construction work, and he is to inspect the house
during and after the execution of the work prescribed. He is not
to have any pecuniary interest in the trade or in any patent connected with sanitary appliances. Clearly a new standard of public
health is being called into operation.

Mr David Bland of 203 Chesterton Road was appointed Sanitary Inspector to the Syndicate, and the Secretary was authorised
to take in the *Sanitary Record*, price ten shillings annually.

A clue to this fervent interest in drainage is given by an item
in the minutes for 1882. A house where there had been a fever
the previous term, 11 Trumpington Street, was ordered to show
a certificate from the Medical Officer of Health stating that the
house was satisfactory from a sanitary point of view, but he declined to issue the document. The architect, W.M. Fawcett, was
requested to inspect the house by the lodging-house-keeper.
After insisting on certain alterations being carried out, Mr
Fawcett approved the sanitary conditions and the licence was
thereupon granted. One wonders how many other cases there
were before the Syndicate felt sufficiently prompted to appoint
their own officer? The 'fever' presumably was typhoid.

Making a change of emphasis, the Syndicate received (in February 1883) a memorial from the Executive Committee of the Women's Union about young servants employed in lodging-houses. The Secretary was given the task of ensuring that satisfactory arrangements were made, both for the proper charge of the house and for the lodging of the young employees. A vast amount of scuffling about in servants' garrets would have been entailed. We next read that Mr Howard's health did not permit him to offer himself for re-election. A record was made of the admirable manner in which he had discharged his duties.

Where, all this while, was the Syndicate's work carried out? In June 1880 they agreed 'to ask the Press Syndicate to allow them the use of the Registry as an office for the following year, provided that the Registrary (if he returns) does not object. The Pitt Press had demolished six inns in Silver Street to make room for their new printing house in 1833 but in fact they made little use of their grand space and at first the Fitzwilliam Museum stored its overflow there. Then the building was taken over by the Registry as the central office of the University, and stayed there till 1936 when it moved to the Old Schools under Dr Keynes.

If the Registrary objected the Secretary was authorised to hire a room and also to engage a clerk at a stipend not exceeding £15 *per annum*. So in December 1881 we find the Syndics agreeing to allow three guineas a year for the use of a room at 4 New Square as an office for the Syndicate. This address is also the home of the Junior University Marshall, John Sheldrick, and the sum of £4 was allowed to him as Clerk to the Syndicate in November 1883 to buy himself a writing-table.

The affairs of the Shallow family occupied the Syndicate's attention on several occasions. First the Proctors reported they had a complaint about his shop. Thomas Shallow kept a tobacconist's at 2 Rose Crescent, and in 1879 'the Secretary was directed to caution him and to inform him that if occasion for complaint should arise again, his licence would be withdrawn'. The warning must have sufficed and no word is heard for 18 years when the licence was transferred from Thomas Shallow to his widow, Flora Shallow. Flora must have got sick of the tobacco business and longed for something more fragrant, because by 1902 she is running a florist's as well as a lodging house. Being so named she perhaps thought it more appropriate.

Let us take a look at some of the occupations listed in the eighteen eighties. There were 10 lodging-houses in Willow Walk. William Carpenter at 2 Willow Walk was a Pindar, that is the man appointed to take care of straying animals, lock them up in the Pound and charge their owners for restoring them. There was of course a Pound near Pound Hill, over in the Castle Ward of the Borough, but maybe, living at that address he looked after a nearer enclosure somewhere on Butts Green or Midsummer Common. In 1885 Mary Ann Nichols of 5 Brunswick Place is described as a cow keeper: presumably she escorted cows on to the Common and home again. She also looked after three students. Dennis Greenwood of 59 Jesus Lane describes himself rather poetically as a yeoman. Caroline Stanley was a cork cutter; Henry Morgan a bath proprietor in St Andrew's Street. Alfred Edwards of 18 St Edward's Passage a billiard-table keeper and Edward Broom of 2 Portugal Place a boot closer.

But new forms of employment are making an appearance. H.J. Adams of Melbourne Place was a telegraph clerk, Thomas Metcalfe of 5 Earl Street an Assistant at the New Museums, Thomas Applin of 4 Clare Terrace a Rifle Instructor. and yet three more Thomases, Thomas Crowhill of 10 Brunswick Place is a Sanitary Inspector, Thomas Woods a bit further along at 17 Brunswick Place a soda water manufacturer, and Thomas Stearn a photographer at 72 Bridge Street.

In 1891 James Flitton, living at 4 Norwich Street, describes himself as a colliery agent. A lodging-house keeper in Tennis Court Road has the splendid name of Kerenhappuch or Clark. Henry William Hardy of 2 Little St Mary's Terrace is a swimming-master — the Terrace was along the river at the bottom of Little St Mary's Lane, where the Graduate Centre now stands and he was conveniently near the water for early morning swims. Emmeline Bays appears as a hatter and hosier at 11 King's Parade in lists after 1886, and many readers may remember Mr Bays at New & Lingwoods. By the turn of the century, we raise our eyebrows as the new woman enters the scene: Blanche Maud McPherson is a gymnasium proprietor at 9 Peas Hill.

F.E. Thomas of 1 Malcolm Street was 'a philosophical instrument maker'. His enviable peace of mind was disturbed however by events of Michaelmas 1902 when he was admonished for taking into his house a lodger, formerly a member of the University, without asking leave. Apparently the visitor celebrated too carelessly his return to Cambridge: 'a disturbance took place in the house and a bottle was thrown out into the street'.

As early as 1880, the Vice-Chancellor had been requested to communicate with the Heads of Colleges as to the returns of students residing in lodgings: this was to help the Secretary to know exactly who and what number of lodgers was in any given house. In addition a lodging house keeper was required to obtain the permission of the Syndicate and of each of his undergraduate's Tutors before taking as a lodger anyone who was not a member of the University. 'A proposed arrangement whereby Nurse Paterson, when not engaged on her professional duties, should board with her friend Mrs Law at 1 Green Street (a room being placed at her disposal) — was considered to constitute her a lodger and to be undesirable in a licensed lodging house'.

Thomas Hubbard of Prospect House received a lodger (in the locked book the 'lodger' turns out to be 'Madame Blondini) without permission and was summoned to appear before the Syndicate to make his explanations. The Vice-Chancellor, Dr Searle, let him off with a caution but when Mrs Bowyer of 2 Earl Street had appeared on the same charge on three occasions, she had had her licence suspended for the Easter Term and thus lost the income from three sets, a not inconsiderable sum. In 1895, Mr Vokes was hauled over the coals for taking two lady lodgers without permission, but they were allowed to stay for the rest of the current term. Perhaps it was May Week. This charitable view did not last till May 1900 however, when T. Mason of 76 Trumpington Street asked if he could take as a lodger a lady engaged in research in Cambridge. Permission was refused and a printed notice was sent out reminding lodging house keepers that they were not allowed to take non-members of the University into their houses.

Landladies were expected to take on a great deal of responsibility for the students under their roof. Two examples from the nineties come to mind. 'March, '92. A licence was granted to Emily Wagstaff of 15 Portugal Place after she had given explanations as to the misconduct of one or more of her lodgers in getting out of her house one morning in January last at 3 a.m. and breaking a street lamp. Mrs Wagstaff was admonished to be more careful in the future'. Was she expected to stay up all night? And in April 1894 we read of a more complicated incident, not a prank at all. 'Mrs Scruby, lodging house keeper 50 Bridge Street appeared before the Syndicate in consequence of a complaint through the Proctors that she had allowed the lodgers to leave the house about 12.30 (a.m.) to assist a helpless man in the street, and that she had not reported the same. Mrs Scruby having been heard was considered justified in having let her lodgers out of the house, but was seriously cautioned for not complying with the Regulations and reporting the same.'

Interestingly enough a letter to me from a Caius *alumnus* of 1943-5 describes a very similar incident: J.A. Robinson writes: 'the other event concerns the very rigid rule which allowed us to enter the house up to midnight but under no circumstances to leave between 10 p.m. and midnight. On one night about 11 p.m. I partially witnessed a knife fight in Park Street which left one man injured and groaning on the pavement. In no way would the landlord (a Mr Holmes) allow me out to see what might be done. Nor did the police really want to get me involved in giving evidence and were very glad when I had nothing useful to offer'. And that was in the height of World War II.

Before moving into the twentieth century we ought to take a look at the various kinds of cases for permission to reside exceptionally that came before the Syndicate.

The question of the student's means is raised in this specimen: 'S.H. Fullerton of Queens' was given permission to keep terms while residing at 25 Emery Street, together with his brother-in-law A Atkinson, a married non-collegiate student and graduate of the Royal University of Ireland, Fullerton being an orphan and in needy circumstances'. This was followed by a stern note: 'This permission is not to be taken as a precedent'.

In 1891, a non-collegiate student (for whom you remember there was always more free dispensation) was allowed to live out of licensed lodgings 'with Mr Orriss, noted to be 70 years of age and married'. The student in question is 'a minister of the Countess of

Huntingdon's Connection', a religious sect of the time. The Syndicate were extremely scrutinising about the owners of houses where students were allowed to live. Clearly Mr Orriss is deemed not to present a threat of any kind, and H. Knowles of Corpus Christi was permitted to keep terms while residing 'with his sister who is many years older than himself' and not presumably a nubile flighty girl who might lead him into temptation. It is odd to contrast this strict care with the state of the town described in the Spinning House chapter.

Unusually, two Sedgwick brothers were given special permission to occupy two sitting-rooms and a common bedroom in licensed lodgings. This relaxation of the rules was followed up in the next year (1894) by a printed note to all lodging house keepers spelling out that under no circumstances are less than 4 rooms to be let to two undergraduates unless they are brothers, in which case full information must at once be sent to the Secretary at 1 Mill Lane (note new address).

Permission was rather grudgingly given to R.H. Connolly of the Downside Benedictine Monastery, Bath, to keep the Michaelmas term at the house of and under the charge of Baron von Hilgel, M.A., in Barton Road: the Syndics refused to commit themselves at that stage for a longer period. Anatole von Hilgel was Curator of the University Collection of Archaeology and Ethnography.

Even brothers were not always thought to be safe: R. Narayanam of King's was told he could share a bedroom for one term only with his brother (not a member of the University) at 14 St Edward's Passage and the Tutor of King's was to be notified that permission would not be extended. Nevertheless here he is a year later applying for permission for Narayanam to live at 44 Park Street, and the Syndics unbent sufficiently to approve of his sharing a sitting room with this brother as long as they had separate bedrooms. It was agreed (October 1895) that the Secretary should be allowed, at his discretion and with the assent of the Tutors concerned, to grant permission to a married undergraduate to reside with his wife in licensed lodgings where other undergraduates were keeping residence.

In the penultimate year of the century the question arose of the Syndicate being empowered to grant permission for residence while students were in Addenbrooke's Hospital or in recognised nursing-homes, the institution to have first obtained formal recognition from the Syndicate. This was put to the Senate and by Grace of February 1900 Ordinances were amended to permit such residence where approved by the Syndicate.

Dr Searle had been Chairman of the Syndicate for many years as deputy for the Vice-Chancellor but is himself made Vice-Chancellor in January 1889. The Secretary (Mr Huddlestone for much of this period) and his sanitary inspector have been active on the water improvements, and can report that of 736 houses licensed in 1891-1892 678 are connected to the waterworks. It was agreed not to accept applications except where the Company's water had been laid on. When a new Secretary, H.G. Fuller of Peterhouse, took over in 1892 he was given the following general instructions:

1. that houses with but one, and that an outside W.C., where the approach was through any room in use, or the back outside premises permit of egress, will be considered unsatisfactory;
2. that in all cases the waterworks must be laid on to the W.Cs;
3. that the tenants in St John's Road be given notice that an inside W.C. will be required;

When there was a change of tenancy sanitary requirements of a more stringent character would be insisted on before a new licence could be granted.

Mr Fuller could report that improvements had been carried out in 86 houses in accordance with Syndicate instructions. But then he falls ill and a temporary secretary acts during his absence. In June 1895 Mr W.W. Chawner of Emmanuel, who had sat on the Syndicate for several years, is elected Secretary and the Deputy Vice-Chancellor conveys to Mr Fuller their appreciation of his services and sympathy with him in his ill-health. But that October Mr Chawner announced that he wished to resign the office at an early date, and the Syndicate has to go through the appointing process all over again, electing W.W. Buckland to the post. He is to advertise for a new sanitary inspector to replace Mr David Bland who has died. But no appointment. was made and the Secretary was authorised to arrange for freelance sanitary inspections as and when needed.

Nevertheless, W.W. Chawner, now Master of Emmanuel, signed the Minutes in 1896 as Deputy for the Vice-Chancellor and Chairman of the Syndicate.

In June 1899 he resigned from the Lodging House Syndicate and was Vice-Chancellor himself for the following academic year. Meanwhile Mr Huddlestone has been made a member of the Syndicate. The office at 4 New Square is open from two to four o'clock and the Secretary is available during Term in his room at Caius from noon to one thirty daily and from six to seven thirty on Mondays, Wednesdays, and Fridays.

It would have been Buckland who had several tricky situations to deal with: Robert Tyers of 2 Malcolm Street had his licence suspended till the end of the academic year for employing a girl of bad character and, compounding his fault, for continuing to employ her knowing of her misconduct. Mrs Tyers was called to appear before the Syndicate and would be required to submit testimonials of character before the licence could be renewed. Mr Sadler was said to be not sober in his habits and his wife an habitual drunkard. He was summoned to account for the pair of them, and admitted the truth of the charge. The Syndicate adjudged that he was not to take lodgers and not to apply for a licence till they could produce clear evidence of reformation. In Sidney Street Mrs Mutimer had been another to employ a servant of extremely bad character without making proper enquiry of the girl's antecedents. But as her employment had only been outside term, Mrs M. got away with a warning.

Mr Buckland must have pursued this theme with vigilance: at 8 Bene't Street (in recent times, Hockeys Estate Agents occupied these premises and a director described them as 'a warren of staircases'), T.F. Stanley had his licence revoked for employing a girl knowing her to have had two illegitimate children and to have been dismissed from a lodging house a year before on the grounds of immorality. Stanley worsened the case by having a cousin who was a betting-agent frequent the house. Another lodging house keeper got mixed up in the business: A.T. Roff of 17 Botolph Lane admitted employing the same servant and only dismissing her after finding out her second misconduct. He was reprimanded only, not having any dubious cousins on the premises. These several cases were enough to cause the Chairman, in February 1899, to direct a circular to be prepared advising lodging house keepers that they would be required to produce to the Secretary satisfactory written 'characters' (i.e. references) for any servant in their employ. In the Minutes of the Proctorial Syndicate for March 1900, Mr Buckland signs as a Pro-Proctor.

In the course of Buckland's inspection of houses in the Long Vacation of 1900 he made out the following table:

> 350 houses employed no servant
> 53 had a day girl
> 248 had a resident servant

But maid-servants would often have been dismissed at the end of the Easter Term and the figures would be affected by this.

Mr Coward of 21 Maids Causeway is reported as having refused to have his child vaccinated (against smallpox). He had covered himself by obtaining a certificate of exemption, but the Secretary was ordered to communicate the fact to his lodgers' Tutor(s).

A severe case of doormanship revolved around 17 Park Parade where the Syndicate approved of Henry Hall entrusting the front door key to his daughter after 11 in case of necessity. He is partially paralysed and requires attendance at night, and on that account Mrs Hall is sometimes unable to go to the door. Miss Hall is 32 years old.

Letting lodgings at the turn of the century is described as having become less profitable: the number of sets remaining unlet had gone up considerably and the reason is that so many young men had departed for South Africa to take part in the Boer War.

The Syndicate must have been somewhat startled in April 1901 when it was reported that Buckland too had left for the Cape, with no prospect of his return for at least a year, though his motive is on health grounds: they expressed their sense of the loss sustained and appointed J.H. Gray, M.A. of Queens', to fill the gap. He is sent off to ascertain from Mrs Scott at 15 Park Parade whether her husband is to return to the house or not, on his release from gaol. No licence will be forthcoming if he does. Walter Scott had been convicted of embezzlement.

6

The Firm Rule of Pollock

Here begins the long reign of the Rev. C.A.E. Pollock, of Corpus Christi, appointed in June 1901 and destined to stay till 1913, when he became Bursar of Corpus for 15 years and President from 1921-28. Charles Archibald Edmund Pollock had been sixth wrangler in 1881, was made a Fellow, ordained deacon and then priest at Ely in 1888, and was college Dean (1895-1901). Born at Holly Lodge, Vale of Health, Hampstead in 1858, he married at the age of 38 Grace Isabel, daughter of the late Canon G.B. Blenkin, and they lived for many years at 19 Chaucer Road.

He served Cambridge in many capacities, as Councillor, Alderman, Chairman of Addenbrooke's Hospital, and in 1942 had the honorary freedom of the Borough conferred on him for 50 years of public service, being then the oldest member of the Council. On that occasion he was described as 'a little austere and unapproachable to those who did not know him but possessed of many human qualities and by no means lacking in a sense of humour'.

One needs to reconcile this somewhat grim image with the news that he was an ardent cyclist and won fame as a young man by travelling all the way to Nice on his penny-farthing. At the Cambridgeshire Collection in the City Library are stored all his wedding journey bills in Switzerland. He died in 1944 aged 86 and his obituary records that:

> In 1901 he was appointed Secretary to the Lodging House Syndicate, a post for which his knowledge of the town peculiarly fitted him, and his inspection of the houses was sufficiently drastic to lead to great improvements in their sanitary arrangements.
>
> He was a man not easy to know, but his heart beat warmly and affectionately beneath what appeared to be a cold exterior and in times of trouble, undergraduates and colleagues were perhaps astonished at the tenderness of the sympathy that poured out from such an unexpected source.

Pollock did sterling work in the fields of elementary education and youth training, but I can imagine that he struck terror in the hearts of erring landladies.

However, let us return to those empty sets and note the Syndicate on that account relaxed the rule about permanent lodgers. For example, two elderly ladies, the Misses Haslop, are given permission to occupy a set at 10 Downing Terrace (in Lensfield Road), and, even more daring, an 18 year old elementary teacher is to live with the family at 1 Earl Street, it being understoood that Mrs Beale, the landlady, is held responsible for Miss Bendall.

There is another change in the staffing that November.

> Mr Sheldrick, the Clerk to the Syndicate being no longer able to perform the work, it was agreed to appoint F.W. Cowles as Clerk at £20 *per annum*, subject to a quarter's notice, to include all work done by him and attendance at his father's house, 8 Christ's Lane, to distribute forms and give advice to applicants for licences. Certificate forms to lodging house keepers to be sent out by messenger at the beginning of the Michaelmas Term instead of being distributed to applicants at the Clerk's house as hitherto.

Mrs Esther Pratt made an application to be licensed at 69 Jesus Lane but was refused in accordance with the Regulation of February 1899 that a licence should not be given to a woman permanently employed out of her house for a substantial part of the day.

Mr Pollock had to visit Francis Cherry in Clarendon Street although the Chairman had already been to see him about his unfastened window and had noted his unsatisfactory character: now he is reported as several times the worse for drink. (Remember that Pollock has married the daughter of the Senior Proctor). Mr Cherry is warned he will forfeit his licence if it happens again.

Another licence is in jeopardy in Earl Street. The wife of C.W. Jarvis has left her house and her husband in consequence of his continued drunkenness. Mr Jarvis stated he was going away to sea so that his wife could return to the house (and thus be assured of a livelihood). Desperate remedies, but the Syndicate instructed Mr Pollock to recover the licence, or if refused, to notify its cancellation to all colleges.

In his annual report for 1902, the Secretary notes that he had permission to use the records of the public health committee. Mr Burwick had been employed to report on the sanitary condition of newly-proposed houses to see if they qualified for licensing. The improvements in standards are impressive. The number of licensed houses has decreased to 639, but only 193 sets have remained unlet this year, partly because Caius are making extra use of lodgings while their building operations go forward in Rose Crescent. They opened St Michael's Court the following year.

A fine of one shilling is to be levied on a lodging house keeper who is late in sending in a certificate, or claiming a licence or making a return of the lodgers resident in his house. The Syndicate is prompted to make an exact interpretation of the rules and decides that a lodging house keeper may admit friends of an M.A. to his rooms after 10, whether they are undergraduates or not.

There must have been a smallpox scare because a circular is sent out, requiring all non-University residents in a lodging house to be vaccinated and a formal list returned to the Secretary. But this is not enough action and letters appear in the *Spectator* complaining of sanitary conditions in University lodgings (November 1902). The Secretary is urgently instructed to employ a competent sanitary inspector, not resident in Cambridge, to prepare a report on houses appearing to him unsatisfactory.

Dr Collingridge of Christ's, Medical Officer of Health for the City of London, seemed the man for the job, and had agreed to report on sanitary conditions. He visited 21 houses pre-selected by the Secretary and Mr Hills, a sanitary inspector, had looked at others under Dr Collingridge's instructions. Six houses were singled out as inadequate by Collingridge and three licences were not to be renewed, all in Trumpington Street. Mr Hills was to be employed to inspect every lodging house and the University made a grant of £50 for his remuneration.

In the midst of all this sanitary fervour comes an outcrop of incontinent daughters: Mrs Bragg's daughter at 63 Jesus Lane is about to have a child, the father a former University lodger, and two other lodging house keepers' daughters — in Bene't Street and Market Street — are said to be living immoral lives. All three mothers state their intention to give up their licences at the end of the Lent Term, Mrs Bragg having no alternative.

A note refers to an epidemic of smallpox in the Long Vacation of 1903 as a result of which the emphasis on re-vaccination is renewed. But no case of smallpox occurs in any lodging house.

The Secretary had cause to send out the following notice under his own signature:

> The attention of the Syndicate has been called to the fact that commissions are sometimes offered to lodging house keepers and others in connexion with the supply of caps and gowns to freshmen. The Syndicate desire to warn lodging house keepers against accepting any gratuity from tradesmen in this and similar cases.

At this period, the Syndicate fixed nine meetings a year and had the dates printed on a special card. They met usually at 2.30 on Mondays, and on one occasion they placed on record their grateful appreciation of the services rendered by Dr Peile, Master of Christ's, during his long tenure of the office of Chairman (till May 1904).

Mr Coward's licence at 21 Maids Causeway is not to be renewed. We have met Mr Coward before, having set views about compulsory vaccination: now it appears that he, his wife and five children have not been re-vaccinated and three other children have never been vaccinated at all.

Three M.A.s residing in the Market Place were refused permission to have latch keys because an undergraduate was also resident. Presumably the trio could come in at what hour they chose, but had to ring the bell and await entry. After a discussion, the Syndicate recommended to the Senate two amendments to Ordinances; one that regulations for advanced students be relaxed as regards residence; two, that lodging house keepers should be required to give notice to the Secretary of any resident suffering from T.B.

In January 1905 the Secretary is able to report that Mr Hills has spent ten days in Cambridge. The Town Inspectors had also been active and an additonal inspector had been re-appointed. Houses in and around Park Parade had been thoroughly overhauled and defective outside drains reconstructed. The 614 licensed houses afforded 1481 sets, of which 264 were unlet, with a large number of rooms vacant in Jesus Lane and Malcolm Street, many of them desirable apartments.

The following Michaelmas he brings the sad news that A.W. Cobbett, whom he had employed over Easter to make a sanitary inspection of a large number of houses, had fallen. from a window ledge while inspecting a house in Portugal Place, and fractured the base of his skull. He had had to spend some time in Addenbrooke's and at Dovercourt (a convalescent home) but was still not fit for work (six months after the accident). Mr Cobbett had been attempting to block a ventilating shaft although at the time of his engagement Mr Pollock had impressed upon him that he was to test drains without blocking ventilating shafts. So the Syndicate was assured that it had no legal liability for the accident. Nevertheless it benevolently agreed to vote him six guineas in consideration of the expense of his accident.

In the absence of any system of social security or sick pay, what, one wonders, did the Cobbett family live on during the summer of 1905? However, he is reported back at work in the New Year and the large entry the previous October means an unusually high number of undergraduates in lodgings. The Secretary warns that if there is a similarly big intake the following academic year, it may be difficult for men to find rooms. He hopes the Syndicate may therefore consider it desirable to allow two men to share a sitting room, a privilege at present only granted to brothers, and in a a few cases, cousins.

In fact, there was a shortfall thanks to the large freshmen entries of 1905 and 1906. Many of the houses formerly licensed would not, as they stand, come up to the present more stringent sanitary standards, and the Secretary was forced to insert a paragraph in the *Cambridge Express* to recruit more lodgings. He also wrote to parish priests asking them to notify him where licences might be granted.

The Senior Proctor reported a complaint from the police about Miss Kempton of 25 Jesus Lane, who had refused to give the names of her lodgers when requested to do so by a police constable whose helmet had been knocked off by a magazine thrown from the window. The Secretary was instructed to censure her.

The Syndicate went on to discuss whether the water supply had possibly been contaminated by sewage from Fulbourn Asylum, where lately there had been an epidemic of typhoid fever. The Chairman was to alert the Council of the Senate to this danger. Evidently the Senate listened because, after a meeting of the

Bursars and Stewards, the Vice-Chancellor issued a memorandum on these lines:

> 1. The Town Council was to be asked to examine water supplies to the town and reports to be open to inspection;
> 2. The meeting did indeed think there was danger of contamination;
> 3. The Colleges and the Lodging House Syndicate were advised to take precautions re supply of water and milk.

A mysterious note in the Minutes reads as follows:

> Some discussion took place with reference to means of escape from lodgings in the event of fire; and also with reference to organ grinders, Mr Macaulay mentioning that the police would take action upon the application of any lodging house keeper at the request of the Syndicate.

What on earth was the connexion? Anyway, the Secretary was to notify lodging house keepers that it was intended, where necessary, to require the provision of means of escape in case of fire. Jumping out of windows was no longer adequate protection.

Some of the many permissions granted are a little out of the ordinary. On the application of the Master of Magdalene, Prince Leopold of Battenberg was allowed to keep terms at 15 Fitzwilliam Street 'until his rooms in College were ready'. Perhaps he was having them magnificently painted. And L. Wolff of Caius. an advanced student and French lector, was given permission to live at 'Oak Lea', a house in Oxford Road on these grounds: 'he suffers from sleeplessness and his medic advises his residing on as high ground as possible'.

By 1908 the Syndicate was saying publicly that it would receive applications from houses beyond the ordinary limits of previous years and an article in the newspapers drew attention to this. Just enough lodgings were forthcoming. The Secretary reported that nearly all houses in the central district suitable for lodgings had already been licensed. Some properties were lost on account of University expansion; two houses had been pulled down in Free School Lane so as to extend the Cavendish Laboratory, and one in Silver Street to allow the University Pitt Press to expand. A large number of people were on the look-out for a suitable house in which to set up as a lodging house keeper. New buildings at Pembroke and King's were expected to ease the situation.

The list of licensed lodgings for that year takes up 19 pages, and the number of sets goes up yearly by 100 or 150, the figures testifying to Mr Pollock's industry and the willingness of town residents to make their homes available.

The Secretary is instructed to have printed a form of bill for use by lodging house keepers to record termly charges for coal, gas, electric light etc. More and more amenities are gradually being regarded as indispensible. But Mr Pollock must take care not to be too precipitate in his eagerness to license. B.A.s of Sidney Sussex had to leave the house of Mr Judge at 147 Chesterton Road on account of his drunkenness: his licence just granted was hastily withdrawn and the list was printed without including his name. Although expressly forbidden to do so by the Secretary, Mr House at 30 St Andrew's Street had allowed a young female servant to sleep in a room at the top of the house while he and his wife slept on a lower floor. Mr House was called to a meeting and cautioned.

A hint of the growing professionalism of the office is given by the instruction to Mr. Pollock to have a form of bill printed for use by lodging-house keepers to record charges for fuel and electricity. By 1907 a printed form appears, on which the details for the granting of individual permissions are to be entered. In November 1909 the Syndicate sent a report to the Council of the Senate asserting the need occasionally to issue provisional licences, e.g. where a lodging-house keeper dies during the course of the term, and requesting authority to give permission retrospectively in appropriate cases, with a forfeit payment of £1 to the Common Chest if a Tutor sought permission on behalf of his pupil for a period longer than the Term in which he remembered to apply.

Special arrangements were made for listing licensed houses for the sole use of non-collegiate students, and in 1910 the Council of the Senate saw no objection to an increase of up to twelve in the number of residents at St Edmund's House and Cheshunt College if so desired by these institutions. The Syndicate approved a total of twelve at St Edmund's, and the junior Proctor and the Secretary were detailed off to inspect Cheshunt and report back. The inspection proved satisfactory and no objection was made to the residence of twelve undergraduates there.

The Priory Nursing Home in Newmarket Road was approved as a place in which undergraduates could, with permission, keep terms.

Keeping a lodging house is clearly both profitable and socially acceptable: a lodging-house keeper waiting to retire is able to make most favourable terms with his successor and a price is paid for furniture greatly in excess of its value. This compulsory purchase of the house contents was a custom. long to continue: I myself well remember the groans and bitter complaints of incoming tenants to houses in, for example, Jesus Lane, who had been forced to pay perhaps a couple of thousand pounds 'key-money' for racketty old washstands, shattered cane chairs and grisly worn 'old-gold' carpets that were, very soon after their arrival, conspicuous in skips at the road-side.

Mr Cowles, the Clerk to the Syndicate must have impressed others with his efficiency because he was also appointed the 'Vice-Chancellor's Clerk and clerk to the Financial Board'. (One wonders how many assistant staff members carry out these functions nowadays?) This was not thought permanently desirable but the Syndicate permitted the plurality till the end of the year. His pay was £25 *per annum*. By December 1910 he was no longer able to act as Clerk and was replaced by Mr. Southcott of 7 Green Street who as a new boy came cheaper at £20.

Mr. Pollock, ever vigilant, had cause to censure Mrs Camham of 4 Rose Crescent who had allowed letters and telegrams to be sent to her house for forwarding to a bookmaker in London. And he reported Mrs Catleugh of 11 Bateman Street who allowed her lodgers to be on terms of intimacy with her daughters: the Syndicate requested the Chairman to interview Mrs Catleugh and point out to the erring woman that this conduct could not be approved. Another dangerously tempting daughter appears at 70 Trumpington Street and her father F.S. Sheldrick, is only to be given a licence if he arranges for her to be absent from Cambridge in term time.

In January 1911 it is reported that 831 houses are licensed, affording 2,040 sets: an increase of 35% in houses and 40% in sets over the previous six years. But the following year 395 sets are unlet and supply exceeds demand. New accommodation has been built at King's and Magdalene and 60 sets are in course of erection at Emmanuel and 30 at Queens'. Fewer men than formerly now stay up after completing 3 years of residence and this is especially so as regards medical students (who no doubt had to go off to London and Edinburgh to complete their clinical training).

The standard of lodgings is improving all the time; bathrooms have been added to a great many houses in the last few years and sanitary conditions have steadily bettered. But the Secretary remains alert to matters of public health. Mr Izzard, a lodging-house keeper at 2 Tennis Court Terrace, is diagnosed as suffering from an early form of phthisis. Dr Humphry, whom we have met before, is consulted and says that the sputum should be examined from time to time, and a report made to the Syndicate if tubercle bacilli are found to be present. The lodging-house keeper and his doctor were so informed.

A licence may be granted to Mr Coward of Maids Causeway but is to be withdrawn if smallpox occurs in Cambridge: the attentive reader will remember Mr Coward was the one with strong objections to vaccination. 1913 sees a great many infectious diseases about, mainly scarlet fever and diphtheria, but there is no evidence of any undergraduate catching infection from the family with whom he lodged.

The Granta Home for Nurses at 70 Hills Road is approved as a nursing institution where residence may be permitted.

An addition is to be inserted in the licence:

When a student is temporarily absent from Cambridge during Term, the lodging-house keeper is authorised to lock up his rooms and will be held responsible for any disorder or mischief arising from neglect of this precaution.

7

The Shadow of War

At Michaelmas 1913 our benevolent despot was appointed Bursar of Corpus and resigned his post. It was advertised in a printed notice put out by the Chairman, Edward Beck. Twenty candidates were considered and in December M.R. James, the Vice-Chancellor and Provost of King's, announced the appointment of F.M. Rushmore, M.A. of St Catharine's, for three years, still at the old salary of £150 *per annum*.

Mr Rushmore's first year in office seems marked with action against immorality or even conviviality. Mrs Field of 15 Norwich Street was severely reprimanded for leaving the house open after 10 and, what is worse, for entertaining a party of undergraduates. at supper. In May 1914 the Senior Proctor reported that two girls of loose character had spent an hour one afternoon in the rooms of an undergraduate at 5 Market Street.

Mr and Mrs Moden appeared before the assembled Syndicate and were warned to be more vigilant. So was Miss Lofts rebuked for allowing a girl of doubtful character to spend two-and-a-half hours upstairs at 8 Earl Street. Did the Senior Proctor stand outside with a stopwatch? The Chairman informed the Syndicate that non-University visitors were known to have remained in licensed rooms long after midnight, and as there was no regulation against it, the lodging house keeper was powerless to cause them to leave. The Secretary was to consult Dr Keynes, the Registrary, in this matter.

On complaints received from the Senior Proctor, the Secretary had secured dismissal of one maid-servant at 25 Fitzwilliam Street and had allowed another to continue on sufferance until the end of term only, at 5 St Mary's Passage. This Senior Proctor was indefatigable in office: he informed the Secretary that Mr Cook of 69 Jesus Lane was guilty of immorality with a servant formerly employed in the house. On being challenged, Mr Cook admitted the charge was true. Mrs Cook was then informed that her licence would be continued only on condition her husband left the house within ten days. Mr Rushmore's intervention was so successful that he was able to report Mr Cook had left Cambridge altogether. Next on the list comes Charles Hermges, a waiter, keeping a lodging house at 50 Maids Causeway: he was admonished for using insulting language to a lodger.

Meanwhile the Non-Collegiate Students Board put in a proposal to receive at 25 Fitzwilliam Street not more than twelve undergraduates under the charge of an officer appointed by the Board. The Syndicate looked into it and sent a memo to the Senate (May 1914) who agreed that the Syndicate was within its powers in granting permission for a limited group of students to live in the premises of the Non-Collegiate Board, provided that the names of students and particulars of the circumstances were laid before the Syndicate in each case. Thus was conceived Fitzwilliam College, though no-one realised it at the time, and all such pettifogging matters paled before the advent of war.

Events happened so quickly that by October 1914 the Secretary was reporting 770 houses licensed, 447 of which had no university lodger in residence. They had all gone to the front. That November Rushmore worked out an interesting breakdown on the ownership of lodging houses:

85 were owned by the lodging house keepers themselves.
528 were owned by private persons and let.
136 were owned by colleges of the University.
8 were owned by Cambridge Corporation.

In January 1915 the Secretary reported that 'soldiers were billetted in approximately five sevenths of the houses and this to a considerable extent made up for the loss suffered by the absence of University lodgers'.

At Michaelmas 1914 only 1700 undergraduates were in residence: by 1916 only 575. The billetting was to continue through the Lent Term of 1915 and only five lodging-house keepers had applied to the Borough Distress Committee for relief. But as the war moved into its second year, the Secretary was to report that 100 lodging house keepers had given up their vocation because of the war and at least another hundred should be advised to give up in view of the uncertainty of the future.

One senses a very real social problem here, and many suffered great distress because all their capital had been sunk in furnishing the house, and it was impossible in the circumstances to realise their money by selling the furniture (since no-one wanted it) and beyond their means to store it. Many lodging house keepers were elderly and had no other chance of employment. The worst cases were notified to the local relief committee and sustenance grants were made, to keep their heads above water. But the old social pride at being an independent lodging-house keeper must have been sorely wounded.

Poignant signs of the times come in the list of permissions granted; Stephenson, an undergraduate of Clare, is given permission in 1916 to keep terms at the Leys where he is appointed resident music master 'owing to the dearth of masters in consequence of the war'. And Harrison, a third-year undergraduate at Caius, is allowed to keep terms at Addenbrooke's where he is acting as Assistant House Surgeon 'on account of the great difficulty in obtaining the services of a qualified doctor for such work'.

In January 1916, Mr Pollock's name appears again in the Minutes, this time in the guise of a Syndic: he raises the question of allowing certain undergraduates to share a sitting room and this is informally discussed. Surely when eighteen-year-olds were daily being thrust into positions of vast authority and habitually in danger of losing their lives, these minor restrictions on conduct must have seemed singularly incongruous? But it was to take another war to make that point finally.

Some of the poor victims survived and came to Cambridge to study, like B. Hardwick, an undergraduate of 25, wounded and discharged from the Army in 1917 who appears as a candidate for holy orders. In June 1918 a research student was allowed to count as residence nights spent by him in charge of patients suffering from gas-poisoning at the Balfour Laboratory: and many invalid officers in the army were given permission to live outside the licensed system, by now hugely depleted and reduced.

A meeting of the Syndicate was held on 12 November 1918 but no note of relief or joy at the cessation of hostilities creeps into the Minutes. In the New Year the signs of revival are manifest. The Syndicate held an earnest discussion on how to increase the number of lodging-houses and on providing lodgings for overseas students, a new source of intake. It was thought advisable that no such students should come up until lodgings could be procured, so the necessity was urgent. An advertisement appeared in the press urging townspeople to renew lapsed licences and new lodging house keepers to apply, the Syndicate promising to extend the area beyond that hitherto fixed.

College tutors were invited to a special meeting called for May 1919, at which Syndics convinced them of the need to raise the price of lodgings if enough accommodation was to be secured. A charge for services in lodgings, not exceeding one quarter of the licensed rent was to apply from Michaelmas. One particular need was to house officers from overseas troops of the U.S. Forces, who were sent to Cambridge to carry on their studies for a short period. Householders were sought willing to receive such officers as paying guests: it was stipulated that they would dine in College. Dozens of married men, presumably ex-servicemen, were given permission to reside in hired houses.

A Royal Commission reported on Oxbridge in 1919 and the whole University must have felt under review and on parade.

Mr Rushmore, who had served faithfully throughout the war, perhaps found his energy flagging and retired in June, before the onslaught arrived. His place was taken by Dr T.A. Walker of Peterhouse, whose first task for the Syndicate was to define the limits within which lodging-houses could be licensed, a power last exercised in 1879.

After an immediate review, it was announced that licences might be granted for suitable houses anywhere within $2\frac{1}{2}$ miles of Great St Mary's. These limits now matched the precincts as laid down by the Council of the Senate in 1914. Walker was faced with an unparalleled situation and must have improvised wildly. He was able to report himself in receipt of applications under unprecedented conditions, ranging from bedsitting rooms (the first time the word has been used) to large premises let on special terms to lodging house keepers or managed by college caretakers, and to huts proposed to be erected within the precincts of the University. Cambridge must have conditioned itself to makeshift erections and emergency plans — was not Neville's Court at Trinity adapted during the War as an open-air hospital for wounded soldiers, with wards along the cloisters?

In the present dearth, Cheshunt College offered to house under-graduates. We sense the strain on the office. That October, in view of the increased demand for accommodation, it was agreed to make more frequent inspections of lodging-houses, to check on cleanliness and proper supervision. Syndics first thought such in-spections would be most effectively carried out by a woman and re-commended the appointment of a woman inspector, but at a later discussion, they produced a set of objections to such a step.

To secure a satisfactory officer it would be necessary to offer at least £150 *per annum* (i.e. the same stipend as that paid to the Secretary), her visits might be resented 'especially by new lodging house keepers of a superior class' and it would be difficult to distinguish between the duties of the Inspector and those of the Secretary. Thrown by contemplation of such embarrassing difficul-ties, the Syndics resolved to postpone their recommendation 'In view of present unsettled conditions' — a comfortable excuse. However, the proposition that a woman's competence at house-keeping might be useful and profitable had got into the composite Syndicate mind, and was to emerge later, as we shall see.

Next came Mr Southcott, the Clerk, asking for an increase. It was agreed to pay him £5 for recent extra work and to raise his annual stipend to £30. In similar spirit, a petition arrived from fifty lodg-ing house keepers seeking an advance of 50% on room-rents. The Syndics dismissed the claim as unreasonable but rooms were to be reassessed with an eye to present-day conditions.

Dr Walker had busied himself in investigating the circumstances of non-collegiate students residing with Mr Joseph at 28 & 29 Trumpington Street. Mr Joseph is an M.A. of the University and occupies with his wife the two lower floors at 29 Trumpington Street. A married undergraduate, too badly wounded to come up alone and unaided, lives with his wife in two rooms at 28 Trump-ington Street. Ten other undergraduates occupy rooms in the two houses. In addition, Fitzwilliam Hall has acquired seven other houses in the neighbourhood (in Fitzwilliam. Street) and has instal-led lodging-house keepers to look after these non-collegiate stud-ents. The Chairman undertook to lay the facts before the Council of the Senate and seek their instructions, first interviewing the Chairman of the non-Collegiate Board. He and the Censor were invited to a meeting of Syndics to discuss the status of 28-29 Trumpington Street and the Council of the Senate (which had set up a committee to investigate) was considering a change of Ordinances to cover the residence of students in houses provided by colleges: they recommended treating these houses on the lines followed in the case of St Edmund's Hostel and Cheshunt College.

Over 100 undergraduates and non-collegiate students were given permission to keep terms in unlicensed accommodation in October 1919, another 30 that December, and for Michaelmas 1920 the list of permissions takes up $4\frac{1}{2}$ pages of the Minutes. Cambridge must have been bursting at the seams. Among those granted approval was, Henry Morris of King's later to be Director of Education for Cambridge and originator of the Village Colleges; as a graduate of Oxford he was allowed to keep terms at 2 St Andrew's Terrace.

An application was received on behalf of G.W.L. Darwin (later Sir George Darwin), an undergraduate of Trinity, to count as residence seven nights (28 February — 5 March 1920) at the house of his aunt, Lady Darwin, at Newnham Grange, while suffering from water on the knee: this was approved, subject to the production of a Medical Certificate. The Master of Christ's wrote about the case of some Benedictine monks, who were undergraduates, living in a Benedictine establishment now removed to 13 Park Terrace under the care of an M.D. The Syndicate ruled that Heads of Colleges were to apply on their behalf in the usual way.

Sympathetic Mr Pollock raised the question of the Secretary's stipend in view of the hugely increased workload he was forced to carry, and when this was put to the Financial Board, they replied that the Syndicate should recommend an increase to the Council of the Senate. As a result, Dr Walker's salary was increased to £250 *per annum* as from March 1920.

8

Into the Twenties

In June 1920, 573 lodging-house keepers combined together and signed a petition asking for a further increase of 25% on present permitted charges, due to the increase in the cost of labour and of household commodities. The Syndics could not consent but directed the Secretary to revalue the older licensed houses, and increases of the order of 10 to 15 shillings per week were suggested. Notices warning of rising charges were to be sent to all colleges. Meantime, Mr Southcott, the Clerk, asked for more pay and got a bonus of £10.

At Michaelmas the University population (of undergraduates) reached 5733, many being helped to afford their course of study by state scholarships and ex-service grants. (Since the October of 1891 County Councils had been enabled to award scholarships to poor boys, but the War vastly accelerated the process.) By the New Year, 1828 licences had been granted. In spite of the whirl of getting all these men under cover (women undergraduates had of course arrived now[1] but were safely ensconced behind their college walls and made no claim on lodgings) Dr Walker finds time to comment on the laxity of lodging-house keepers over the rule about locking up by ten.

These householders are still not happy about the income they are making from letting: now they argue that room rents should go up because their own rent has been raised, by at least two of the colleges, under the Rents Restriction Act. They get the answer that no advance could be made in mid-year and they should so inform the estate agents. Bursars might be invited to take some action, it is suggested. The role of Colleges as landlords is becoming more of a factor.

The President of Magdalene informed the Syndicate that the premises lately known as the Nursing Hostel, Thompson's Lane would in future be ranked as part of the College buildings, and known as Neville's House.

---

1 Girton 1873; Newnham 1875. Women were awarded the titles of degrees in 1921 but not admitted to full membership till 1947.

Eliza Jane Mason ran a huge house at 16-21 Market Street, affording 18 sets for Caius men, but she was discovered to be engaged in other undertakings in the town; distracting her from her occupation as a lodging-house keeper. The Secretary was instructed to write to the College to suggest another arrangement be made. A letter was sent to him complaining of the character and career of Mrs Ellen Elizabeth Smith of 81 Mill Road and since the police confirmed this adverse report, her licence was withdrawn. So standards were maintained even though space was vital. But maybe Dr Walker is exhausted after licensing 1610 houses in 1921, providing the University with 3003 sets of rooms. Certainly his post is advertised and the applications of four candidates are considered, 'the present Secretary not offering himself for re-election'. Two candidates were invited to a special meeting and of these Captain J. T. Baines, M.A. of Trinity, was elected.

He proceeds to tidy up a few lodging house keepers: Mr Taylor's wife at 7 Regent Terrace is a confirmed drunkard so their licence is promptly cancelled. On the other hand when it is discovered that the Vincents' unmarried daughter of 28 has an illegitimate child dating from the war and living with her in the parental lodging at 14 Earl Street, their application for a licence is granted on the grounds that Mr and Mrs Vincent are thoroughly respectable people with good references. Perhaps Captain Baines was going to apply more enlightened standards?

The Secretary of the Financial Board proposed raising the licence charge from a shilling to two shillings and sixpence and the Syndicate set up a sub-committee to ponder so radical a move, the charge not having been changed for 40 years. The list of lodging-houses is to have a different format: the rents are to be quoted on a termly basis, not weekly; the addresses are to appear in alphabetical order throughout; without reference to districts, and the parishes are to be omitted altogether. No doubt with the changes in local government, the old role of the parish in administrative matters had weakened to vanishing-point.

A second sub-committee is to prepare a report on changing Ordinances to cover residence in houses other than lodging houses. Here we see the beginning of the Syndicate's power to authorise hostels, and when the recommendation was passed by Grace in

January 1923, the first applications rolled in from Colleges seeking to use given premises under the new dispensation: Gonville & Caius were given permission to house not more than 11 undergraduates at 26 Green Street; Magdalene to use Neville House, Thompson's Lane for 14; and the Non-Collegiate Board to put men into 3 & 19 Fitzwilliam Street.

Decisions such as these raised the question of the proctors' authority over unlicensed houses where students had been given permission to keep terms: Syndicate permission was to be conditional on the proctors' having the same right of entry, (i.e. in the event of disturbance) as they possess in the case of licensed lodging-houses. As for the licence fee, that was to remain at a shilling until the end of the present academic year. The salary of the Clerk was raised by £10, giving him a salary of £40 plus a bonus of £10 as from the New Year, 1923.

That March a lodging-house keeper lost his licence on unfamiliar grounds; W.A. Plumb of 22 Sleaford Street must have appeared in Court as being concerned in a case of 'welshing' at Cottenham Races, and his son was convicted of the offence. Mrs C.J. Taylor of 6 St Clements Gardens had failed to report a case of measles in the house. Hauled before the Syndicate, she was interviewed and the Secretary instructed to write a letter of severe reprimand.

The Syndicate sent a report to the Senate on an addition they thought it advisable to insert in the undertaking given by lodging-house keepers, to the effect that they would report to the junior Proctor when any undergraduate proposes to keep a motor bicycle or other motor vehicle at his lodging.

The recommendation was passed by Grace in June 1923 and marks the control the University still exerts over students and the traffic problem. lodging-house keepers were also advised to ask their lodgers at the division of term whether they required their rooms for the following term or not. This was intended to prevent misunderstandings in future.

Maybe the postwar boom was beginning now to subside and thus the pressure on lodgings was easing? Word went out that licences granted to houses in Cherry Hinton, Romsey Town, East Road and adjacent streets would not be extended except in cases where the present lodgers wanted to continue for another year.

What plumbing and a pure water supply were to the 'nineties so the securing of doors and windows became in the 1920s. The Syndicate became obsessed with security. The first hint comes in October 1923 when the Secretary is directed to prepare a circular letter on the use of Yale locks on outer doors. Next the Syndicate recommended to the Senate an amendment to the form of declaration signed by lodging house keepers on receiving a licence: they proposed that the words 'and securely fasten the shutters of the ground floor of my house' be omitted in future since fewer and fewer houses had shutters at that time and it was against modern health policy for students to sleep always with the shutters closed. But the amendment was referred back by the Council.

At the November meeting Syndics agreed to send out a circular letter reminding lodging-house keepers that they had a duty to prevent anyone entering or leaving their house between the hours of 10 and 6. Yale locks are useless in achieving this since no key is required to open the door from the inside, and University members could not be prevented from slipping out at all hours. Syndics were appalled and pronounced that outer doors must have a lock that could only be opened by a key from the inside as well as out. A week later the Syndicate is back gnawing the bone again. This time two Syndics and the Secretary are detailed off to meet the Tutorial Representatives and discuss the revision of the regulation as to locking ground-floor windows.

By March 1924 the Syndicate has prepared a new amended report to the Senate recommending 'and securely fasten with a locking device . . . the ground floor windows' leaving out all mention of shutters. But this too is thrown out by the Council of the Senate and in May a long and impassioned discussion is recorded in *Reporter* on the subject. The Rev. C.A.E. Pollock asserted it was totally impossible for lodging house keepers to effect one hundred percent security at night, and impractical for every room on the ground floor to be made secure against midnight escapings. As a present Syndic and previous Secretary he is full of sensible and pragmatic arguments: thousands of windows, he says, would have to be fitted with these expensive locks, and the strain on the Secretary to check every one would be intolerable. But he is strongly opposed by a fellow Syndic, Mr Crawley, who brings his former proc-

torial experience to bear and is alarmed at seeing undergraduates
all over Town sitting on their ground-floor window-sills and
chatting to their friends. University discipline will be set at naught
unless it was spelt out to lodging-house keepers what their responsibility entails.

Dons are clearly aghast at the publicity the issue is receiving. The
Chairman urges tact and discretion lest iconoclastic ideas be ar-
oused in the student body. All this talk of getting out of windows
and friends letting in their fellow lodgers in the early hours — why,
it will lead to anarchy. The prisons of several thousand young
males must be securely locked up all night, the better to achieve
their education. Sir Arthur Shipley, the Chairman, goes so far as to
admit he supports Mr Pollock in this discussion, but was induced to
vote against him. He actually says he hopes the Council will keep
referring the report back so that no decision can in fact be taken
until such time as someone else is appointed to the Chair. At long
last a new amendment meets with Council approval and is passed
by Grace in June. Under this the lodging-house keeper promises
'to fasten securely the ground floor windows of rooms occupied by
lodgers *in stat. pup.*'. No mention of padlocks, nor shutters, nor of
furtive exits via the kitchen window or from the outside lavatory.

As I finished making notes on the Minutes of this period, a letter
arrived from a Clare undergraduate of the early forties who had
been one of Mrs Gare's lodgers in Thompson's Lane and had felt
the weight of her thumb. 'Behaviour was important. You might not
be thrown out but life would be very uncomfortable if you transgressed. With regard to the 'after 10 gate fine' Mrs Gare was very
strict. However the dodge was to find out when her elderly
mother-in-law was on duty. You then rang the front door and entered through the back door.' It is certain that there always was a
'dodge' and that circumventing the rules added a great deal of
spice to the night's jaunt.

But there were matters other than security that Syndicate was
concerned with too: for instance, public health. The Secretary was
instructed to prepare a circular letter urging vaccination against
smallpox, for immediate despatch in the event of an outbreak, and
a flurry of disquiet followed the news that Mr R.J. Cross, a lodging
house keeper at 4 Jesus Lane was being treated at Papworth for

T.B. Mrs Cross had had the sense to get the house disinfected but was reprimanded for neglecting to report the infection. The licence was transferred into her name on condition her husband did not return home until he could bring a medical certificate to say he was free from infection.

In November 1923 the Principal of Wesley House sought recognition for his new buildings in Jesus Lane. It was decided to approve them for residence purposes, both for undergraduates and graduate students, and to accept the Principal as the responsible authority, to be resident in person at 32 Jesus Lane. They added the suggestion that the front railings on to the pavement be made higher than in the plan submitted, so as to make them incapable of being climbed.

At this date, 1323 houses are licensed, offering 2665 sets.

A place of residence appears for the first time when W. Aron, an undergraduate at Jesus is given permission to keep terms at Hillel House in Glebe Road: he was working as assistant to Mr I.H. Hersh, M.A., a master at the Perse. Hillel Houses are always establishments set up for the housing of orthodox Jews. In my own day, I often regretted that Cambridge did not have one.

Complaint was made that control over the residence of non-collegiate students was extremely lax. The Acting Censor penitently gave the Secretary an assurance that this would be remedied. Capt. Baines visited Cheshunt College and St Edmund's House to inspect the accommodation and arrangements for discipline, and must have given a positive report on what he found, since the Syndicate granted recognition, referring to the Council of the Senate the question whether a maximum of 20 students at each establishment was appropriate.

A report from the women police claimed that Mrs Aplin's daughter of 20 had been seen at various times in the company of undergraduates. The girl admitted that this was so and was warned by the Secretary that such conduct was undesirable and not to be pursued at Jordan's Yard. Several other disciplinary matters kept the Secretary occupied. Mrs Ayres was detected in the theft of money from a Sidney Sussex student at his lodging in 16 Portugal Place, and her licence was cancelled. Mr Baines called at 8 Victoria Street and found Mrs Law in a state of intoxication. Her licence was not to be renewed but the present lodger was considered not to be in great moral danger and was allowed to stay until the end of term. Mrs Cornell overcharged for gas and lighting: she was ordered to produce her gas bills and attend a meeting to give an explanation. As she did neither, her licence was not renewed. The Senior Proctor reported (March 1926) 'that he had received information from the Police to the effect that Mrs D.J. Hayward, 125 Oxford Road, had been concerned in a dispute on Coe Fen with a man, both of them being intoxicated; and that her house had been raided by the Proctors since undergraduates were resorting there for the purpose of drinking'. It was decided to cancel the licence forthwith.

Another licence was not renewed thanks to the Tutor of Clare who reported that Miss Hancock's house at 13 Park Street was dirty and unfit for undergraduates, and that Miss Hancock had proved difficult over cooking invalid food for a sick lodger. Undergraduates who would, at a a later period, go into a college sick bay when they were taken ill were commonly looked after by their landlady, and no doubt the standard of nursing varied considerably.

Two other landladies had daughters too attractive for safety; Mrs Thurgood had two girls fond of consorting with undergraduates at 32 Grantchester Street, and Mrs. Newman of Emmanuel Road joined in the fun herself and went drinking with her daughter and her undergraduate lodgers at the Lion Hotel, leaving the house in a generally unsatisfactory condition'. They were both put on parole. More larks were going on at The Croft in Primrose Street, a house run by A.E. Longley, a Captain in the Royal Engineers. It was alleged that the outer door had been found open after ten and a dinner party held, the guests not leaving till after midnight. Undergraduates had been present at dances held in the grounds. On being interviewed, Capt. Longley pleaded that he had been ill on the night in question 'as a result of his work in the recent strike' (presumably the General Strike). Nevertheless he was reprimanded and dances were prohibited during term.

The Vice-Chancellor himself took the Chair in Michaelmas 1926: G.A. Weekes, the Master of Sidney Sussex. The Syndics decided to authorise the payment of office rent to the Clerk to the Syndicate, up to a maximum of £11 p.a., the office having been moved, owing to the death of the Clerk's wife, from his old house 8 St Clement's Gardens to 16 Park Street.

Mr Baines' nose for liquor led him to Free School Lane at an unguarded moment where he discovered Mrs Lawrence in a state of complete intoxication and withdrew her licence.

The Cambridge University and Town Gas Light Co. wrote offering to make an annual inspection of all geysers fitted in lodging houses, free of charge. There had been a serious accident recently, thanks to defective fittings and the offer was accepted.

Let us at this point hear a living voice tell what it was like to be in lodgings at this date. Here is a correspondent, Mr Geoffrey Young, recalling his first year at St Catharine's, October 1926: the Head Porter has sent him to his 'best landlady', Mrs Flitton at 59 Grantchester Street.

> She was the daughter of someone who worked on the land at Linton and she had worked as a maid in one of the better Cambridge hotels. She married a Mr W.L. Flitton who was manager of Baily Grundy & Barrett, the electrical shop opposite Great St Mary's Church. In those days the electricity system in Cambridge came from different sources and there were four different voltages (I think 25, 50, 75 and 100). We had no electricity at No. 59 and there was gas downstairs for lighting and a gas geyser in the bathroom (baths were 6d each) but otherwise only candles upstairs.

> There was a wash stand with large china basin and ewer in the bedroom and hot water came in a small copper can in the morning and evening.

> I was her only lodger and had the front room downstairs. This had a large bay window with cased frames and sashes all of which were fitted with padlocked brackets of College specification and bought from a designated shop and were on each side of each sash so that they could not be opened more than about six inches.

> There was a large table, a small table in the bay, two dining chairs, an easy chair, a sofa plus a sideboard, an aspidistra in a pot on the bay table a marble clock and two ornamental vases on the mantelshelf. Linen and cutlery etc. were kept in the sideboard. Under the slate mantelshelf was a tiled fire-surround and

hearth with a grate plus fire-tools and a coal scuttle. The charge for a scuttle of coal was officially fixed at 6*d*. The other charges, e.g. rent, were also fixed.

One bought one's cakes, fruit and the like but commons[2] (bread and butter, tea and such things) came in the rent.

I forgot to mention that above the mantelshelf were two gas brackets for the illumination of the room and there were lace and material (heavy) curtains in the windows.

I had a cooked breakfast, lunch (extra) when I ordered it and dinner was usually in the College Hall.

My bicycle was stored in a back shed for we were not allowed cars until our second year. Mrs Flitton used to get up early on Sundays and get me a cooked breakfast so that I could leave the house at 6 a.m. which was the earliest permitted time so that I could ride to the Peterborough area where I had several relatives by bicycle in order that I might have a long day there. After the first year I went by car still leaving at 6 a.m.

Unless we had college permission, we had to be back in 'digs' at 10 p.m.: between 10 p.m. and 11 p.m. the gate fine was 1*d*. and between 11 p.m. and midnight 2*d*. After midnight arrivals were reported to the College.

After I finally went down I kept in touch with her, sending her a Christmas parcel of food each year and writing at intervals. When I had business in the Cambridge area I used to stay with her and after I was married she put my wife and myself up for our holiday so that we could go around Cambridge and the region round about which my wife did not know . . .

The Tutor of Emmanuel made an unusual request on behalf of his pupil, D.R. McCullagh, a research student and graduate of the University of Manitoba: he wanted a latch-key, pleading the necessity for a walk late a night, due to his constant insomnia. Very reluctantly the Syndics gave their permission 'for the present term only, and as an exceptional case'. That was at 18 Clarendon Street and presumably he sauntered around Parker's Piece in the dark.

---

2. How one traces the continuity from the mediaeval world in that use of the word 'commons'.

In December 1927 a letter arrived from the proctorial Syndicate insisting on the outer doors of lodging houses being provided with locks other than Yale. As it was, the proctors were prevented from testing whether the lodging house keeper was complying with regulations or not. The Syndics resolved that from the next licensing date (November 1928) no house was to be licensed where the outer door was fitted with a Yale or similar lock (i.e. one that could be opened from the inside without using a key). The use of a door key and a door knob inside and out are to be substituted, no latchkey is to be given to a lodger and gate-hour regulations are to be strictly observed. All lodging house keepers are circularised to this effect, and on top of that, houses not considered satisfactory in the event of an outbreak of fire are to be warned. For instance, in the case of 17-20 Market Hill, a big house, the Secretary is to inspect it, accompanied by the Bursar of Caius and an expert from the Town Fire Brigade.

The status of B.A. research students is discussed with reference to residence requirements: the Board of Research Studies were currently considering the general question. The Syndicate sent their opinion that senior research students in their fourth or fifth years of residence should be permitted to reside in unlicensed lodgings.

Early in 1929 we come upon L Wittgenstein, Research student at Trinity and aged about 40 being given permission to count towards residence the ten days he spent during the Lent Term at the house of Mr F.P. (Frank) Ramsey, M.A. of King's, at 4 Mortimer Road; and to keep terms while living at the house of Mr M.H. (Maurice) Dobb M.A. of Pembroke College at Frost Lake Cottage, Malting Lane.

A hint of the shortage of lodgings is conveyed by the following note: 'a suggestion that lodging houses with outdoor sanitation only should no longer be licensed was rejected in view of the amount of accommodation needed'.

The residence of research students again came up for discussion; applications for permission to reside in unlicensed lodgings should be granted in exceptional circumstances only. The Secretary is instructed to write to the Tutorial Representatives asking them to make application as early as possible in each term. To make things quite clear — and *a propos* an enquiry about Magdalene research students — it is spelt out that those who are graduates of the University are not obliged to keep further terms by residence and in such cases it is unnecessary to seek permission.

Some lodging house keepers have evidently complained that their room rents are not sufficiently profitable; applications for increase of rent in rooms, owing to higher rating assessments, must be dealt with on the merits of each particular case.

Local estate agents had come up with a proposal to build a large block of flats for undergraduates in the Town. Later generations would have welcomed such a move, but the Syndics sent answer that the University is opposed to the hostel system and would regard any such initiative with disfavour. We must remember that England is at this period in the clutches of an appalling slump and unemployment must have been rife. Building progress always comes to a standstill in such conditions.

Two disciplinary cases come up for judgement: Mr. Kitchener of 18 Malcolm Street was summoned to appear at the meeting and was severely reprimanded by the Chairman for neglecting to observe the door rules. The year's licence for 55 Victoria Road is made conditional on the absence from the house of Mrs E.M. Hawkes, a daughter of the tenants Mr & Mrs Humphrey. Mrs Hawkes had been the lodging-house keeper previously and a King's undergraduate had been defrauded over the payment of money for washing, so now she is to make herself scarce. The Syndicate had a long memory.

The 1930 list shows E.E. Kenzie as a lodging-house keeper at 7 Tennis Court Terrace, letting 3 sets and a bedsitter; his occupation is given as a college waiter. After the war one of those sets will be occupied by the author's husband, when he came back to Downing to complete his degree. Mrs Kenzie looked after him well but she didn't by then need to run up and down stairs with coal-scuttles, because he had a gas-fire.

An honorarium of £50 and a note of special thanks were awarded to Mr P. Brodby 'for his services as acting Secretary during the illness of the Secretary'.

Mr Baines, back in harness, cancels Mrs M. Ladds' licence at 37 Mill Road because her door was unlocked at 10.40 and she was guilty of a serious overcharge to an undergraduate during the Michaelmas Term previous., but later the Syndicate relents and her licence is to be renewed in October ('30) after testimonials to her excellent character are read. Mr Benstead is not so fortunate at 16 St. Barnabas Road and his licence is taken away for an unlocked door and the offence of borrowing £20 from an undergraduate and not fully repaying it; one of his cheques has been dishonoured.

An exotic character, H.R.H. Prince Chula is allowed to count as residence the 17 days that he spent at the Cavendish Nursing Home. A little later, a familiar name appears — A.F. Blunt, B.A. of Trinity, is to count 3 days spent by him during convalescence at the Malting House, Newnham, the house of Mrs Gordon. Presumably this is Anthony Blunt.

Mrs Aves who lived in that handsome row of houses, 4 Bene't Place, could not keep out of hot water. First she took a man into the house without permission who was prosecuted for the theft of an undergraduate's shoes. Mrs Aves was ordered to attend the next meeting and was severely reprimanded. But in May '31, she made out false gate bills, and left the control of her front door to her 'house boy' (sic) who of course failed to secure it. So the licence is cancelled, 'as from this day'.

The charge for a bath was not to exceed 6*d* and the licence fee went up to 2*s* 6*d*. 12a Market Hill was thought to be unsuitable for licensing because a restaurant The Scotch Hoose Café was on the first floor. When the Senior Tutor of Trinity Hall wrote querying the signing of the Syndicate's permission forms, authorising lodging-house keepers to let rooms, he mentioned 'the fact that the majority of tutors themselves engaged rooms for their pupils during the vacation'.

Undergraduates did not themselves always go round checking their choice of rooms: one wonders whether tutors tried to match the personality of lodger and landlady, or dabbled much in the selection of residents to form a compatible group under one roof? The nannying implications are striking.

The Dean of Gonville & Caius was admonished when he sent in an application for permission on behalf of one of his pupils; Mr. Baines pointed out that the Ordinances require applications to be made by heads of houses or tutors: not mere deans. In another

context the Syndicate became informal: 'at the Chairman's suggestion it was decided that in future the wearing of cap and gown at
Syndicate meetings should be optional'.(Jan.'31) It certainly wasn't
optional in the writer's day. Though the cap had gone, gowns were
firmly in order till 1992.

A letter from the Vice-Chancellor stressed the importance of
undergraduates wearing gowns at night, but the Syndicate felt it
had done enough in pointing out the obligation to lodging-house
keepers in the licence.

Mrs Howard's licence at 4 Earl Street is not to be renewed after
reports were received from neighbours, (including a University
Constable), 'of frequent visits from Newmarket men and others late
at night, and the house known to be unsatisfactorily conducted'.
She has also been previously guilty of false gate returns, no doubt
extending to her lodgers the same tolerance she evidently applies
to her own life-style. It is alleged that theatrical touring companies
put their actors (and actresses.) up in licensed lodgings, and the
Senior Proctor is detailed off to obtain a list of addresses to check
whether lodging-house keepers are indeed taking theatrical lodgers without first applying for permission. Newmarket men and
theatricals are loaded words.

When a Chinese research student, C.C. Wang, who is non-collegiate, asks permission to live in unlicensed lodgings on the grounds
of economy, he is refused and told that cheap licensed lodgings are
readily available. A report of overcrowding sends the Secretary to 6
Jesus Terrace, New Square, to investigate (Nov. '31). He finds 8 inmates including 1 undergraduate, sharing 4 bedrooms, with 4 of
the family sleeping in one bedroom. Jesus Terrace houses are tiny
and I am surprised that there were as many as 4 bedrooms in such
a small space. The undergraduate is removed 'pending a decrease
in numbers', and the landlady reprimanded.

This year, '31-'32, 1300 houses are licensed of which 871 contained bathrooms, and 370 had outdoor sanitation only. Syndicate
policy is to reduce as far as possible the number of houses without
indoor sanitation. The reader should remember that washing arrangements in college were similarly stringent and spartan and involved sparsely-clad men sprinting across open chilly courts to
frigid bath-houses.

W.C. Kerr sent a photograph and wrote in fascinating detail about his first year at Christ's in 1928 when he was allocated rooms with Mrs Dickerson, the landlady at 12 Earl Street.

Mrs Dickerson, Earl Street

The house had not been modernised. I had a gas fire in my sitting room but there was no heating upstairs. The w.c. was outside at the back of the house and the house had no bathroom. This added to the novelty of my situation since in order to have a morning bath I joined a little procession of undergraduates clad in pyjamas and dressing gown walking across Christ's Piece to the College bathhouse; strangely I never caught cold doing this even in the depth of winter.

As it happened the winter of 1928-9 was severe and the outside w.c. in Earl Street was frozen up for some days, so we not only had to go to college for our bath, but for those few days the college toilets were our only resort. I don't recall being put out by these circumstances; for me this was Cambridge life, and that was sufficient.

The academic year '31-'32 starts off with a finger-wagging for the Senior Tutor of Downing. He is to be told that the Syndicate deems it unsuitable for the Head Porter to engage rooms on behalf of undergraduates, and further advised to consult the published list first to see whether a given address is licensed or not. The Senior Tutor evidently sent a pained, perhaps indignant reply, because at a later meeting, the Secretary is directed to reply that 'the Syndicate in no way desired to interfere with the freedom of action of colleges, but to point out that the system at Downing had proved faulty, the Head Porter having engaged two sets of rooms that were not in fact licensed'.

Head Porters, of course, went on being invaluable sources of information about lodgings, a tradition upheld by Mr Monument of St. Catharine's to this very day. So the Downing men were no doubt hastily moved into more legitimate accommodation as were two other undergraduates who had to leave 3 Victoria Street rather suddenly owing to the insobriety of their landlady. When the police confirmed her reputation, her licence was cancelled forthwith.

The landlady of 137 Chesterton Road also lost her licence but for a different reason. She had been overcharging for gas and electricity and was called to attend a meeting but failed to produce a reasonable excuse. The Senior Tutor of Trinity had just complained to the Syndicate about this malpractice, to such good effect that circular letters went out to all lodging-house keepers laying down permitted charges:

> *Heating*: Normal charges for gas or coal fires should be 30s to 50s — on average 40s per term or 5s a week.
>
> *For Lighting*: 15s to 25s termly but half that price in the Easter Term and extra could be charged for new lamps and mantles supplied.
>
> *For the hire of plate and linen*; 15s to 25s would be appropriate, an average 2s 6d a week.

The class of lodging etc. was to be taken into consideration in determining the precise charge. Lodging-house keepers were recommended to install separate meters for gas, to avoid quibbling.

At this time, the Syndicate is still without a permanent home and the Secretary is instructed 'to make inquiries at Stuart House (in Mill Lane) as to the possibility of always securing a room there for meetings, it being felt that repeated changes of venue led to confusion. A distinguished new member of the Syndicate is Mr D.A. Winstanley of Trinity, the historian.

Spikes are to be put up at No. 5 St Mary's Passage to prevent undergraduates living in No. 4 from climbing in through the windows. Then begins a tortuous rigmarole about a certain Mrs S. in Park Parade, thought to have a man sleeping in the house, not a member of the University (and not presumably Mr S.) The tutor of St. John's has information on this and is to confer with the Syndicate in person at the next meeting. He did indeed attend, to explain. why undergraduates were removed from the house at the behest of the college. His allegations having been substantiated by the police report, the Syndicate determined to consult the Commissary of the University as to what would be the legal position if the licence was cancelled without assigning a reason. Francis & Co. (the University solicitors) advised not to revoke the licence, to avoid possible trouble or unpleasantness. However, Senior Tutors were to be advised that the licence might not be renewed and asked not to engage the lodging. Pembroke can't have read the letter, or decided to ignore it.

Three fourth-year undergraduates booked at the fatal address and the Secretary had to interview the Senior Tutor and spell out the moral danger. The licence was indeed not renewed for '32-'33 and the Chairman acquainted the Vice-Chancellor with the facts and told him the Syndicate was not in a position to give reason for their action. He reported at the next meeting that the Vice-Chancellor approved of the Syndicate's handling of the case but 'was anxious to avoid the possibility of legal proceedings and any repetition of the Spinning-House case'.

Mrs S. brings the matter to a head by applying for a licence. She obviously hasn't taken the hint. The Chairman is sent off to consult Sir John Withers and Mr Collin as to the exact powers of the Syndicate and the final decision is deferred until they have pronounced. Sir John Withers was M.P. for Cambridge at this date. He advised that the licence should not be withheld 'unless Mrs S. were confronted with the charges and were allowed to answer them, and unless the charges were subsequently substantiated, possibly by reference to her husband, as to the grounds on which he left her'. The Junior Proctor abstained from voting. The outcome was that they renewed the licence and informed the Senior Tutor of each college accordingly.

I spell out the case in some detail because it is fascinating to see the care taken to avoid a confrontation that might cause all Cambridge Town to fall upon an overweening University body. The puritanical concern for morals is still as ardent as ever but the arrogance has gone. However, no such qualms seem to have been felt over two other cases of this period.

Mrs Huckle lived at 13 King's Parade and had a son who is often seen driving about at night in a car, accompanied by rowdy under-

graduates. The Secretary is to ask Mrs Huckle to see that this practice ceases. He receives two letters about the conduct of certain
lodging-house keepers; one is anonymous and the other from
someone whose licence had been cancelled in a previous year. (One
wonders whether neighbours often took revenge by writing anonymous allegations about one another). He is to consult the Chief
Constable about the people named and to request the Police to
keep an eye on the houses in question.

After his talk with the Chief Constable, Mr Baines notes 'Mrs
Brewster, 6 Tennis Court Road, had lost her position as instruc-
tress at the Jesus Green Baths, (these were on the Pitt Club premises) owing to her open association with a certain man with whom
she frequented public houses'. No action is to be taken except 'to
inform Peterhouse so that, if they thought desirable, another tenant could be found'. Mrs Brewster has lost her job, and now she's
likely to lose her home as well.

Mr Piggott of Park Street makes a refreshing change, asking to
be de-licensed, since his only lodger, a Caius B.A., does night work
at the laboratory (and therefore the gate-rules cannot be observed).
His application is granted providing the man's Tutor sends his
written approval. Concurrently, the Council of the Senate are considering the question of residence by research students and debating proposals to allow those of age 27 or more certain privileges including living in unlicenced lodgings and certifying their own residence. The Syndicate want to study the report but don't care to be
loaded with the task of assessing the merits of each individual case.

Mr Baines should have continued in office until June 1934 but a
letter from him is read at the May meeting of 1933 asking to be allowed to resign. He is not present at the meeting, no reason is
given, but his resignation is accepted as from that date. The minutes are written by Mr L.C. Van Grutten, a member of the Syndicate who now acts as Secretary: he had been junior Proctor in 1931.

I myself remember Mr Van Grutten well, and used to visit him at
the White House in Trumpington Road, where he rented rooms to
selected postgraduate couples. I wish I had asked him to explain
Mr Baines' precipitate disappearance. Evidently the Syndicate is so
startled it feels the wind of change whistling and embarks on a long
discussion on the theme that a woman could carry out inspection

duties more efficiently. The Chairman of the day, J.A. Venn, the President of Queens', is to put these three options to the Vice-Chancellor.

1. To appoint a male secretary;
2. To appoint a male secretary at a lower salary, with the additional appointment of a woman to assist in inspection;
3. the appointment of a woman secretary.

The post to be advertised by the Chairman according to the Vice-Chancellor's decision, and candidates to be seen at Senate House in June. The Council of the Senate agreed to the third proposition, the appointment of a woman, and the Grace went through in time for an advertisement to be inserted in *Reporter* and in the *Cambridge Daily News* for Monday 19 June 1933. It offered a two-year appointment at a salary of £250 and asked for the names of three referees. 'Preference will be given to applicants with a special knowledge of Cambridge'.

Thirty-two candidates applied and three were selected for the final short-list, Mrs Culverwell, Mrs Hainy (? or Harry) and Miss Kennett. At the interview the Master of Sidney proposed that Miss Kennett be appointed, and the vote was carried unanimously. She lost no time in staking out her territory: offices were found at 31 Trinity Street and approved by the Master of Sidney. She was given £20 to furnish it and a telephone was to be installed. At her first meeting she reported a lodging-house keeper at 4 Hertford Street had tried to prevent her inspecting the house, and the husband had called at the office and been insolent. The Chairman promised to reprimand the culprit.

The problem of Mrs S. in Park Parade rears its head again with a report that she is immoral and unfit to have a lodging-house. This time the Syndicate is firm — is it not in the keeping now of a maiden lady? — and decides Mrs S. is not to be granted a licence. She writes asking permission to appeal but is told the Syndicate's decision is final and no interview can be granted her. The new firmness extends to the plumbing: In future no house is to be licensed that has not a bathroom and indoor sanitation.

9

Under Feminine Guidance

A photograph of Miss Kennett hangs to this day in the reception of the Accommodation Office. It shows a cool, languid, gentlewoman with that long, English, slightly horsey face, whose dress droops discreetly over her person. You guess she sits with her ankles crossed, and the gown was probably beige. Professor Thistlethwaite first Vice-Chancellor of East Anglia, remembered her from his days as a Tutor at John's and described her to me as 'very much a *grande dame*.' Landladies recall her with respect and holy terror. She would enter houses as of right and march into rooms to thump the mattress with judicial air. She was to rule the Lodging House Syndicate for 24 years. The University gave her an honorary M.A. in 1955 and she retired at last to Felixstowe where she lived to a great age.

Here she is at work in October 1933; Mr Jones at 19 Silver Street employed a daily servant supervised by his sister of the Belle Vue Hotel. Any change in this arrangement is to be reported to the Secretary. The two unspoken elements in this innocent statement are that Mr Jones must be a widower (or a bachelor) and the girl does not, and must not, sleep in the lodging-house. This same Mr Jones lost his licence the next summer for overcharging and falsifying his accounts. At 4 St Andrew's Street a similar situation arises after Mr C.W. Clark's daughter was married. While she lived at home the proprieties were observed, but as there was now only a young maid alone in the house with her father, who was asked to engage a housekeeper. A contemporary report sets out that lodging-house keepers employ girls as daily servants, pay them low wages and dismiss them at the end of term when the young men go down. A scheme of registration of servants by the Secretary is discussed but the Syndicate ends up deciding not to interfere.

We have met Mr Longley of the Croft in Primrose Street before, giving jolly dances in his garden. Now a porter from Trinity gives evidence that an undergraduate had left college after hours but was noted as legitimately within doors on Mr Longley's gate-list. The lodging-house keeper volunteered as an explantion that he must have got out of his window after 10 p.m. He is 'ordered to have the windows on the first floor locked and barred so that egress and ingress shall be impossible" and Miss Kennett is to see the work is done. In spite of this second warning, Capt. Longley is in trouble again the following year. A note in the locked black book says that he 'was absent from the house when the Proctor went at 12. 10 a.m. on November 14th. He was charged with leaving the house in charge of his son, sending in false gate bills and having the under-graduate's chauffeur as lodger without permission. Licence rescinded 4 December 1935'.

Mr Daldry, late of the Hermitage (now part of Darwin College and once licensed as a large lodging-house) applies for a licence at his new house, 7 Holland Street but it is not granted because 'he was much given to dog-racing and to low company'. As for Miss Hoppett at 21 Jesus Lane, she is soon despatched — 'House filthy, licence cancelled'. The Dean of Caius gave evidence against F.W. Constable that he was unfit to run his lodging-house at 12 Mill Lane (now the office of the Society for Visiting Scholars). Three Caius men were removed from this address on the grounds that their landlord refused to show his fuel bills, that men were not al-lowed to use the bathroom after 10.30, and that he was guilty of in-solence and physical violence towards them. Constable was sent for and questioned and his licence was not renewed.

The Ordinances were overhauled and a draft for changed word-ing sent to the Registry. The word 'woman' is to be substituted for 'lady' in the amended clause about not allowing anyone except the undergraduate's mother in his room after 10.

Three thousand copies of the new regulations on permitted charges are to be circulated by the college tutors to their pupils in lodgings. Miss Kennett has been working on the manager of the Gas Board and he has undertaken to instal rotary meters for gas stoves at a hire of 1s a quarter plus a fixing charge of 2s 6d.

A report of the Proctorial Syndicate for January 1935 on certain charges in the Edicts demonstrates that tradesmen could still be discommuned at this date. The University had the power to forbid any trade with members of the University for a given period where a tradesman or shop-keeper caused an offence, as for example, in allowing an undergraduate to run up bills of more than £5 without notifying his Tutor. In a town like Cambridge such restrictions, even for a brief time, could spell financial ruin since the University was so pre-eminently the important customer. A man not allowed to sell his wine or hats or hire his horses for a term or two could easily go out of business.

Maybe all this emphasis on the tightening-up of regulations provoked a hostile reaction from the recipients. Certainly the Chairman reported that a Lodging House Keepers' Association had been formed and asked for instructions to be given to the Secretary in the event of their sending a deputation. It was agreed that the Secretary was to arrange for not more than three to attend the April meeting — the Syndicate had no wish to be out-numbered — and they were to be asked to send memoranda of the special points they wished to discuss. Evidently the discussion proved amiable and the Syndicate acknowledged the reasonableness of their point of view; for one thing, the Chairman undertook to write to the Tutorial Representatives about the need for Colleges to co-ordinate their differing instructions to the lodging-house keepers as to the sending in of gate-bills, and the rendering of accounts.

A clause is to be added to the list of lodging-house keepers' obligations about parties for more than 5 needing prior permission from the householder. All regulations on the licence are to be printed in the same type, but the Vice-Chancellor's notice is to be printed in Clarendon type (momentous decisions these). The Syndicate recommended to the Council of the Senate that provisional licences may be granted for a period of less than one year and operative from the first day of the term in which the licence is granted. Lodging-house keepers are to be instructed that if students take the rooms themselves, they must give a written undertaking to confirm the reservation, and must ascertain that college permission has been given for their residence at a given address. A Mr Spittle wrote asking if lodging-house keepers could be supplied with printed slips for re-engaging rooms at half-term. One of the Proctors is deputed to design with the Secretary an appropriate form, and the specimen that was then approved was identical with the slips in use in the present writer's time.

Miss Kennett called at 32 Trinity Street and found the householder absent and her daughter and a housekeeper alone in charge. It proved that Mrs Hibbitt the lodging-house keeper was ill at Liverpool. The Secretary wrote to her and received an apology and a medical certificate, but nevertheless the house was not in recognised hands. Mrs Kitt the housekeeper is to be asked to provide two letters of reference and she is to have the regulations spelt out to her. By November (1935) Mrs Kitt has failed to send testimonials and Miss Kennett warns her that she could not be left in charge unless the letters are forthcoming. Enquiries are made about her in her native town, and when at last a favourable reply arrives from the Chief Constable of Folkestone, Mrs Kitt is allowed to remain till the end of the Michaelmas Term.

The Senior Proctor reported seeing a man climb up by the projecting sign above Barrett's china shop, and walk along a ledge by the first floor windows of 5 St. Mary's Chambers. Miss Kennett makes it her business to see that the lodging-house keeper there had locks fitted on all the windows, and that she takes the trouble to lock them each night at 10.

Mr Telfer, the assistant tutor of Clare, writes to ask if landladies could be instructed to see an undergraduate's tutor if he has women visitors and the propriety of his conduct is doubted. But the Syndicate could not agree to this — direct sneaking to Tutors was not to be condoned.

One of the proctors, the assiduous Mr Heywood, reports that F.E.A. Welford pleaded guilty in court of obstructing a University constable at the Maypole Inn. The Chairman is to send for him and give him a reprimand. When Mr Welford appeared, he made an apology and promised loyalty to the University for the future. A Russian lodging-house keeper at 5 Richmond Terrace is discovered to be running a restaurant in a room on the ground floor, serving lunches and dinners. Unless the practice is given up, his licence is to be revoked.

King's proposed to open a new hostel at Peas Hill, and Mr Donald Beves came to represent the college claiming that the permission of the Syndicate was unnecessary. The Syndicate referred the case to the Council of the Senate who must have reinforced Syndicate powers, because a little later the Provost of King's wrote to ask approval for the hostel. This was granted for 5 years for occupation by 20 students, but King's was to undertake responsibility for discipline arrangements, and to take steps to assure the safety of inmates in the event of fire.

Fire is the issue again when Miss Kennett visited Basing House, a lodging house used by Magdalene men. She thinks the house unsuitable and highly dangerous in case of fire. Mr Cox the landlord is to be informed that rents will be reduced, and that he must provide some means of escape. The Chief Fire Officer is to be asked to make recommendations; two fire extinguishers and two automatic Davy lines must be installed. The Senior Proctor and Miss Kennett put their heads together and re-assess the room rents and in the course of their colloquy, come up with even more stringent demands for new fittings, for a fire escape and for a large refrigerator (surely a great novelty and a luxury at this date) and a service lift. When in the following October the Fire Sergeant carried out an inspection, a further automatic fire escape and extinguisher were suggested, and ordered to be installed shortly.

The Junior Proctor asks whether there has been any change in the regulation forbidding the letting of rooms to other than University members and whether that prohibition applied in May week. Though the point was discussed, the Chairman ruled that the regulation applied till the end of term, and a leaflet was to be sent out to all lodging-house keepers reaffirming that no person who is not a member of the University may be received as a lodger in May Week or at any other time during term when students were in residence, without written permission. Even as late as 1953, a correspondent describes the risk his landlady took on his behalf.

'She would certainly have been drummed out of the club if the college authorities had learned that she had given accommodation (in the spare bedroom of course.) to my girl-friend for the night of the Cardinal's Ball (an annual Cath's function at the time); it was all entirely innocent (at least, that is what I tell my wife.)'.[1]

And toleration went a stage further in the case of the ex-lodger who remembered that: 'There were indeed some lovely landladies — those in Portugal Place ('Will there be an extra pillow required, sir?') to those bringing up partners for the Pitt Ball.'[2]

In the thirties the Syndicate is still discussing the expediency of licensing houses with basements: the Secretary obediently went off

---

1. See letter (Walters), p.260.   2. See letter (Carver), p.295.

to investigate and must have had an athletic time clambering up and down stairs. She came back with the figures: there are 216 houses with deep basements, 179 with semi-basements, most of them dark and airless; and 64 with shallow basements, for the most part bright and airy. The Syndicate decided not to license houses with deep basements unless they could be satisfied that they were for storage only and not for cooking or for habitation. This new requirement was to be gradually imposed and not to take effect till October 1937.

The Syndics were of course animated by a concern for the living quality of the landlady; there would not have been any question of putting an undergraduate into a basement, shallow or not. Soon we find the Bursar of Corpus voicing his anxiety at this new regulation about basements, and the Chairman gallantly offers to attend a Bursars' meeting and explain the Syndicate's reasons. The Chairman at this date, by the way, is still J.A. Venn, President of Queens' and the membership has been very stable, with the same names listed as present meeting after meeting, Turner, Burnaby, Guillebaud and the Master of Sidney.

Miss Kennett has been asked to prepare a list of houses that might be dangerous in case of fire. In her going about the town, she realises that the entrance to 2 Petty Cury is through the yard of a public-house, and as this is clearly unsuitable, putting thoughts of drink into innocent undergraduate heads, this address is not to be licensed after the present year. To help her, the Fire Sergeant sends in his report on what he considers to be vulnerable licensed houses in the centre of town, and she is directed to write to the lodging-house keepers concerned and inform them of his recommendations.

Another of her tasks is to send to all college bursars a list of licensed houses with deep basements. Now it is not only Corpus that is worried but three representatives from the Bursars' Committee came to meet the Syndicate raising five points in defence of houses with basements. In return, the Syndicate explains its policy of slowly bringing about an amelioration in standards, as has largely been achieved in the matter of sanitation. The Bursars are asked to communicate with the Secretary whenever a house belonging to their college falls vacant so that they may profitably discuss what structural alteration or internal rearrangements may be necessary before a new tenant moves in. While this sounds only reasonable to us, no doubt the Bursars at that date saw this as an astounding infringement of their freedom of action. Some whiff of their concerted bristling must have made itself felt because it is recorded that the Chairman 'very strongly pointed out the absolute power of the Syndicate to grant or withhold licences, as the body appointed for that purpose by the University'. The Bursars concurred.

Two disciplinary matters arise, one rather unusual and sad. Mrs Fennemore of 15B Malcolm Street has been admitted to Addenbrooke's with self-inflicted wounds and it seems that a future breakdown is possible. She is to be allowed to continue if a satisfactory certificate can be obtained from a psychiatrist. L.C. Hornsby has had an actress from the Festival Theatre lodging at his house at 35 Newmarket Road, without seeking permission. Indeed the Senior Proctor reported having seen a girl entering the house even after a visit of remonstrance from Miss Kennett. Although summoned to appear before the Syndicate, Mr Hornsby failed to turn up and his licence was cancelled from the end of the term.

Among new edicts issued by the Proctorial Syndicate in January 1935 was one that prohibited the giving (or joining in giving) 'in any licensed lodging house without the permission of his Tutor and the Junior Proctor a party or other entertainment at which more than 20 persons are present'. A month later the restriction was tightened up to apply to 15 persons. This must have put a dampener on many hospitable occasions, but there was the following concession:

> April '37: The Secretary was told that, if one were asked by lodging house keepers, she might say that on Coronation Night the 10 o'clock rule for locking-up might be relaxed except in cases where there was a man confined to gates.

So no doubt George VI's formal arrival to the throne was celebrated at Cambridge in a mood of unprecedented laxity.

The Syndicate could be liberal enough when the student's intellectual needs dictated exceptions to rules: R. Weekes of Magdalene, a research student, was given permission to have a key at his lodgings in Magrath Avenue because of experiments in ionospheric research which require to be watched continuously for twelve or fifteen hours. And two years later a Caius research student working on atmospheric electricity was similarly given permission to have a key of his lodgings in order to be at the Observatory whenever there was a thunderstorm, but with the injunction that the Tutor of the second lodger in the house (if any) should be told of the arrangement. With hindsight, considering the date, June 1939, that student was soon to have more to observe in the sky than just thunderstorms.

The Fennemore case came up again. Dr Noble had seen her and reported she was well and fit to carry on her work, but the Chief Constable had said that her husband was given to bad drinking bouts which were the cause of her nervous depression. The licence was nevertheless continued, at least provisionally since Tutors professed themselves willing to leave their pupils there. In another case the pupils took matters into their own hands: all the Pembroke men lodging at 59 Lensfield Road left at the end of the Michaelmas Term (1937) because their landlady, Mrs Hughes was drinking and causing great trouble in the house. She was not to be relicensed.

The controversy over deep basements goes on. Corpus enters the lists, demanding that a licence for 6 Trumpington Street be continued, notwithstanding its abnormally deep basement, as they are contemplating certain improvements. But the Syndicate refuse to comply, after the lapse of the present tenancy. Again, the Bursar of Trinity is required to put kitchen and living rooms above ground if the new tenant of 11 Green Street is to be allowed a licence. (Was that, one wonders, the house of the barber who used to keep a live, but sad, bear in his basement as proof of the genuineness of the bear-grease he supplied to young gentlemen to add lustre to their hair?)

The Syndicate stood its ground in the interest of the lodging-house keeper. Trinity strongly disputed the Syndicate's decision over its property, but it was upheld, the firm reply saying that it chose not to allow a landlady to work in a kitchen entirely underground. For this, the Secretary said that the new Medical Officer of Health fully approved their policy. When Lord Butterfield made a speech about preventive medicine some time ago, I reflected on the influential work of the Lodging-House Syndicate in raising public standards of health and hygiene, in so far as they affected the lodging of undergraduates.

Mr Salter makes his first appearance as a Syndic in the year 1937-38: he was to play a prominent role in Syndicate affairs and would become its Chairman in 1941 and rule over it till 1958. A photograph of him hangs in the Accommodation Office and he lived to a very great age.

Religious groups are demanding the right to establish their own households about this time: first the Franciscans appear, taking over 17 Trumpington Street for some of their novices, who would be members of various colleges. This move contradicts, of course, the essential collegiate spirit, so before granting a licence the Syndicate thought it wise to report to the Council of the Senate for a guiding principle. They must have given the go-ahead as permission was granted (1938) for Bene't House on Mount Pleasant to be used as an approved house of residence for Benedictines and 17 Trumpington Street for the Franciscans, which, following on the establishment of St Edmund's House in 1896 began to redress the balance so dramatically upset on the abolition of the once-powerful Cambridge monasteries in the sixteenth century.

The name of M.F. Perutz of Peterhouse flies out of the page. Described as an Austrian research student, he is given leave to reside in unlicensed rooms at 35 Leys Avenue on grounds of economy. How far-seeing of the Syndicate to facilitate the studies of a future Nobel prizewinner. Another permission case is interesting enough to quote. In April 1939, the Syndicate considered the request from Downing that H.W.H. Kennard be allowed to reside in his own flat with his younger sister, a girl of 19. The application was refused and his Tutor was to be told 'that if his pupil liked to keep terms in a two-set lodging house, the Syndicate would be prepared to give permission for his sister to be with him'.

Complaints about landladies who sent in excessive bills led to exhaustive discussion and give us illuminating glimpses of pre-war costs. Two men lodging with Mrs Risley at 14 Alexandra Street (which disappeared in the Lion Yard redevelopment) disputed their bills and were told that total charges should not have exceeded £5 for coal and £2 10s for electricity for them both, over the Lent and Easter terms of 1937. £5 to cover providing coal for two study fires for sixteen weeks — the landlady had to stagger upstairs with buckets of coal and firing, light and tend the fires and clean out the fireplaces daily, not to mention the cleaning of floor and staircases, constantly dirtied by coal dust.

Horrified undergraduates found extra charges of 25 or 28 shillings added to their bill at the end of term for baths and this prompted the Syndicate to lay down a specific reasonable sum for hot baths, 'in no case exceeding 6*d* where gas is employed or 4*d* where water is otherwise heated. An inclusive termly charge, not to exceed £1 may be made but only with the consent of the lodger, obtained at the beginning of the term [to avoid unpleasant surprises presumably]. No other charge may be made for the use of a bath or bathroom.' When Tom Wood sent me a copy of his 1947 lodging bill, he amusedly points out how Mrs Fuller circumvented this sort of dictum by charging '1*s* 6*d* for toilet'. He adds, 'I was never certain if this was the proportional cost of the toilet paper or just a charge for wear and tear — or perhaps it should be called 'depreciation'.[3]

About this late thirties date we begin to hear more about bedsits or 'half-sets' as they were commonly referred to. When Mr Burnaby of Trinity (a Syndic) asked whether a hostel only offering bedsits would be approved, for reasons of economy, the Syndicate debated the point and agreed to 'license any building set up and approved by the college'.

The Borough of Cambridge was now expanding so fast that some students living within its area were in fact beyond the precincts and the Council of the Senate received many applications from students to live just outside in villages such as Shelford and Girton. Many lodging houses had been demolished in the centre as town improvements had been carried out in accordance with slum clearance and higher standards and as most licensed rooms were noted filled in 1938 and more would be required for the following academic year, the Syndicate voted to forward a request to extend the precincts by half a mile.

All nursing homes in the Borough registered by the Medical Officer of Health were to be recognised by the University for res-

3. see letter (Wood), chapter 4, p.151.

idence. But perhaps some stood higher in public estimation than others? In October 1939 the Secretary is directed to tell Tutors that it is not necessary to apply for permission to count residence in The Grove or Brooklands Avenue Nursing Homes, and that if matrons of nursing homes asked to be put on 'the list', they should be told that the choice of a nursing home for an undergraduate rested with his Tutor.

The first indication of the outbreak of war comes with a request from the Chairman to waive normal regulations affecting hygiene, etc., and to license retrospectively any houses that Tutors might have secured for their pupils. More urgently, a notice is to go out to lodging house keepers permitting them to unlock doors and windows between 10 p.m. and 6 a.m. when an air raid warning was given, on the understanding that they would be responsible, after the All Clear was sounded, for seeing that all undergraduates were in their rooms; if not, they were to report the absence to the Tutor by 9 in the morning.

By November 1939 it was reported that 2014 men were in licensed rooms, other rooms in the system being occupied by military, or by evacuated civil servants or by members of London colleges. The writer's husband remembers the envy with which members of the London School of Economics in particular were regarded since they were exempt from the discipline and restrictions that Cambridge men had to observe. L.S.E. men were all assumed to be 'living it up' in flats with women, in a scene imagined to be one of untramelled debauchery. In emulation, several Tutors proposed that their pupils be allowed to hire a house of their own 'in which they would do some of the domestic work themselves, each man having only one room'. A senior member of the University could, if required, live there to be responsible for its proper management. But the moment was not ripe and the Syndicate thought such a scheme impracticable on financial grounds. However, it was agreed that lodging house keepers already licensed might apply to let single rooms in their houses as bedsits 'during the present emergency'.

When in January 1940, the Chief Constable asked the Secretary to notify all lodging house keepers of their obligation under the Aliens' Order to keep registers of all lodgers, whether British or alien, the Syndicate directed her to refuse, with regret, saying they had no machinery to circularise. As new regulations or instructions had always been all too promptly sent round whenever the Syndicate saw fit in the past, I find this reply a little disingenuous.

Further echoes of war: Mr Clarke, landlord at 74 Trumpington Street (now the home of the Department of Estate Management, but then a large lodging-house catering for Corpus men) is reprimanded for having his door open at 10.30 one evening when an undergraduate belonging to the house told the Pro-Proctor that he had unlocked the door to let out a lady visitor. Clarke explained that his lodgers had been instructed by Corpus to go to shelters in the college in the event of an air raid; they had to be pretty prompt in getting themselves (pyjama-clad?) across the road, as the gate of the college would be shut three minutes after the siren sounded. That being the case, he had hung the key in the hall so that men could unlock the door and have a speedy exit. But this reasonable explanation was not acceptable and the Syndicate ordered him to keep the key in his pocket in future. The possible consequences — of seven men trapped in the house while bombs fall — don't bear thinking about.

When a Trinity man sought permission to count nights spent at the Labs. on duty in the Fire Squadron, the Syndicate agreed it was not in their province to determine so critical a question, and referred it to the Council of the Senate. And so a formal decree is issued, that 'persons *in statu pupillari*, absent from their rooms at night while engaged on work of national service under the local authorities, and with the approval of their respective Tutors, should count those nights as residence'.

Early in 1941 the Secretary was asked to keep and publish her office hours every day in the week preceding full term for the convenience of Tutors, and it was arranged she should be in the office from twelve to one o'clock every day. The Syndicate agreed to pay 15s towards fire fighting appliances for the A.R.P. scheme in Trinity Street where the office was, and a month later the Committee of the fire-watching scheme demanded (and got) 5s a week towards expenses.

The Syndicate Office was classed as business premises for firewatching purposes and they were obliged to provide a firewatcher.

The Secretary had been taking her turn in the voluntary scheme for the street, but as there had been many bombs dropped near her own home in the country (this was October 1941) she perhaps thought her duty lay rather to her village than her office.

Evidently there were rebellious murmurings about the fire-watching scheme: Mr Kitson Clark the ARP warden was consulted and wanted the two sides of the street to collaborate in one scheme, partly to save expense, but Matthews refused to join in, no doubt having set up an elaborate plan to protect their own valuable premises. Five shillings must have loomed as a large contribution and the Secretary wrote asking for details of these 'expenses' to which she was forced to contribute. Answer came that they needed mattresses, blankets and more water tanks but that once these had been provided they expected to reduce the subscription to 3s a week.

Miss Kennett transferred her attention to conditions in lodging houses and reported a number with a wooden staircase to two or three bedrooms on the top floor from which there existed absolutely no means of escape in case of fire. She was urged to visit those houses deemed to be specially dangerous and insist on having a knotted rope fixed for escaping from the top storey; without such an installation the house was not to be licensed.

It is interesting to note that disciplinary control was still exerted even where a Cambridge undergraduate is not concerned: Miss Adcock, of 93 Chesterton Road, had accused a London student of stealing a cushion, and had sent him a solicitor's letter asking him to leave the house. 'As she had caused trouble on previous occasions, the Syndicate decided not to renew her licence next year.'

Mr Southcott, who had been Clerk for nearly 30 years, had suddenly died. The Secretary had paid to his daughter whatever was due as salary and expenses. The Syndicate agreed not to appoint another Clerk until 'next summer' and when in April 1942 the subject was raised, Miss Kennett expressed her willingness to continue the work and the appointment was left in abeyance, she being given a free hand to employ temporary clerical assistance whenever necessary. Mr Salter undertook to apply to the Divisional Petroleum Office for extra petrol for the Secretary's use, and she was allowed 10 gallons, to last from June till the end of August.

That Michaelmas a laconic entry records tragedy. Two lodging-house keepers were reported killed in a recent air raid, Mrs Rattle of 4 Jesus Lane and Miss Johnson of 4 St Clement's Gardens.
It may be of interest to list the London institutions that evacuated at least some of their students to Cambridge in 1942: The Bartlett School of Architecture, Bedford College, London Hospital Medical School, London School of Economics, Queen Mary College, Barts Hospital Medical School and the Faculty of Law at King's College, London and University College, London.
A lodging house keeper wrote a letter to the V.C. suggesting that undergraduates should be required to return to their lodgings by 11 p.m. (rather than 10 as in the Regulations) as a move to save light and fuel. No such amendment was made but lodging-house keepers were to be sent a letter encouraging economy by every possible means (other than that one). The allowance to each man was 3 cwt of coal for the Michaelmas Term and 4 cwt for Lent. Since coal must have been delivered indiscriminately to the landlady's coalhouse or bunker, one wonders how on earth she worked out the just allocation to each student.
Miss Kennett must have used her petrol ration to good effect because in January 1943 she is able to give a full report on the fire precautions:

> 51 houses with parapets
> 132 with ropes fixed
> 42 where there is a way of escape on to a roof
> 7 with Davy automatic escapes
> 4 with ladders
> 2 with rope ladders
> 4 with communicating doors to the house next door

As the call-up rate intensifies, there are fewer and fewer men actually studying at Cambridge and consequently lower numbers occupying licensed rooms. The 884 undergraduates of 1940-41 are down to 785 living out in 42-43, but pressure from elsewhere fills up the empty spaces. Up to 200 naval cadets will be coming on a course in April (1943) for whom rooms must be found. The Chairman advises that the cheaper rooms should be booked if possible, as the amount allowed by the Admiralty would not pay the rents of large sets. He will apply for a special allocation of petrol to help

Miss Kennett in her search and if this is refused she is to hire a car or taxi. By March she has booked 147 rooms. Later, we hear that Mr M.M. Daldry overcharged the five naval cadets sent to lodge at 6a King's Parade, in spite of the agreement made over terms. He was summoned to a Syndicate meeting to explain his greedy behaviour, but as he refused to come his licence was revoked.

The Camp Reception Station in Storey's Way and the Sick Bay at Emmanuel are to be recognised as places of residence during the present emergency. But not every military excuse proves adequate: when G.B. Cook, aged 22 and a graduate of Birmingham University, asked to count residence at 22 Maids Causeway, an unlicensed address, on the grounds that he was engaged on Secret Research Regulations, he was told that as one enjoying the privileges of the University, he ought not to be exempt from the regulations applying to an undergraduate. He was to move into licensed lodgings forthwith.

A threat to requisition some licensed lodging houses as hostels for foreign workers turns out to be groundless. The Syndicate panics anew at the risk of the Secretary being called up for nursing; she had registered some time ago and the Ministry of Labour sent a demand for her services to the Chairman. It is agreed that he should write to say she could not be released from her present duties.

Miss Webb of 7 Park Parade is given permission to let rooms to two 'girl students' (sic) from L.S.E. notwithstanding the fact that one set in the house is let to a Trinity undergraduate. The Adviser to Students at the Colonial Office wrote complaining of a rebuff to an African student sent by the Nigerian Government to L.S.E. As an evacuee, he had gone for lodgings at 20 Aylestone Road and had been rudely turned away. The offending landlady was sent for, and alleged the illness of her brother was the prime cause of her refusing to take the Nigerian student. But she went on to admit strong prejudice against the black races. While reprimanding Mrs Platts, she was told 'to find out the nationality of lodgers from the college in future, before promising them rooms'. In other words, she was entitled to exercise racial discrimination, but not face to face on the doorstep because that is unkind. Laws prohibiting such a response did not to come into force until much later. Record-cards in the office in my own day still bore a pencilled A.N. in the corner, indicating the more liberal landladies who were prepared to take lodgers of 'any nationality'.

Mrs Taverner may hold a licence for the duration of the War only, because her house at 17 Botolph Lane has an unhealthy deep basement. Today it is the headquarters of the YTEA and old files are stored in the basement. They certainly don't keep a landlady down there, I have been back to check.

At last a hopeful note is struck: in January 1944 the Chairman raised the question of finding accommodation for undergraduates after their demobilisation. Letters are to be sent out to all those holding licences at the time when war broke out. Soon a letter arrives from Sir Hubert Sams, read at the request of the Bursars' Committee, asking the Syndicate to waive restrictions on the licensing of houses, such as not accepting those without bathrooms or indoor sanitation, or with basements, ready for the large influx of undergraduates expected once the Germans were defeated. While the Syndicate were anxious to maintain pre-war standards, they would be willing to grant temporary licences for below-standard houses 'during the bulge period'.

Another helpful initiative was to allow undergraduates to reside in bed-sitting rooms, subject to obtaining their Tutor's consent. Miss Kennett having sent out 255 letters to ex-lodging house keepers had only 52 replies, and was busily visiting the houses of possible candidates. In re-appointing her for a further three years, the Syndicate voted her an honorarium of £50 for the present year, and wanted Tutors to be told of its exertions to provide for the future.

One ex-Army man must have been working hard on his landlady: I wonder did he dictate the letter that Mrs Hicks of 32 Hobson Street wrote to the Syndicate, asking 'that M. Loftus an Oxford graduate and late Captain in the Scots Guards, be allowed the use of a latch-key and whether his lady friends might stay until 11 p.m.' This is January 1945 — maybe Loftus had been invalided out with war injuries? Surprisingly, the Syndicate capitulated over the key, provided he gave an undertaking to use it only for himself (and not admit undergraduates by its means), but they stipulated that he must keep to the 10 o'clock rule for his visitors.

By July the War in Europe was over. A special Syndicate meeting discusses the proposals of a sub-committee set up to consider rents and agreed to increase rents by an average of 10%, to operate as follows:

Sets up to and including £10 to be raised £1
Sets between £10.10.0 — £12.5.0 to be raised £1.5.0
Sets between £12.10.0 — £15.10.0 to be raised £1.10.0
Sets between £15.15.0 — £19.10.0 to be raised £1.15.0
Sets £20 and over to be raised £2

Lodging-house keepers have already been allowed to charge from 15s to £1 a term for the hire of linen. Evidently peace has already brought a rising cost of living. Also the City has put up the rates.

10

A Busy Peace Returning

At first a sprinkling of applications arrived for married men to be given permission to keep terms with their wives in unlicensed lodgings, but this soon became a flood as demobilisation accelerated. By December 1946, 2511 men were living out of college, 723 in unlicensed rooms and 66 beyond the precincts; 358 married men had been granted special permission to reside with their wives, and because of the pressure on central town accommodation, men were allowed to live as far out as Swaffham Bulbeck, West Wratting, Oakington, etc.

The Tutorial Representatives were asked 'to impress on any of their men who may be in unlicensed rooms the importance of being in by midnight' but obviously it would have been impossible to patrol the whole neighbourhood as in the old days. Men whose wives were living elsewhere and could only visit them occasionally had to ask special permission to receive them at their lodgings from time to time, or for ecstatic honeymoons at the Blue Boar.

In discussing the question of residence outside the precincts Syndics argued that if men were too far away, they would forego the advantages of residence in Cambridge to the detriment of their studies. They decided that they would not normally give permission for residence at a distance beyond 10 miles, only in very exceptional cases.

In accordance with this, they refused a man permission to keep terms at Wimbish near Saffron Walden, a distance of 16 miles or so. But on appeal and at a special meeting to which the Registrary was invited, they agreed to be willing 'to give favourable consideration to any strong recommendation from a Tutor that leave be given to a married man entering or returning to the University after approved national service to reside with his wife during 1946-47, provided his Tutor certifies that the applicant is in a position to attend the formal instruction appropriate to his course'.

At that meeting the Registrary must have caused some eyebrows to rise by announcing that the Council of the Senate had agreed to allow three undergraduates — neither married nor ex-servicemen

— to keep their third year by residence 18 miles from Cambridge in a house belonging to one of them. In fact, the Syndicate agreed to consider favourably any application in closely similar circumstances.

The office must have been incredibly busy with seeking out roofs to cover the hordes and processing all the permission applications. Miss Kennett had orders to engage a part-time clerk to be paid £75 *per annum*: the Bursar of Trinity offered a lease of three rooms at 31 Trinity Street at a rent of £45, the Syndicate paying the rates. The college was to clean and decorate and wire the attic, put in a gas or power point, and give permission to sublet. This was to be the office for some years.

The attic was to be offered to D.T. Piper, M.A., who asked to use it as a study, but by the end of 1946 the tenant was Mrs Keogh, a dressmaker, given the room for 10s a week. As for the supply of housing, a letter from Lord Annan tells us how a young tutor was expected to ride about on his bicycle in search of lodgings for his men.[5]

Attempts were made to secure huts for married undergraduates at Wimpole Hall Camp or Oakington W.A.A.F. camp, or at any other within easy distance, but the Ministry of Works delayed so long in answering appeals that nothing in the end came of it. The Council of the Senate was enlisted to induce government departments to release as much accommodation as possible and the Borough M.P. gave the information that the 1400 Civil servants living in Cambridge in 1939 had turned by successive evacuations into about 2600 in 1946, all taking up potentially useful student rooms. Those private residents who had taken London students were to be asked to house the Cambridge men as London colleges returned to what was left of their own institutions in the capital.

To give an idea of prevalent crowded conditions, let me quote a brief note after a home-visit by Miss Kennett. 'The Secretary said she had been to the A.A. site in Long Road where Hoole of Emma lived with his wife. there was only one large room and no water laid on, but there was a closed stove and it was fairly comfortable.'

By 1947 a proposal came from the Cambridge University Accommodation and Grants Committee that a new committee should be

5. See his letter of 25 September 1993, p.285.

formed to explore possibilities of finding further accommodation possibly in conjunction with the Borough Housing Committee. The Secretary and Mr Salter, the Chairman, the Senior Proctor, and the Registrary, Dr. Spooner, and Mr Crawley (this is the first mention of Mr. Crawley, who was later to play an important lead in Syndicate affairs) all agreed to serve.

When they met in June they expressed appreciation of all the extra work undertaken by the Syndicate and voted it be given powers to deal with the abnormal conditions. Dr. Alec Wood, the Medical Officer of Health, was to be invited to join future discussions and one or two undergraduates from the Accommodation Grants Committee.

When this amplified committee got together, the undergraduate representatives asked for pre-fab and requisitioned houses to be made available to students, whereupon Dr Wood painted a moving picture of the appalling overcrowding in the town: all requisitioned houses were filled immediately. The city had on its books 6,500 applications for houses for people already working here and 500 of these were urgent cases.

So far 500 new homes had been built of which 300 were pre-fabricated; another 400 families were temporarily housed in huts or requisitioned property. With such claims on its resources from the townspeople there was evidently little hope of diverting any housing in the direction of the University. The Committee was apprised of how much was achieved by the efforts of the Syndicate and its members were advised to keep in touch with the Secretary to avoid wasteful overlapping.

Rents were reviewed, ready for the academic year 1947-8, and were to be increased in the same proportion as in July '45, reflecting a steady rise in the cost of living post-war. Landladies are free to charge 10s termly for shoe cleaning and baths are to cost 1s if heated by gas or electricity and 8d if by other means. alternatively a charge not exceeding £2 may be levied termly if the lodger's consent has been given in advance.

The minutes give up many whole foolscap pages to the record of applications from married men and single research students for permission to keep terms in unlicensed premises. The Secretary's statistics for that December are worth quoting in full:

830 licensed houses, containing 1508 sets, 119 extra bedrooms and 230 bed-sits. Of these, 124 houses are without bathrooms and 109 have outside sanitation only.

2,883 men are living out of college, 58 with their parents, 117 in theological colleges;

450 married men have been given permission to live in unlicensed lodgings. 94 of them beyond the University precincts.

Fitzwilliam House complained that they experienced particular difficulty in finding rooms for Indian research students, but the Syndicate firmly ruled that they could make no difference in the licensing rules for British and foreign nationals. Magdalene and Corpus Christi sought permission for large properties they had each acquired to be licensed by the Syndicate for use as hostels. Some good lodgings were lost to the University because their elderly owners were debarred from earning a bit of extra income under the old-age pension rules, and the Chairman offered to take this up with the National Insurance administration.

Hitherto, it had been obligatory for those intending to apply for a licence to get their applications countersigned by a member of the Senate, as evidence of their respectability: but with the growth of the town, many applicants had no personal acquaintance with senior members of the University. In future, anyone qualified to endorse a passport can sign for the lodging-house keeper. Later, Mr Crutchley at the Pitt Press drew up a new form of certificate for applicants and this was adopted.

Mr. Dewey the eccentric chaplain of Pembroke joins the Syndicate at this period and is full of helpful and liberal suggestions. His first recorded act is to draw attention to the bad condition of the office and the staircase leading to it and to propose that it be painted and distempered. The Secretary is to obtain estimates for the work; Mr Rooke's of £25 is accepted, and the college is to repair the roof — cheerful portents of all the renovation and refurbishments that were going on all over England to make up for wartime neglect and damage. In November '48, three hopeful undergraduates asked if they could rent the attic at the office, but were sadly refused and the Secretary told to find a suitable tenant, preferably an M.A.

In spite of the pressure on space, standards are not to slip altogether. Mrs Parker's house at 6 Tennis Court Terrace is so dirty she is refused a licence, and Mrs Strange is called to meeting to account for her door being open at 11, not issuing gate-bills and taking as a lodger someone not a member of the University. She admits all the charges but explains that part of her house at 25 Grange Road was let as a flat, and other rooms were occupied by M.A.s and B.A.s. The Syndicate told her to operate as a lodging-house wholly or not at all: she is not to be given a licence but as her record is good, she may apply later if she mends her ways.

Mrs Docking was also sent for, to attend a meeting and account for allowing an undergraduate to come in after midnight and falsifying her gate record to his college. She didn't appear but her son and daughter tried to represent her and under cross-examination admitted that the key was 'always left under the dustbin'. As the house is at 271 Cherry Hinton Road they must reasonably have expected that the Proctors were most unlikely to call and certainly not to go fumbling under their dustbin. However, the Syndicate refused to deal with these deputies, saying their business was with the licence-holder, and they refused to renew her licence.

At the following meeting (Oct. '49) kind-hearted Mr Dewey pops up over the question of summoning delinquent lodging-house keepers before the Syndicate. He thought — as was no doubt true, faced with that barrage of black-gowned figures — that they were put at a great disadvantage and that their humiliation led to bad feeling between the University and the Town. He must have won Syndics round to his way of thinking since they decided their minor disciplinary cases would be dealt with in future by a visit or a warning letter from Miss Kennett — herself sufficiently alarming, if not intimidating — and only in serious cases was a personal appearance in the dock to be required. If a lodging-house keeper was so summoned and failed to appear, the licence was to be automatically revoked.

The very next February an offence so heinous that it could not be ignored occurred and Mrs A.E. Riseley of 14 Alexandra Street was ordered to come before a special meeting to account for overcharging on her electricity bills: she had charged 3 men £49 for one term, a very large amount for that date when electricity was only used for lighting. Her two best sets at this time rented for £22 10s a term each. She refused to appear and so lost her licence. Although her undergraduates and her solicitor pleaded for its restoration, the Syndics stuck to their resolve.

For an eloquent description of life in lodgings at the house next door but one, 12 Alexandra Street, at the beginning of the war, see the letter from Professor J.R. Lander, then a Pembroke freshman (March '93).[6]

Now for a fascinating piece of detective work. None of these three cases, Strange, Docking and Riseley, is recorded in the locked minute-book covering discipline-cases for the period. Their names are entered in Miss Kennett's handwriting in the alphabetical index at the beginning of the book, with page numbers 49 and 51 indicating where the entries were made, but the entries are not there and the preceding page has been renumbered. Pages 50 to 51 do not exist and subsequent pages are not numbered and refer to cases after Miss Kennett's time.

The page coincides with a place where the stitches of the book's binding come through in the middle, so it would have been possible to extract a double sheet without leaving trace. Is it possible that someone destroyed the record, not noticing that the names had been entered in the index?

In fact, there are no entries at all for the period 1945-1959. I checked the numbers of double-pages making up each section bound into the little book: a normal section comprises six double sheets or twelve pages. The one in question only contains five double pages, which proves that two pages have been extracted. A mystery. The Syndics would have been inexorable about Mrs Riseley because she had already been disciplined for excessive charges in 1938.

Back in the office, Miss Kennett's allowance for expenses goes up to £35 from £25 and the Chairman is to enquire if she could be permitted to put in a claim based on her mileage, like other University Officers. The lower room in Trinity Street is sought by Mr Rowe as a showplace for furniture and antiques etc. and she is to get permission from Trinity to sub-let to him on a quarterly tenancy.

---

6. See page 251.

By January 1950, 3589 men are living out of college, 1534 of them in unlicensed rooms, and Mr Norman St John Stevas is given permission to count nights at 6 King's Parade.

The Syndicate begins a controversy with the Council when the Town Clerk writes to ask it not to license Council houses on account of the desperate shortage of houses for families. The Chairman and Vice-Chairman of the Borough Housing Committee come to a Syndicate meeting (June 1950) and explain that they propose to move childless couples into smaller dwellings. They would allow council tenants to take civil servants or artisans as lodgers, but not University men, arguing that workers were citizens and rate payers whereas undergraduates are not. The Secretary, called on for the facts, had found only 28 undergraduate lodging in council houses out of 5936 *in stat. pup.* In the outcome, no action was taken over council house tenants already licensed as University lodgings but the Syndicate was to refer fresh applications to the Council for their prior permission.

Trinity tried to dodge Syndicate supervision of its property by insisting that 35-36 Sidney Street, 20 Trinity Street and 14-17 Green Street didn't need permission but were all extensions of the college itself and incorporated in it. The Syndicate swallowed some of this but queried the inclusion of the Green Street houses, and ultimately decided that they should be regarded as a hostel, needing a licence for a given number of years in the usual way. We might usefully compare this decision with the bid by Jesus in the late seventies to have their Jesus Lane lodging-houses recognised as 'outdoor staircases'. With the help of expensive London counsel, they won their case in the Courts and henceforth administered their property across the road without Syndicate interference or the presence of a lodging-house keeper. But this is to anticipate.

Leading the way to a future emancipation is our liberal Mr Dewey again, asking permission for five undergraduates, with degrees already from other Universities, to keep terms in unlicensed rooms, three of them in a flat of their own. The Syndicate was quite prepared to discuss the whole question of whether it might be expedient to relax the rules about gate-bills and locking doors at 10.00, and the Chairman put it to the Registrary that the time might be ripe to waive certain regulations.

As a result, the Council agreed to authorise the Syndicate to permit those *in stat. pup.* recommended by their college to keep terms in unlicensed lodgings; tutors were to state the age and academic standing of the pupil concerned, and apply for permission as sparingly as possible and only for fairly senior men.

For the year 1951-52 882 undergraduate and research students were given permission to keep terms in unlicensed accommodation or with a resident M.A. Each case had to be individually processed and presented to the Syndicate and the tutor notified of the decision, and the amount of administrative work it caused the office was colossal.

The years 1947, '48, '49 and '50 have seen increasing numbers of women students from Girton and Newnham being given permission to live in these special conditions; it was no longer axiomatic that women all lived in college, since quite a few married women are now appearing, and more women were staying on after graduation to pursue research.

A further initiative taken by the Council of the Senate was to invite the Lodging House Syndicate and the Proctorial Syndicate each to appoint two members to a committee to review the rules applicable to licensed lodgings. In January 1952 the body so formed recommended that the door-shutting hour should be 11 p.m. not 10, and that the clause in the regulations about window-locking be deleted. They thought it a hardship for the lodging-house keeper to be compelled to sit up to admit a man with a late pass and proposed he be given a key. The Tutorial Representatives were to be consulted and in the following year the lodging-house keepers were circularised to give their opinions on the subject of changing the hour to 11.

By April 1953 the question had become controversial and so was to be dealt with by a report rather than merely a Grace. Mr Crawley now joins the Syndicate. Tuesday 9 June was Coronation Day for our present Queen and the Chairman and one Syndic met in solitary state to dispatch pressing business. The Secretary was delicately instructed that, if any lodging-house keeper asked permission, she was to give them a dispensation to ignore the 10 o'clock rule on that particular night, in the name of general patriotic fervour and rejoicing.

At the end of that year a Trinity undergraduate complained of £4. 10s stolen from his rooms at 69 Maids Causeway, the house of Mr A.E. Neal. Men had complained over the previous two years of petty losses of money, cigarettes and wine and twice men had asked to be moved. In April 1952 Mrs Neal had been convicted of six cases of theft from unoccupied cars in New Square. Now there was evidence that she was opening her lodgers' letters so Trinity refused to send any more men to that house. The Secretary had visited the couple and advised them to let outside the University and the rooms were presently taken by a civil servant. The Syndicate agreed that Mr. Neal should be told in June that the licence could not be renewed, and when he did re-apply he was refused. But it is interesting to compare this treatment with the harsh and automatic penalties dealt out in earlier times to lodging-house keepers with criminal convictions.

A similar leniency attaches to the case of Mr Butcher in charge of a lodging-house at 14 Mill Road and of the Post Office at No. 16, next door, who was also convicted of theft. The Secretary is to see Dr. Wild as it was a Downing house, and Dr. Wild said he would not send men there again. Miss Kennett called on Mrs Butcher who admitted her husband's offence and announced she no longer had Downing men but took people from Christ's. As long as the Tutor at Christ's raised no objection, the Syndicate agreed that they would relicense the house.

All through these years of nationwide University expansion, the licensed system keeps growing. More and more houses are newly licensed, Miss Kennett adds hundreds to the stocks and her car allowance goes up by leaps and bounds as she motors relentlessly around the residential roads of Cambridge. Figures for the year 1954-55 show 3284 undergraduates living out of college, 2197 of them in licensed rooms. But Miss Kennett is getting elderly and the Syndicate prepare to make a new appointment. They are unanimous in wanting a woman again but they prefer not to advertise: the Chairman is to see the Treasurer and get a definite figure for the salary to be offered and an allowance for a car.

Suddenly the University must have brought in a new ruling as to the age at which officers had to take compulsory retirement, for in the new year we find the Chairman writing to all the Syndics to enquire whether they would like Miss Kennett to continue in office for another year 'under the extension of the retiring age'. They all elected for her to stay on, and to celebrate, decided to buy the office a typewriter through the Treasurer. In fact, this extension was not the last as in June 1956 Miss Kennett was again re-appointed, to serve until Michaelmas 1957.

We hear intimations of a rise in the cost of living: Jesus and Trinity tenants have their rents raised by the colleges, and Syndicate rents are to go up, with a proportionately higher charge for sets to encourage landladies to let two rooms rather than proliferate the bedsits. Sets go up by 10% whereas bedsits gain only $7\frac{1}{2}$%.

Trinity give notice in October 1955 that the office (at 31 Trinity Street) may be required by the college. The Secretary is to enquire of the Treasurer if any suitable room is available in University property. His answer was to suggest a room on the top floor at 1 Rose Crescent and the November meeting was held there, for the Syndics to see and make a choice of two rooms. Miss Kennett thought she could manage with one room as there was a lobby where people could wait, and agreed to have the office there if a large cupboard for stationery were installed. The room was to be decorated and a gas fire installed.

Before the move was accomplished, a momentous event occurred although no mention of it is made in the Minutes: Miss Kennett was given an honorary M.A.. A Grace was submitted on 2 March 1955 'that the degree of Master of Arts, *honoris causa*, be conferred under Statute B, IV upon Mary Cecilia Domneva Kennett' and she received the degree at a congregation on 5 March.

In this academic year ('55-'56) comes the first mention of New Hall, the third foundation for women, at first finding a home in the Hermitage, now the central building of Darwin, 19 New Hall students were given permission to live with an M.A. if undergraduate or in unlicensed accommodation if they were research students.

The Syndics discussed the times at which colleges shut their gates: most do so at ten, a few at eleven and liberated King's at midnight. Some hostels in St Peter's Terrace kept open till eleven. The Chairman was to see the Master of Peterhouse and put to him that the Syndicate thought hostels should observe the ten o'clock rule in line with licensed lodgings.

Noel Annan wrote, asking if the new second hostel on Peas Hill could be treated as if it were part of the college. When the question had been brought up originally, the Council of the Senate had ruled that the present building be licensed (by the Syndicate) as a hostel, and this would seem to apply also to the later addition. The whole question of hostels was discussed and doubt was expressed whether a building could be deemed part of a college unless there were not only a porter but a Fellow in residence. They stuck to this resolution when King's again applied in the following year, and refused to allow Peas Hill and the West Road hostels to be treated as part of college.

That deep basement at 17 Botolph Lane is causing trouble again. Mrs Lowe is the new tenant and has not been told that the basement could only be used for storage. The Secretary and the Bursar of Caius went over the house and the Syndicate insisted that the lodging-house keeper should have a living room on the ground floor even if cooking were allowed in the basement. Caius must have grumbled because a letter arrived from the Bursars' Committee asking the Syndicate to revoke their decision to refuse licences to houses with deep basements.

It was an uneconomic policy, they said, and many lodgings are lost thereby. But the Syndicate stuck to its principle 'that they could not allow lodging-house keepers to live in unhealthy rooms underground', and to illustrate this would grant a licence at 30 New Square only until June and not thereafter, unless the kitchen and living-room are put above ground.

This brought Jesus into question and the Bursar wrote protestingly, saying that because of the Syndicate policy, hundreds of sets would be lost to the University. The Chairman replied that the living-room of this house was completely underground and did not satisfy the requirements of the Ministry of Health for living standards. Far from colleges losing 'hundreds of rooms', there were only 54 houses with deep basements in the University lodgings system.

This time the appointing mechanism went ahead and early in 1957 the Syndics considered the qualifications of several possible applicants for the Secretary's post: two candidates were interviewed at a special February meeting and the Chairman was to offer the appointment to one of them. The person chosen was a Mrs

Deuchars, who wrote to accept the post in March, whereupon the Syndics spent some time debating how long an overlap there should be while Miss Kennett initiated her into her duties. They determined to install her by mid-September or preferably, even earlier, bearing in mind that Miss Kennett's appointment expired at Michaelmas.

There must have been consternation when a telegram arrived in April to say that Mrs Deuchars regretted she was unable to take up the appointment. No hint of a reason is given, and although Mrs Deuchars was given time to reconsider, she stuck to her decision to refuse. So the job went to the second candidate, Mrs Storr, who accepted the offer, probably with some surprise, and arranged to take over for the Michaelmas Term. The telephone directory for 1957 lists a Mrs S.M. Storr as living at 53 St Barnabas Road.

While all this was in the melting-pot, a deputation arrived from King's bearing a request signed by more than 300 undergraduates for lodging-houses and hostels to be left open until midnight. The Tutorial Representatives, asked to comment, were unable to reach a concerted opinion and suggested, in a novel spirit of liberty, that closing time be optional. The Secretary reported lodgings were being lost because of the locking-up rule, and that new householders on the outskirts of town commonly made a practice of giving their lodgers keys; nor were windows assiduously locked as in the past. The Proctors actually proposed that keys be given but that men should be in their rooms by midnight, with the lodging-house keeper obliged to report on returns to the house after that time, or absence overnight, or visitors after midnight.

As yet another proof of the air of freedom blowing, the Syndicate agrees to ask the Council of the Senate for authority to let fairly senior undergraduates live in unlicensed lodgings. The Tutorial Representatives' reaction was to welcome the unlicensed option for people recommended by their college; they evinced some resistance to the free issue of keys, and suggested a class of 'approved lodgings' where more relaxed rules could apply. The Syndicate ignored this last idea.

As for the Council of the Senate, it saw no objection to 'each college having discretion to close its outer doors at such time no later than midnight as might be convenient'. As for generations, men and more recently women too, had always found means of entering their college late at night without going through the gates and 'disturbing the porters', this close attention sounds a little academic.

That summer Miss Kennett in one of her last acts inaugurated a new tradition, one that was eventually to link Cambridge with every British University and lend a new professionalism to its housing practice and expertise: she was authorised by the Syndicate to represent it at Sheffield University in July at a conference of those engaged in accommodating university students, and her travelling expenses were paid.

What began as a social meeting-ground for a few colleagues at Midlands universities was to develop through the 1970s into a fully-fledged professional body, the Association of University Accommodation Officers. As governments played a more leading part in determining university policy and housing law became yearly more complicated, the Association took on the role of advising and indeed training its members, and became a vital forum for the exchange of views and information.

Miss Kennett is visible still in the background, initiating Mrs Storr, and she gave an interesting account of her Sheffield conference where nearly 20 universities had sent representatives. Cambridge was the last to continue the licensing system, Oxford having already given it up, although they continued a list of approved addresses supervised by the Delegacy of Lodgings.

Mr Garth Moore reported that the son of a lodging-house keeper at 14 Portugal Place had been convicted of housebreaking and theft and sentenced to 3 years imprisonment. His wife, with four previous convictions herself, was thought to be still living at the address and the Syndicate was clear she should leave and Trinity be told. Miss Kennett was to take a letter to the lodging-house keeper and ask for written assurance that this woman had left.

Mr Prior of Trinity is to be told that it is not possible to revoke a licence because the lodging-house keeper has refused to accept a coloured student as lodger, however regrettable that may be.

New Hall was growing fast as we can see from the grant of permission of the first President, Miss Rosemary Murray, to operate three premises as hostels till 1962: Bredon House, Selwyn Gardens, St Chads at 48 Grange Road, and the Old Granary in Silver Street.

By the end of the year the Secretary was able to report the land-ladies were very satisfied with an increase of twenty per cent. Tutorial Representatives had had no complaints from undergradu-ates and no-one had asked to move: the increase had simply been absorbed. The only dissident voice came from a meeting of the Chairman with the Bursars who would have preferred an even higher rise. Better liaison was recommended for the future in case it was desirable to make further increases.

As a final enconium: 'everyone joined in wishing Miss Kennett great happiness in her retirement', and so her sway of over twenty-two years comes to a close.

At this point Mr Kenneth Berrill (later Sir Kenneth and Bursar of King's) joined the Syndicate and as his first contribution said that rents in the centre of town would have to be greatly increased if they were to remain economic, and then only wealthy under-graduates could afford them and landladies might have to concen-trate on commercial lettings. If this were to be so, the Chairman felt, lodgings would have to be found away from the centre of town as had already happened at Oxford.

One hundred men were living in unlicensed lodgings while 68 licensed lodgings stood empty and applications for 30 new ones had been received. The Syndicate is to apply to the Council of the Senate again to give leave for senior persons *in stat. pup.* but such permissions will not readily be granted if a substantial number of licensed lodgings are left unfilled at Michaelmas, the Syndicate being anxious to encourage new applicants for licenses. Obviously if a landlady doesn't get a lodger it acts as a strong deterrent to ap-plying again for a licence and she will start to look elsewhere. The time when the University was the only market for lodgings has gone by and now they are one among other eager customers. An extra 250 men are expected to arrive for the year 1958-59.

Permission is not to be given in future for undergraduates to live at Alexandra House or the Central Hotel, so there must have been complaints. Mrs Storr has occasion to visit—in reprimanding stance—two landladies, one of whom, a Mrs Cushing in De Freville Avenue, is not subsequently relicensed, but no entry appears in the locked book until 1959. The reader will remember the suspicious absence of record between 1945 and 1959 detailed eariler.

Like all new brooms, Mrs Storr busies herself with the wording of instructions to lodging-house keepers, first in connection with the giving of parties in lodgings, but more generally a redrafting of rules is carried out, of course with help from the inevitable sub-committee. They decide to send out a printed leaflet with the licence, showing the dates of each term to facilitate landladies' letting rooms through the vacation. The Lodging House Syndicate is to have an imprest account like other University departments, and effect economies over printing; they estimate the first year's budget under the new arrangement at £350-400. June sees the last meeting chaired by Mr Salter: Mr Crawley takes over at Michaelmas ('58) and his first duty is to send the unanimous and warmest thanks of the Syndicate to Mr Salter for his devoted work as Chairman for so many years.

Several discussions focus on married undergraduates living out in the country and Mr Berrill suggests they thereby miss out on the advantages of University life. Tutors are to be warned that permission for such residence will be given for one term only unless there is an exceptional due cause. If possible, these married students should be urged to find accommodation within the precincts: failing that they should live not further than five miles from Great St Mary's.

John Broadbent then a go-ahead Senior Tutor at King's, wrote to suggest an updating of pre-war regulations was overdue, and Dr Lapwood felt time could be saved at meetings if letters requesting permission were only read out in full where any discussion was needed. As there are pages of special permissions, it must have made weary work if each case was spelt out minutely and aloud. The yearly certificates signed by the landladies are to be abolished except for new licencees, and a simplified licence and certificate are to be printed on one sheet. Permitted charges are to be printed on a leaflet. Dr Broadbent sends in another volley on the question of charges for electricity, but the Syndicate decided 'it wouldn't be practical to make a fixed charge'. Instead the leaflet will suggest charges of 5s to 15s per term and an additional 5s for the use of a radio. When senior members put pressure on the Syndicate to permit their sons to live at home beyond the precincts, they agree, but not beyond a radius of five miles.

A novel request comes from an undergraduate's wife to be given a licence at 18 Maids Causeway, but she was refused and the two men lodging with her were allowed only to count four weeks in October as residence.

Mrs Storr is clearly not so versed in University ways as Miss Kennett, and her minutes are scored with crossings-out and corrections. She writes 'license' for 'licence' and 'principle' for 'principal' and dates a meeting on 24 November as 'Lent Term' 1959. She persists in listing a new Syndic, (later to be my first chairman, Ernest Frankl) as Mr Frankle. But she does at last produce her first statistical tally, (Oct. '59): 1223 licensed houses providing 2,528 sets. No doubt she has been very busy and £100 is allowed in the estimates for the year '59-'60 and £250 for the year '60-'61, to pay for extra secretarial help. The Syndicate give her permission to attend a wardens' conference at Queen's University Belfast in April. The provision of accommodation in universities was very much bound up with welfare and many of her colleagues would have worn another hat as wardens of hostels, being themselves resident in University-owned student residences. This of course was never a function at Cambridge.

The landladies themselves have been engineering change, wanting more precision about their obligations, and on three issues the rules are clarified:

1. Oil heaters may only be used with the permission of the lodging-house keeper.
2. A man may not claim the use of his room in the vacations, but can leave property at his lodging, with the lodging-house keeper's consent and at his own risk.
3. The room is taken by the term: unless the lodger signs at mid term the form his landlady gives him, he is not committed to occupy or pay for the room in the following term. This puts the responsibility on the lodging-house keeper to obtain his written intent.

The expansion of the women's colleges is causing a new battlefield for the landladies as women undergraduates flock to Cambridge and assert their equality with men. First a mandate goes out that women visitors are not to be allowed in lodgings before 11 a.m. —

flirtatious breakfasts are not to be encouraged. But the Syndics themselves can't agree over curtailing the time for women visitors in lodgings. The landladies make loud complaints and some invent their own rules, but these are told 'where there is any restriction on women visitors the landlady must inform the lodger before he engages the room'. Hence came the many stories of a belligerent landlady confronting the undergraduate on her doorstep with the warcry, 'Remember now, no girls, mine's a decent house', before even showing him the room. The colleges, asked to aid the Syndicate's indecision, reply that few of them put any special restrictions about time on women visitors, and all of them would strongly resent landladies being allowed to make their own rules.

The first hint of a new role for the office comes in a letter from the Treasurer (March 1960) proposing that a charge should be made for help given to the students in finding unlicensed accommodation. Debating this, the Syndicate decided that to do so would appear to be undertaking the work of an agency, and would involve the office in more work and more expense. They did accept the Treasurer's offer of two rooms nearer street level at 1a Rose Crescent, however, and from this time the office was possibly more accessible and more visible as a port of call for student. Perhaps with this role firmly in view, these rooms proved less than perfect?

The minutes give no clue to the move but the list of lodgings granted for the year ended 30 September 1961 prints the address as 18 Silver Street and this remained the office headquarters until Easter 2006 when it moved to Tennis Court Road.

All through the sixties there was a frenzy of college-building and expansion as more and more accommodation was made available to house the fast-growing student population. Hints of this fall as the Syndicate approves of new premises for hostels, the licensing of Wychfield for Trinity Hall, and of the Orchard, Huntingdon Road, and Beaufort House, Storey's Way, for New Hall are examples. Churchill College makes its first appearance in the lists of college members given permission for exceptional residence. H.R.H. Princess Margrethe of Denmark was given permission to keep terms at 76 Storey's Way. Much later, as H.M. Queen Margrethe II she was elected an Honorary Fellow of Lucy Cavendish as well as of her own college of Girton.

At one meeting the Chairman felt that Tutors were ignoring his earlier letter regarding the precincts and several requests for permission were refused, notably that of a married research student, to live in unfurnished accommodation rent-free at Elsworth in return for his help on the farm. He was allowed to stay only till the end of the Lent Term, but this was later extended till the end of Easter Term on the grounds that the whole question of residential limits is being reconsidered and 'because he was given wrong advice by his tutor'. The outcome was for the Lodging House Syndicate to increase the limits of residence for married research students living with their wives from five to ten miles, 'on account of the extreme difficulty in finding suitable accommodation'.

So impressed was the Syndicate by the seriousness of this dearth of homes that it sent out letters of considerable import to the Registrary, the Treasurer, the Secretary of the Board of Research Studies and the Secretary of Tutorial Representatives. They recommended that the whole question of married accommodation should be considered before the position worsened, and advocated the provision of furnished flats for a fixed period for newly arriving students. Quite inspired by this novel initiative, Syndics came up with further suggestions, for example that the University might acquire existing houses and convert them to flats for research students, or arrange a central source of information about available accommodation.

Another result was that the University might promote an arrangement for the loan of bulky nursery equipment (cots, prams, playpens, highchairs etc) to research students and visiting married dons from overseas. The Chairman engaged to write to the Registrary detailing these suggestions which he thought 'interesting and useful even if the last of these was not strictly within their province'. (It was to be taken up and implemented most successfully by the Society for Visiting Scholars, but not for some time.) A far cry from early Syndicate days and how the academic mind had broadened in the interval.

By May 1961, the Syndicate has agreed to press for transit flats, possibly converted houses, the number put forward being 15 to 18 flats to be let at an economic rent and to go to the more deserving cases on application from Tutors, a few flats being reserved for late arrivals. And the Chairman agrees to speak at a discussion in the Senate House on 6 June.

From a perusal of *Reporter* dated 14 June 1961, we first observe the decision 'to submit a Grace to relieve persons of standing of B.A. from the obligation to wear academical dress in the streets after dusk'. The main discussion must have attracted a great deal of previous interest because many came to speak, having prepared their case in careful detail beforehand. The subject was the provision of accommodation and common room facilities for graduate students, and some speakers stressed one or other of these topics, wherever their interest lay. Much was made of the fact that Oxford was already preparing to build flats for 200 married couples.

Cambridge at the end of 1960 had 1500 research students and other graduates on the Residents' List, with social needs and housing needs that undergraduate facilities within college were inadequate to satisfy: there was on top no provision for post-doctoral fellows and overseas visitors who had not been given membership of any college. A central meeting-place would also be an attraction to the many Cambridge graduates employed in the Town. Mention was made of the Women Graduates' Club, which had existed for the last twenty years in a house in Mill Lane, and which provided rooms for ten residents, a drawing room and a dining-room that served 40 lunches daily. Graham Hough came out with a strong idea when he said that the real ideal would be a move towards a Graduate College.

So here on that historic occasion are the germs of two amazing innovations that we with hindsight can see heralded the foundation of the Graduate Centre and the run of graduate colleges starting with Darwin and going on to Clare Hall, Wolfson, Hughes Hall and St Edmund's.

Our Mr Crawley's contribution was about accommodation for married students only: about 100 married undergraduates were in residence. He suggested Southacre in Chaucer Road off Trumpington Road, as a site already belonging to the University, where a number of furnished flats could be built, suitable for small families. Alternatively, the University could acquire and adapt a few private houses within two or three miles of the Centre. He emphasised that such a pool of accommodation could only be provided by a central

University initiative such as was beyond the scope of an individual college.

The Chairman must have gone triumphantly back to the Syndicate when it next assembled, to tell them how these resounding notions had been floated and were now echoing round the academic world. He also described Churchill's tea-party for landladies at which the Senior Tutor had made an address, and showed them the stamped addressed cards the College supplied for landladies' use instead of making them run round with gate bills.

That same Michaelmas (1961) the Secretary had to report great difficulty in finding sufficient licensed lodgings, and quoted figures that showed a steady drop over the preceding three years. She gave, as reasons for this dearth, more competition as other educational institutions sought rooms for their students, higher rents and rates for the householder to bear, and a strong dislike on the part of present-day landladies for having their room prices fixed. She actually urged the Syndics to consider the de-control of room rents in licensed lodgings and plan an entirely different approach to landladies.

One probably popular move might be payment by the week instead of making the lodging-house keeper wait for his money till the end of term. Undergraduates might be allowed to live in houses kept by married graduates of other Universities. So draughty a wind of democracy started blowing that the Syndicate thought the time had come to reorganise the whole situation.

That did not save the landlord of 25 Victoria Street whose licence was not renewed. An entry in the locked book alleges reports of very disorderly parties and visits by Police and Proctors.

Almost immediately the Council of the Senate takes up this new area of concern so well demarcated at that June discussion and the Deputy Registrary writes to the Syndicate inviting it to accept responsibility for finding accommodation for married graduates and overseas visitors. Under present conditions the Syndics feel unable to take on full responsibility, but they are willing to become more officially the channel of information regarding vacant houses and flats. So in future files of information are to be kept. Such accommodation will not be inspected and the Syndicate is in no sense to be regarded as an Agent. They will not be asking for extra staff as they intend to employ one full-time assistant instead of the two present part-time assistants, but authority will be needed to pay for additional part-time help at peak periods. There must have been news in Mr Melville's letter that the University had a long term policy of erecting a block of possibly 30 flats and in the meanwhile Syndics urged the Council to consider acquiring suitable houses for conversion to relieve the more urgent cases of hardship.

Some 230 cases of special permission were considered and granted at the October meeting and supplemented by a further 350 in November. The system is being totally flooded and Syndics having considered a report from their equivalent institution at Oxford, the Delegacy for Lodgings, determine on a six point report to the University incorporating the Secretary's reforms above mentioned and recommending permanent instead of yearly licences and a request to Colleges that they should not use licensed lodgings for graduates or for short-term lets while the shortage continues. They first try the new ideas out on the Tutorial Representatives, and find the majority of tutors are dead set against any de-control of rents, so the move is dropped for the time being. They turned down the suggestion that a member of the Lodging House Syndicate could give an unbiased opinion in any case of gross overcharging in married accommodation, holding that it was for a man's college to defend him in such an event, and deeming the Rent Tribunal much more experienced. This is the first recognition of an outside body empowered to lay down rent levels, not answerable to the University and set up on a nationwide basis.

A Mr Rose has evidently had some disciplinary problem giving him cause to propose that the Syndicate 'should seriously consider circulating a document to undergraduates on behaviour in lodging houses, especially quiet after 11 p.m.'. Instead they decided to brief tutors on inconsiderate behaviour.

Permission was given in January 1962 to an undergraduate couple, aptly enough called Hope, to live with their baby in a caravan 'provided it was properly sited'.

A tricky case turned Syndicate attention to colour prejudice. One landlady gave notice to her lodger at 6 Harvey Road; objecting to the colour of his friends, and the affair attracted a great deal of publicity in *Varsity*. The Secretary heard evidence from the undergraduate and from a representative of the paper. A report in June 1962 tells us that the Senior Proctor visited the house, finding the landlady highly emotional and probably unreliable, but she convinced him that there was no question of assault and no real colour prejudice. Nevertheless the licence was not renewed as there had been previous complaints. The Chairman felt sufficiently impressed by the incident to write a letter on the subject of colour prejudice to Lord Walton.

More difficulty was experienced at the following Michaelmas in placing coloured students in lodgings. A landlady of Langharn Road accepted a Nigerian but then changed her mind and turned him away: as she was not letting, she was not licensed for that academic year, but no further action was taken. The Syndicate advised tutors in confidence not to send men to lodgings where they might be refused and several colleges asked for extra copies of this briefing.

In those pre-Race Relations Act days, it is heartening to note that Dr Cargill Thompson of King's urged the University to set an example by refusing to license houses which would not accept all nationalities, but this the Syndicate felt to be not practicable. Why so is not clear since the Secretary at this very moment was able to report a surplus in all types of lodgings, including furnished houses and flats.

Let us not forget that these are the swinging sixties: the Chairman brought news of a party in Newnham Terrace where the men had got Tutors' permission for 80 to 90 guests, although their landlady had not given consent for more than 15. Her floors must have been sagging. In future, a tutor would be well advised to see the landlady's written consent before giving permission for a party of more than fifteen.

The Secretary kept note of how many people made use of the office in Silver Street for accommodation other than licensed lodgings:

Research & Certificate of Education	701
Married men (callers)	225
Correspondence	108
	1034

At Michaelmas 1962, the office had to deal with more than 460 cases of special permission for residence.

Meetings of the Syndicate are usually held at 1a Rose Crescent, and new members include Dr Gay of Downing and Miss Murray, President of New Hall. A suggestion of Mr Frankl's that charges for hot water, electric light and bicycle storage should be included in the rent, led to the landladies being canvassed for information on what they did actually charge. Their replies were reasonable for the most part but they were afraid of undergraduates being extravagant if electric light were to be an inclusive charge. One remembers all those little scribbled notices stuck. to peeling wallpaper, asking the inmates to switch off staircase and corridor lights, and all the stumbling about and swearing that gave rise to. The minutes actually record Mr Frankl's first coining of that immortal cliché: 'In this day and age a man taking lodgings could reasonably expect . . . (these charges) included in his rent', and so by unanimous consent it was agreed.

The minutes for the April 1963 meeting are in a different handwriting, presumably that of Mrs Baker, the office assistant. First she records that 'an apology for absence was received from the Junior Proctor, Mr Bainbridge', a name we shall come across later. Then with surprise we read that the Chairman spoke of the great loss the Syndicate had suffered by the death of Mrs Storr on 16 April 1963. Her family had been written to, and a wreath sent to the funeral and members were now asked to stand in silence as a tribute to her memory. The March 1962 meeting had been cancelled because of her illness, but no other reference prepared us for this news.

The Chairman, Miss Murray and Mr Frankl form a sub-committee to consider applications for the post after placing advertisements in *Reporter* and *The Times*. Mrs Baker is to be given additional payments while she takes interim charge of the office, and to employ an extra temporary assistant for as long as necessary during the summer.

Luckily she must have been extremely competent because for May 1963 we have the first typewritten minute, noting that the office daily received requests for help from landladies faced with increased rates and sometimes higher rents as well. Inflation is making itself felt, and Mr Frankl is quick to urge that rents for assessed rooms be increased next year. A short-list has been drawn up and the whole Syndicate meets specially to interview them. Mrs Baker is offered the opportunity of coming for interview but declines it, since the Syndics are already acquainted with her and she has no need to ask questions about the duties. This is not to prejudice her chances. Four candidates are interviewed, and the vote goes unanimously to offer the post to Mrs Rita M. Phipps of 317 Hills Road, at present in charge of the Cambridge Regional Office of the B.M.A. She is to have £1050 *per annum*, and the offer is for 3 years to 30 September 1966.

11

'Educating Rita'

The Tutorial Representatives have already recommended a change in Ordinances to permit men of B.A. status or over 24 to live in unlicensed lodgings without requiring their Tutors to apply to the Lodging House Syndicate for approval; and a letter from the Chairman to the Deputy Registrary about finding extra accommodation mentions relaxing the rules still further, for example perhaps allowing third year undergraduates to keep terms in unlicensed lodgings up to five miles from the centre. The need for such relaxation is evident in the list of permissions granted, exceeding the number of 570 and including for the first time members of Churchill College.

The Robbins Report indicates that Cambridge may expect an increase for 1964-65 to 1,352 students for whom a home must be found. The Syndicate hopes that the Vice-Chancellor might make a public statement about the need for many more lodgings and perhaps he will write a letter to the *Cambridge News* inviting householders within the precincts to contact the Secretary with offers of help.

They begin 1964 with a rational move to collect statistics from all colleges as to the exact number of undergraduates, graduates and affiliated students in lodgings. A typed form is sent out under cover of a letter from the General Board of the Faculties, its aim being to help the syndicate to assess the number of extra lodgings needed. The form requires answers as to each college's present use of lodgings and future expectation of use, and we note the new professionalism both in the way it is laid out and in the inclusion in the minutes of important and relevant documents. The firmer grip and diligence are shown too by the much longer office hours now announced on the cover of the list: 9.00–1.00 and 2.30–5.00 (9.00–12.00 on Saturdays).

Perhaps it is rather irreverent of me to quote an anecdote about Mrs Phipps at this point: she was devoted to golf and accustomed to spending one or two afternoons a week on the golf course at the Gogs (no doubt when work permitted). One bright afternoon she was just coming out of the office door with her bag of clubs slung over a shoulder when she bumped into Miss Murray, the Chairman, then intent on coming in to see her. 'Oh I'll just stow these in the boot', she extemporised quickly, dodged round to her car in the Old Press Yard, and was back on parade with slightly pink cheeks before Miss Murray really noticed.

Another workmanlike touch comes with the mention of tables showing average rents in colleges and used as a basis of comparison for licensed rents. The Secretary was to calculate the averages for lodging-rents in the central area. But a letter from the Bursars' Committee protested that college rents are not a fair comparison and that an economic rent should be determined for lodgings. They recommend the Syndicate procure professional assistance and make a periodical reassessment of all rents at intervals not greater than three years.

The Syndicate was highly sceptical of this advice and considers an adequate supply the best test of a fair rent, with constant gradual reassessment by the Secretary. The initial panic over Robbins is somewhat dispelled by a letter from the Vice-Chancellor to Heads of Houses, explaining that the universities in aggregate had offered more places than were originally envisaged. As far as Cambridge was concerned, it could now expect that the total in residence in 1967-68 would be of the order of 9,600, the present figure in April 1964 being 9,000.

This scale of expansion can almost be coped with by the college buildings already projected and begun. To this decade we owe the exciting architectural experiments of Queens', John's, Trinity, Caius at Harvey Court, the high-rise tower of the William Stone Building at Peterhouse, Jesus' new range, as well as smaller schemes on the part of every college.

An overwhelmingly interesting passage in relation to this present work is this from the *A Guide to Cambridge New Architecture*, referring to Sir Leslie Martin and Harvey Court.[1]

> The real needs of an urban community — to meet, to park, to work and to play — had been betrayed by the manipulation of families in isolated towers. In schemes designed since his move to

---

1. *A Guide to Cambridge New Architecture* by Nicholas Taylor and Philip Booth, or see their larger work *Cambridge New Architecture*.

Cambridge as Professor in 1956, Sir Leslie and his colleagues, have made one assumption: that the 'urbanity' of city life is intrinsically desirable — and in the case of student life, that residence itself should be the primary medium of higher education. Bathrooms, kitchens and bed-space — the functional components of residence — Sir Leslie sees not as ends in themselves, but only as a personal survival kit on a communal launching-pad — hence their unobtrusive recession above and behind the dominant places of community life; outside places, such as piazza and terraces; inside places such as 'long gallery' and common rooms.

The Graduate Centre is in full swing as a social focus on the riverbank, two new undergraduate colleges Fitzwilliam and New Hall have joined Churchill, and the graduate colleges Darwin and Clare Hall help to absorb the flow of more mature research students. At the same time massive developments on the Sidgwick Avenue site have afforded badly needed extra lecture-room and library facilities for the Arts Faculties, and laboratories have sprung up all over town to serve the exploding sciences.

Copies of important letters are now stuck into the minute-book, and the minutes themselves are circulated between meetings. The Secretary goes regularly to national and regional meetings of her professional association and brings back news of what her colleagues are doing at other universities. When the Chairman writes his riposte to the Bursars' Committee, he is able both to say that graduate rents form a useful basis for comparison (in setting licensed rents) and that rents at other universities are lower than at Oxford and Cambridge. He states that the present secretary has visited about 700 licensed landladies and called on a large number of households who might be persuaded to apply for a licence, in the nine months since her appointment.

But while we see the parochial, ivory-tower flavour of the office being matured by wider contact with the best of the nation, it was still possible for the Syndicate to turn down an urgent attempt by King's to have 14 King's Parade (which they owned) acknowledged as part of the college. Directly across the road from the Porters' Lodge though it might be, it was not within the college precinct and undergraduates residing there must obtain permission in the usual way.

The Council of the Senate poured oil on troubled waters by urging some informal liaison between the Syndicate and the Bursars' Committee, and when rents were raised by £1 per term per place as an immediate gesture it was seen as sufficient. The number of special permissions approved at Michaelmas 1964 rose to 686, and we have the first mention of competition from language schools, a new phenomenon, and from industrial firms advertising for lodgings for their employees, recruited from outside the area.

In January 1965 Westcott House and Ridley Hall were recognised as houses of residence, and St Edmunds House now became an approved society. The Public Health Department undertook a programme of inspection of lodgings and reported (April 1965) 'all our inspections so far confirm your high standards'.

Underlining all this busyness, the Chairman wrote to the Registrary about the finances of the department, ready for the next quinquennial settlement. He details the work of the Secretary and her full-time assistant and asks for a second full-time assistant to be added to the staff as soon as an office can be provided containing at least three rooms, or four if you count a waiting room, all this to be implemented not later than the beginning of the 1967-72 quinquennium. The licence fee meanwhile has been raised from 2s 6d to 5s by Grace of December 1965, providing a little extra income.

That familiar old phrase 'non-collegiate student' is to be deleted from licence forms as soon as the Statutes of Fitzwilliam College are approved: in fact they got their Charter on 9 September 1966.

H.M. Inspector of Taxes wrote asking to be given a list of licensed lodgings and was denied it, and told that the addresses of graduate and undergraduate students could be obtained from the list of resident members compiled annually by Heffers. 'To send them the Syndicate's list would make for bad public relations,' Syndics said.

The Syndicate was more co-operative towards the Eastern Gas Board, with whom a fruitful relationship now developed round the precautions to be recommended to undergraduates and landladies in their handling of gas geysers in bathrooms. Though the Syndicate hurriedly declared they were not to be held responsible in the event of accidents, they welcomed advice and were delighted when the Gas Board offered free inspection of all geysers in lodgings, and later extended this to graduate lodgings. The Secretary amiably collated the addresses to be visited via the college lists.

Another subject for discussion was whether the time for visits in licensed lodgings from persons of the opposite sex should be extended by an hour. Mrs Phipps said prophetically that the landladies would be opposed.

Mrs Phipps' appointment is to be continued for another three years from October 1966, and she is to work in tandem with a new Chairman, Miss Rosemary Murray, President of New Hall, whose first duty is to send a letter of appreciation to Mr Crawley for his long service as Chairman. Another change in the list of Syndics is indicated by a black box in the minutes of October 1967 round the entry, 'The Syndics stood in silence to remember the late Mr R.N. Walters whose sad and untimely death was a great loss to the University'.

A discussion mentions computerised returns of students in lodgings by the Registry — another sign of the times. — and the Secretary is to consult the programmer about getting her information by this means, though meanwhile she continues to obtain returns (i.e. particulars of students' names and addresses) directly from their colleges. This was to be always an annual exercise that took up a lot of time and work, and much urging of some dilatory colleges to complete their replies. Many of the slack winter months were absorbed in these compilations and checkings, as the present writer painfully remembers.

The cost of living goes on rising as we deduce from the Syndics' recommending an increased stipend for Mrs Phipps and another increase on room-rents of £1 per place per term as from Michaelmas 1968. Miss Murray writes to the Bursars to express her concern over one college's threat to put up rents to tenants of central lodging houses, but there's no chance of halting that inflationary spiral. In reply, the Bursars justified rent increases for lodging-houses under the Landlord & Tenant Act of 1954, saying that if the recent Rent Act had been used instead, the Rent Officer would undoubtedly have fixed higher rents still. They were not at all sure that the

current increase in room-rents would prove sufficient and complained how low the cost of licensed lodgings was as compared with
college rooms.

One fascinating development is the voice of the student in housing matters, foreshadowed by a survey in the *Cambridge Review* for
June 1966 on 'The Graduate and his College'. In 1968 Mrs Phipps
met members of the Student Representatives Council for an informal discussion on residence, and the Syndics invited members
of the Committee to their March meeting together with representatives of the newly formed Graduate Council which was also preparing a memo on lodgings. They were evidently quite impressed
by the 'useful and fruitful discussion' they all had after official business had been despatched. How odd that they never before seem to
have consulted the opinions and preferences of the consumer.
However, they preserve their paternalistic role and although a sub-
committee of the Tutorial Representatives recommended 2.00 a.m.
as the latest hour for entering the gates of colleges and hoped this
would apply in lodging-houses too, the Syndics considered that the
outer doors of lodging-houses should continue to be locked at midnight: landladies are encouraged to give their undergraduates keys
but not obliged to do so.

Dr Bertram, Senior Tutor of St. John's, raises a new and significant question in writing to the Syndicate about 'the Sweet *v.* Parsley
case, still *sub judice*', which starts off a discussion on the possible
liability of a lodging-house-keeper if her lodger smoked cannabis
on the premises. At least they hadn't had to worry about that in the
19th century.

The summer of 1968 shows work for graduate students building
up. The pressure is on to have that extra assistant and another
room for her to assist in. Luckily just at that time the fourth room
at 18 Silver Street was vacated by the retiring Adviser to Overseas
Students and allocated to the Lodging House Syndicate. Mrs D.M.
Ker, widow of Alan Ker of Trinity, had started work at the office
ready for Michaelmas and was to be paid out of the departmental
accumulated balance until her employment could be put on a permanent basis. The Secretary has enterprisingly collaborated with
members of the Council of the Graduate Society to draw up a leaflet under the heading, 'Notes for graduates seeking accommoda-

tion', and copies were given out to graduate students consulting the office and circulated to Graduate Tutors. The office also produced a simplified form of tenancy agreement (still used in my own early days) but the Department of Estate Management were rather disparaging and advised caution in its use.

Mrs Phipps reported a meeting with 'Mrs Hill and Mrs Keynes who were responsible for an advisory service for graduates'. They did not go so far as to keep a separate register of lodgings, but sent their clients on to the Syndicate office and notified it of any useful addresses that came their way. Contemporaneously, the Society for Visiting Scholars under Mrs Burkill would continue to assist Senior members to find accommodation. With good humour, the Syndics hoped for excellent liaison between the three bodies, but there was always a little confusion as to who dealt with whom and where people of a given category should go for advice.

Syndics went on discussing participation by junior members, following a letter from the Registrary, and thought it preferable to have them as full members not just observers. They agreed to invite two or three representatives, to include one or more graduates *in statu pupillari*, thinking that graduate students had a more realistic view of problems in lodgings. It would be necessary to alter the present quorum of five to avoid the embarrassing possibility of being out-voted.

In a spirit of generous free-for-all, they even went on to suggest to the Registrary that it might be advantageous to be able to co-opt other interested parties, even landladies! They foresaw the possible effects of new legislation consequent upon the Latey Report on the age of majority.

In fact, the change of law giving the vote at 18 instead of 21 came about in 1969, and the implications of that took some time to penetrate society. Certainly the idea took root that the undergraduate could no longer be manipulated like a schoolboy, and must be given responsibility to conduct his life as he saw fit. This was to infuse many areas and decisions of University life, and had the most far-reaching consequences.

The immediate result was that two undergraduates and one graduate student came as members to the March '69 meeting and the graduate representative gave examples of current rents in all categories: they varied from about £2 10s 0d to £4 per week and it was independence and cheapness that graduates most sought after in their choice. A firm of London property developers planned a group of rooms to be let at £4 10s 0d per week exclusive of other charges and this gave an interesting sidelight on rents in the open market. Several colleges were reported as giving preference to graduates from overseas in allocating rooms.

Junior members continued to attend meetings, and could propose matters for the agenda, and took useful part. A memorandum by the undergraduate representatives was discussed, taking in gatehours, keys, and relations between colleges and the lodging-house-keepers who served them.

We first hear of the difficulty of finding licensed accommodation for women: 'All landladies appear to prefer male lodgers', and Mrs Phipps confirmed that this unfair preference was also found at other Universities. Churchill has announced that it will be accepting women undergraduates in 1972 and proposes to house them in college. Clare first had the same intention but later failed to reach agreement on changing its statutes.

The Cambridge College of Arts and Technology appears for the first time as a formidable competitor for available lodgings. Its students used to be drawn from local residents and lived at home with their families, but now they are recruited from the whole region and live by preference away from home.

Some indication of the University graduate accommodation demand is given by these figures:

number housed in college	300
number housed in college-owned properties	600

The total graduate population being c.2,300 that leaves 1,400 needing housing in the town. Cambridge University Graduate Society had sent out a questionnaire to size up the demand from graduates for college accommodation. To ease residence problems, Syndics agreed in principle that persons *in statu pupillari* could be given leave to count terms of residence in a house occupied by the holder of M.A. status if such holder were recognised by college, and the Chairman was authorised to give provisional permission for such residence, pending a meeting of the Syndicate.

In October 1969 Syndics agreed, though not quite unanimously, to appoint Mrs Rita M. Phipps for another three years. The feminine element was enhanced by the Senior Proctor's suggestion that the lady additional pro-proctor, Dr Christine Kelsey, be invited to attend meetings, her viewpoint and experience being deemed valuable: also, one of the undergraduate representatives is a Newnham woman, not that Newnham sent many of its members into lodgings. At this date, the student members are only present as observers and are not yet admitted to full membership: no satisfactory procedure for nominating or electing junior members to Syndicates had as yet been established.

An NUS enquiry prompts discussion about race relations and the workings of the 1968 Act in relation to lodgings. It was averred that the office never recorded restrictions but noted (if only mentally) the preferences of a resident landlady for a given national. Junior members produced a memorandum proposing that people *in stat. pup.* should be allowed to live in unlicensed lodgings, but some members thought the colleges and the Syndicate would be unable to go on accepting responsibility for providing accommodation if undergraduates were free not to make use of it.

Mrs Phipps was greatly fortunate in securing the services of Mrs I.M. Glyn who joined the staff as a full-time assistant from a background of commercial lettings of furnished accommodation, gained in city offices.

In April 1970 two landladies, Mrs Coe and Mrs Pilsworth, made history when they attended a meeting after formal business had been despatched, and took part in what was described as 'a helpful discussion'. Syndics must have been surprised and impressed by the landladies' sense since they determined to invite four to the next Spring meeting.

They must have found themselves challenged by the U.G.C.'s admitted target for Cambridge of 11,700 junior members by 1976: that gave them 6 years to plan for the expansion but how were they to estimate what the demand for lodgings would be? Everything of course, depended on the colleges and what initiative they took. To encourage them, the University already paid a subsidy of £50 *per annum* per graduate to colleges renting flats to married graduates; but that represented only one minor corner of the market.

The undergraduate members followed up their first and earlier volley for freedom by presenting a paper urging their preference for unsupervised living. The reader must remember that legislation to reduce the age of majority to 18 for voting purposes had gone through in 1969, and the young of the seventies were beginning to have a very different conception of their rights. To understand the mental climate better we should perhaps go back to the anti-authoritarian revolution that came to a head in the Paris student riots of May 1968. As with its eighteenth-century precedent, it was accompanied by disproportionate violence and acts of retaliation, and inspired a fear of similar outbursts all over the Western world. A sit-in at Cambridge in January 1969 was treated very gingerly by University authorities and produced no concrete results, but undergraduates certainly took to questioning the University's disciplinary role. Right-wing dons were determined not to be bullied by the more vocal element that got on to student committees and this culminated in the over-reaction to the Garden House riot (so-called) of February 1970.

What began as a dinner organised as a tourist office publicity stunt to encourage Greek tourism somehow escalated into an occasion thought by the students to support the fascist junta, and a crowd, originally good-humoured, gathered in the grounds of the hotel. A series of unfortunate accidents turned the bitterly cold night into a battlefield, with police opening french-windows and pressing backwards into the crowd, hosepipes drenching the protesters from upstairs windows, and Proctors demanding names and colleges. Some £2,000 worth of damage was done to hotel property and six students were immediately arrested, growing eventually to fifteen charged with 'riotous and unlawful assembly'.

Judge Melford Stevenson (fresh from the trial of the Krays) was appointed to hear the case at Hertfordshire Assizes. The defendants felt they had been betrayed by the university authorities, alleging that the names of known left-wing adherents had been passed to the police. The sentences surprised many: one man was given eighteen months, another fifteen months, four were to serve nine months each, and the two under 21 were sent to Borstal. Two overseas students, a South African and a Brazilian, were ordered to be deported. These last two sentences were subsequently quashed but

Judge Stevenson's opinion of the rioters at the trial was fully shared by the Court of Appeal (Regina *v*. Caird 1970).

C.S.U. held a public meeting at Sidgwick Avenue in October 1970 to discuss their grievances, seeking greater autonomy and representation on Universities bodies. It is against this agitated and unstable background that one must set the actions and decisions of the Syndicate. While Syndics realised the wish of some to live in flats and houses with their chosen friends and without a resident landlady, the more cautious felt that such enfranchisement should be limited to third year undergraduates. Operating a free-for-all system concurrently with the licensed system might, they warned, lead to a complete breakdown of the latter. How right they were, we can say, with hindsight, but it was to take another twenty five years. *Varsity* rushed into print with an article about living in unlicensed lodgings and the Syndicate had to stress the need for confidentiality over what was said at meetings, if junior members were to go on attending.

Much of the expected pressure on accommodation would come in future from women, they thought, and so the office was to write to the heads of the women's colleges for more precise information. In March 1971 two new appointees joined the Syndicate as representatives of the Council of the Senate: Ken Polack, the Bursar of King's and Gordon Wright, Rooms' Tutor at Clare. Significantly, King's would be taking twenty-five women undergraduates a year starting in 1972, and Clare had already admitted women.

Meanwhile rents of assessed rooms are quietly creeping up: by £1 per term for the academic year 1970-71 and by £3 per place per term for 1971-72. As the latter year started, news came of Mrs. Phipps' illness and Mrs Ker acted as her substitute. A concession is made to undergraduates by an amendment to the Regulations governing residence — as well as being allowed to keep term in the house of an M.A. of the University, the phrase 'or exceptionally, in any other house' is added, with the proviso that in each case, the permission of the Lodging House Syndicate has been obtained. Still, it is a big point gained.

The public authorities are increasingly putting a finger in the pie, especially the housing pie, and we hear for the first time the mention of 'houses in multiple occupation', with the hint of public health standards and requirements. But Syndics thankfully agree that they don't apply to licensed lodgings. It might be as well to combine forces though, and they invite two welfare officers from CCAT and Miss M.B. Wallis, Warden-Tutor at Homerton, to come and discuss the lodgings situation with them, and indeed entertain them to tea in the University Combination Room after 'a useful inter-change of experience and views'.

The invited Junior representatives are meanwhile becoming emboldened and put forward four points revising membership of the Lodging House Syndicate as follows;

1. The Chairman should be retained.
2. Five Senior members, one a woman.
3. Five Junior members, one nominated by the Graduate Society, and one should be a woman.
4. Full voting rights to each member and no invited members.

This was more than a self-respecting Syndicate could stomach. The invited members were asked to withdraw while Syndics consulted. It was proposed that the Syndicate should recommend to the Council of the Senate that membership should be increased to include one member of the Graduate Society and two undergraduates. The motion was not carried and no further resolution was put to the meeting. By March 1972 the undergraduate representatives had written withdrawing, presumably out of pique. Syndics said they would be happy to welcome undergraduates as invited members if C.S.U. (as it is now called) wished to renominate, and were glad to see that the member from the Graduate Society continued to attend.

As if to underline the Syndicate's remaining summary powers, thirteen applications from potential B.Ed. students for permission to live, in 1972-73, at distances of between 14 and 30 miles away from Cambridge were all refused on the grounds that such residence could no way fulfil the University stipulation of residence within the precincts.

Mrs Phipps is better, the acting secretary reports, but she does not wish to apply for re-appointment at the end of her existing tenure, that is till September 1972. The Council of the Senate had extended her sick leave until that date, amounting to a total period of 14 months. In fact, Mrs Phipps had lung cancer and a tumour on the brain and was to die aged 59 before the end of May. Action was to be taken to fill the vacant post, and within weeks, Mrs D.M. Ker was with an absolute majority appointed Secretary for three years from 1 October 1972.

The 'seventies of course spelt inflation: already an 8% rise in the cost of living is recorded, and from April 1972 rates went up by an unprecedented and startling 20%. Bad news for the landladies, and the Syndics had no option but to award a flat increase of £4 per place per term for the year 1972-73. This represents an 11% rise in the average termly rent of £35. Dr Wright proposed an annual review of rents, perceiving that the upward spiral was unlikely to be reversed, and this was agreed. Everyone was aware that rents on the open market were considerably higher than in licensed lodgings and this created a difficult economic climate: how to hold on to an adequate supply of lodgings without crippling the individual student lodger? A perennial problem from now on and a further £4 was added to rents for the following year, 1973-74.

C.S.U. relented and decided to nominate members to those committees from which they had withdrawn their representatives. One consequence of the permanent presence of undergraduate members was a decision to treat all applications for permission involving the personal situation of any individual student as 'reserved business', so that discussions on such matters would in future take place at the end of the meeting, after junior members had withdrawn. In view of the increasing number of special permissions sought, the Secretary was to circulate members with an informative list of current applications prior to the meeting so that reserved business can be got through more quickly.

The office was to widen its net so as not to turn away people seeking its help. The following categories are now eligible:

a) post-doctoral graduates whom the Society for Visiting Scholars are unable to help;
b) Graduates from abroad doing research;
c) English graduates whose research forms part of a research project;
d) Foreign doctors at the Language Faculties.

That second rent rise prompted Syndics to take up political cudgels and write to David Lane, the Cambridge M.P., asking him to raise with the Secretary of State for Education and Science this question of the inadequacy of the student grant to provide a just rent to lodging-house keepers, using the argument that it was manifestly unfair to expect them to subsidise their undergraduate lodgers.

They also enlisted David Lane over news that a lodging-house keeper had been charged capital gains tax on the proportion of the house that she let when she came to sell the property. The Secretary had written to the Inland Revenue for confirmation that this was permissible, and had gone so far as to raise the matter at her recent Association of University Lodgings Officers and Wardens conference, urging each University to protest to its appropriate M.P., but she had been over-ruled on this. David Lane replied that he was in touch with the Treasury over capital gains tax being levied on 'people who kept lodgers in a small way'.

Ordinances were amended to enable residence 'to be kept in a house occupied by a near relative, or an M.A. of the University, or the widow of an M.A. or (and this is new) a B.A. of the University, or exceptionally, in any other house; provided in each case the permission of the Lodging House Syndicate is obtained'. The Council of the Senate insisted that the B.A. in such a case must be the resident owner or at least, leaseholder, of any house where undergraduates were to keep terms. The amendment made it a little simpler to house undergraduates other than in licensed lodgings, and a sign of the times comes in the special permission granted 'for two third-year undergraduates at Pembroke to keep terms in unlicensed accommodation on a houseboat 'Goldfin', Rob Roy Moorings, Chesterton Road'.

Familiar (to the writer) names have joined the Syndicate: Dr Cameron Wilson, Rooms' Tutor at Jesus in November 1972, and another Jesus man, Dr. J. Roseblade, in October 1973 when Miss Rosemary Murray's Chairmanship came to an end and Ernest Frankl took over the Chair. His first act was to announce that Diana Ker had given notice of her resignation as from 1 December, after little more than a year in post. He said that he was in touch with a possible replacement and asked Syndics to be prepared to attend an early meeting. As reserved business 102 special permissions were approved, many on the grounds of the acute shortage of licensed lodgings.

In view of the inordinate volume of work involved, Mr Frankl raised the question of a more liberal attitude towards special permissions and made the momentous proposal, young as he was in the Chair, that they should discuss with the Tutorial Representatives that the licensing system should continue, but that instead of individual permission being given by the Syndicate for undergraduates to live in unlicensed accommodation, this responsibility should be taken by the College, authority being given by the Senior Tutor and the undergraduate's Tutor.

Mr Frankl was in a particularly well-informed position to make this revolutionary suggestion, since he was himself Senior Tutor of Trinity Hall and could judge the possible effects of putting power in the hands of those better able to predict the particular undergraduate's use or abuse of freedom, from their greater acquaintance with him (or her).

That 'special meeting' was held in the Board Room at Stuart House, the headquarters then of the Board of Extra-Mural Studies, on Friday 26 October 1973, to interview the present writer. Round the table were Ernest Frankl, Messrs Deakin and Boorman, the Proctors, Dr Roseblade, the Rev. D. Isitt, Dr Gordon Wright and Dr Cameron Wilson, seven black-gowned figures who rose as I came in, looking so funereal, so solemn, so unsmilingly judicious that I felt myself among a chorus of ravens. However, far from pecking me to death, they voted unanimously to appoint me, for two years from 1 December 1973. (Not that they told me so at the time of the meeting).

So that November with two women undergraduates as junior representatives, I attended my first Syndicate meeting as an observer, at the side of Diana Ker, 'to learn the work' preparatory to taking over. And it was on that occasion that the Chairman reported his discussion with the Tutorial Representatives who approved the new amendment to Ordinances, which was now to read '. . . or exceptionally in any other house, provided that in each case the permission of the College authorities has been obtained. Before granting such permission, the College authorities must be satisfied with the arrangements for observing the normal conditions for residence and discipline and they shall inform the Secretary of the Lodging House Syndicate of all such permissions.'

Another forty five permissions were granted at that meeting, but effectively over a hundred and twenty years of Syndicate autonomy came to a stop at that moment. A letter was to go out to Senior Tutors, who would be responsible for reporting the details of all such permissions each term on the Form LHS2 of the College Returns: College approval was to be given by one specified College Officer and if it were not the Senior Tutor, the Secretary was to be notified of the person to whom the duty had been delegated. Of course a Grace had to go through first, but once the Tutorial Representatives were in favour there was little doubt of acquiescence by the rest of the University.

Tragedies of Undergraduate Life

I. THE CIGARETTE ASH

Cartoon from *The Granta*, Doncaster Supplement,
20 May 1932

12

My Own Joyful Sway

A nd so in 1973 the writer's own long and joyful sway began. The Office staff consisted of René Glyn who taught me everything I needed to know and was there every morning. A young girl, Deborah Watson who took over the reception desk for the afternoons but didn't last very long; and a tall thin whirlwind called Benka Yannoulopoulos appeared to act as my secretary, having been appointed by Diana Ker in readiness.

On the Secretary's appointment it had been made clear that her pastoral role *vis à vis* the landladies was pre-eminent. So a round of visits began and in the course of these social and pleasant calls the Secretary set out to collect sample views: did they prefer payment of rent in advance, since undergraduates might prefer to settle their debts early, the grant being payable at the beginning of each term? Should landladies be expected to make beds? While undergraduates in college were moving towards a greater degree of self-service, one had to remember that many landladies hold bed-making as an excuse for securing daily access to the rooms they let.

These 'pastoral' visits developed the skills acquired by the Secretary in her previous career as London social worker and personnel officer. She was at first taken aback by the landlady's almost automatic production of the sherry bottle at the start of every conversation, and equally looked at with consternation when she smilingly said she didn't drink in working hours.

Hilarious those chats often were and she would be asked for advice or comment on everything under the sun, from chilblains to divorcing daughters. More sober trips were to hospital to see people recovering from operations and sitting up gallantly in festive bed-jackets. She learnt soon to have an enormous respect for the gallantry and good-humour of the landladies. A few were mean and spiteful and envied undergraduates their carefree existence, but for the most part, they enjoyed their young and exuberant lodgers, supported them in any trial and took the greatest pride in their achievements, turning up on degree day and beaming as delightedly as any fond parent. It is not sentimental to say that many undergraduates (male ones that is, almost wholly) regarded their landlady with affection and kept in touch long after leaving their lodgings and Cambridge.

Paying the licence-fee (still 5*s* or 25p rather) meant that all land-ladies had to call at the office, each year, usually early in the Easter Term, and this gave the office-staff a chance to get to know them too. 'Hello Mrs Palmer, is your leg any better?', René Glyn would cry out, in her cheerful way, or sometimes, recognising a certain hat or way of carrying a handbag, would call out, 'Oh yes, 24 Tenison Avenue isn't it?' since the address was often more familiar than the name of its proprietor. When the Secretary was given the decision, she opted not to raise the licence fee and to continue levy-ing it for the next two years as it gave a definite advance indication of how many landladies would be making their accommodation available and also served as a pretext for this office visit and its op-portunities for cementing bonds.

When the office came to work out its annual review of numbers in lodgings, the drop in those occupying licensed lodgings equalled the gain in those seeking permission for living in unlicensed lodg-ings. Pressure on space was eased by the news that Queens' would be releasing a hundred lodgings they no longer needed when they started to occupy their new buildings for 1974-75. Rents were to go up by 12% to keep pace with the general inflationary tendencies.

Or so the Syndics intended: but on the day after they took that decision the government stepped in with its declaration of a Rent Freeze. It was first to apply till the end of December, with rents frozen to whatever level was applicable in March '74: this was ex-tended to continue till the end of March '75. A law fellow of Trinity was called in to advise the Syndicate and set out his views on the application of the Rent Act to student accommodation. If there really were to be security of tenure for the lodger or tenant, that might act as a possible deterrent to letting, landlords being unwill-ing to take on a resident in their house if they had no means of getting rid of him.

The Secretary imagined that as members of the University were necessarily mobile, they might be more welcome as lodgers than members of the general public, who would be more likely to seek permanent residence. Mr Frankl proposed asking David Lane to raise with the Minister of Housing the whole question of exempting from these Rent Act provisions all accommodation let to students, in order to maintain a market supply.

Early in 1975, Syndics were read a letter to David Lane from Gerald Kauffman, Parliamentary Under-Secretary at the Department of the Environment, who held out the possibility of a registration scheme whereby private lettings to students would be excluded from full Rent Act protection. Enabling legislation would be required, and it was hoped this could go through for the academic year 1976-77. The Labour Party, in power throughout this period, built up a complicated series of housing laws, prompted originally by the evils of Rachmanism and its exposures.

When Syndics came to discuss rents in licensed lodgings that spring, they were quite in the dark as to whether they had authority to raise them. At a meeting of the Bursars' Committee they confessed themselves helpless to interpret the application of the new Housing & Rent Subsidies Act (1975) and could give no lead to the equally bewildered Syndicate. However, thanks to Kenneth Polack's insistence, they agreed, subject to legislation prevailing in the Autumn, to increase rents by 20% for the next year and to set a minimum rent of £50 for any room. Even that minimum, for the least-regarded lodging, represents double the cost of a room in say, 1960: that gives us an index to the rate at which inflation is moving at this time.

The following year, the Bursar of King's recommended bringing in the Department of Estate Management, who after a survey on the viability of making a living as a lodging-house keeper, came up with a recommendation that rents needed to go up by a further 31% if they were to remain at any comparable level with market rents. The Secretary reported several colleges increasing their rents to lodging-house keepers by as much as 100%, and she sought better liaison with the Bursars' Committee. An increase of 25% was agreed for 1976-77 with a further 5% to go on the year after regardless of any award then made. These swingeing rises brought a protest from C.S.U. who regretted so high an award before the figure for next year's student grant had been published.

The pattern repeats itself at the March meeting of 1977 when yet another 15% was added to rents (to include the 5% mentioned above). The undergraduate representatives asked for it to be minuted that they considered the increase excessive, and at the following meeting the Chairman had to deprecate the publicity given to the rent decision, a report having appeared in Stop Press within 24 hours, with headlines in the local paper.

Those three years of escalating rent-rises were to have serious consequences. Student feelings ran high on the issue, large numbers of undergraduates not receiving the full parental contribution to the grant and being already put to financial hardship by steep rises in the cost of food, travel, books and clothing. The C.S.U. made representations to the Council of the Senate, calling for a reduction in the increase to 10% not 15%, and questioning the constitution of the Syndicate, and its method of determining rent levels.

A special meeting of the Lodging House Syndicate was called for 9 June 1977 at Trinity Hall, and there the C.S.U.'s green paper was discussed for two or three hours. The student observers were asked to prepare suggestions as to the criteria to be used in setting future rent levels.

I have dealt with three years of rent discussions together because of their culmination in such drama. But meanwhile various other matters had come up, such as King's plan for defining the dates within which undergraduates can claim their ten weeks' worth of residence. Formerly they were entitled to any ten weeks during Term, which could effectively trap the lodging-house keeper, if she had several lodgers, each electing for different dates of coming up and leaving, to thirteen weeks of running her lodgings. Some landladies were keen to take bed and breakfast guests as soon as their undergraduates had left the rooms unoccupied, and this gave them some desperately needed extra income. King's, with a parallel need to clear the rooms ready for the lucrative conference trade, allowed undergraduates in college the use of their rooms as follows:

Michaelmas Term: 1 October plus 10 weeks till the Thursday after Full Term
Lent Term: From the Thursday before Full Term till the Thursday after Full Term
Easter Term: The whole Term, which is only 9 weeks long.

Their example was tested out on the Tutorial Representatives and with their approval adopted for use in lodgings. Mention was made in 1976 that Caius were still buying large lodging-houses: Caius were in fact the last college to insist that its members went into licensed lodgings and would not give permission for undergraduates to find flats for themselves. But most colleges were housing their members increasingly on college premises, and a walk around Cambridge courts will soon show how much college building owed its expansion to this decade.

A proposal originating with the Dean of Darwin came via the Deputy Registrary that the Board of Graduate Studies be made the authorising body for granting permission to graduate students to live beyond the ten mile radius. Syndics with some reluctance agreed to hand over their control for an experimental year and review the situation at the end of that time.

A new factor in the accommodation scene was the way that language schools were mushrooming and multiplying, to serve the needs of young foreigners wanting quickly acquired skill in English and imagining that some of the academic kudos of Cambridge would rub off on them if they studied here. The City planning authority was alert to this and tried to restrict their growth, but the language students had money in their pockets and were able to buy up a sizeable chunk of the accommodation market, thereby making it more difficult both for CCAT and the University. One effect was to make the landlady a much more independent body, able to pick and choose her source of lodgers and dictate the level at which she set her rents. The reader will have noticed the complete absence of disciplinary cases appearing before the Syndicate: the days of intimidating lodging-house keepers had long since gone by.

Let us return to the crucial rents issue, discussed finally at a special meeting of April 1978, timed to allow for the announcement by the government of the following year's student grant. An N.U.S. press release — on the very morning of the meeting — gave the news that the grant was to go up by roughly 10%. The local rates had just been announced and were to rise by 15.5%. With the concurrence of the student representatives, a rents rise of 9.3% was agreed for lodgings, thus for the first time gearing the cost of digs to the purchasing power of the lodger.

At the May meeting of the same year the Chairman reported on the progress of the reviewing committee set up by the Council of the Senate under the Chairmanship of Mrs. Jean Floud, Principal of Newnham (and in her absence, of the Master of Clare). They had taken evidence and surveyed the scene and were in favour of continuing the Syndicate, but with a change of name. They recognised the large effort made by the Lodgings Office on behalf of housing graduates. No conclusion had yet been reached about the role of the proctors as ex-officio syndics. It was thought that the Syndicate's role in granting hostel permissions to Colleges might vanish. By the start of the next academic year, a change of key is very evident in Syndicate affairs. Although the present secretary had been unanimously re-appointed for another three years, there was a turn-around of leadership. Mr Frankl retired from a scene that he had long taken part in, and the new Chairman is Dr Richard Bainbridge, Senior Tutor of Corpus, very active in many University circles and an inimitable actor, both at his own college dramatics and with the Marlowe Society.

By Grace of 22 February 1978, the post of pro-proctor for women had been abolished, women's colleges now being included in the cycle for the nomination of proctors. But at his very first meeting the Chairman mentioned that he thought it desirable to have a woman Syndic and that should be kept in mind in considering the reconstitution of the Syndicate. The experimental year being up, they agreed to a permanent transfer of responsibility for graduate permissions to the Board of Graduate Studies.

But their main task, at this and several meetings to come, was to discuss the report from the Committee of Review. Which of their proposals for reform were useful and acceptable, and what still needed further study and amendment? The proctors had no objection to no longer being statutorily represented: one or possibly two lodging-house keepers were to be co-opted, and the licence-fee was to be dropped as no longer appropriate. The use of the phrases 'lodging-house' and 'lodging-house-keeper' was to be discouraged as smacking too much of the penitentiary. Syndics didn't find the title 'Accommodation Syndicate' endearing and preferred 'Lodgings Syndicate' as more fitting to the body managing the 'Lodgings Office', deeming the word 'lodgings' covered any form of student housing including houses and flats, and quoting the Cambridge use of the word in an expanded sense as in 'Porter's Lodge', 'Master's Lodge', etc.

The Regulation about the appointment of the Secretary was revised to read: 'The Secretary is to be appointed for three years initially and re-appointed at such periods not exceeding five years at a time as the Syndicate shall determine'. And so the process of revision and self-analysis ground on, with the Council of the Senate still making minor amendments, until October 1979 when the Lodging-House Syndicate was formally dissolved after 125 years of existence, and the Lodgings Syndicate came into being. It was to be constituted as follows:

> There shall be a Lodgings Syndicate which shall consist of:
> a) The Vice-Chancellor (or his deputy) as Chairman;
> b) Two persons appointed by the Council of the Senate;
> c) Two persons appointed by the Committee of Tutorial Representatives;
> d) One Tutor for graduate students appointed by the Committee of Graduate Tutors;
> e) Two persons appointed by the Bursars' Committee;
> f) One member of the University *in statu pupillari* appointed by the Graduate Society;
> g) Two members of the University *in statu pupillari* appointed by the C.U.S.U.;
> h) One or two persons co-opted by the members of the Syndicate provided that it shall not be obligatory for the Syndicate to co-opt any person.
>
> Those in categories f, g, & h were not to hear reserved business or take part in the appointment of the Secretary.

And so at long last the Syndicate had a structure and a code of procedure and could give its full attention to the task of housing every student who was unable to find a space within his college. Increasingly, these were graduate students from Darwin and Wolfson, and those causing the greatest difficulty were overseas students arriving in England for the first time.

Two landladies made history by attending the November meeting of 1979 as members in their own right and lent a hand with the task of redesigning the licence and re-defining the obligations of those granted it. The phrase 'licence-holder' was adopted as a neutral title, applicable to either sex and causing no offence. The Secretary reported how accommodation was already being lost because the rents permitted within the licensed system were not high enough and it was most useful to have Mrs Bishop, one of the co-opted members, present and prepared with a statement of her housekeeping costs for the coming year in terms of rent, rates and water rates. At the Rents Meeting, now held in May so as to be aware of the level of student grant awarded for the following year, an increase of 17% was agreed by vote, an unusually high award.

The lay-out of the office was causing the Secretary some concern: one of the rooms belonged to the Department of Land Economy and was used for supervisions, and this meant it was impossible to secure complete confidentiality. More space was needed for the interviewing of graduates. Matters came to a head when a gas escape in that room went unperceived, and the Secretary stressed how dangerous it was to have an area of the office not under her constant jurisdiction and liable to be used out of normal office-hours.

The Secretary had the honour and privilege of being given an M.A. at a congregation on 26 April 1980, under Statute B III.6, and was delighted to receive the Syndics' congratulations. Her Chairman was beside her throughout the ceremony in the Senate House and when she confided to him that she wasn't sure whether she was being married or confirmed he whispered back, 'You are being wed to the University'.

We catch the up-to-date tone of the new Syndicate from items of her report at the beginning of the academic year 1980-81; the new college, Robinson, not having its full complement of junior members yet, is housing Fitzwilliam and New Hall undergraduates in their empty rooms. She is able to comment, 'the ease of letting outside the University makes the threat of revoking a licence laughable'. The Proctors have of course disappeared and with them the last trace of overweening University authority. In its place come 'market forces'.

A spectacular change has happened in that overseas students rarely arrive now with several children in tow. Those with families either do not apply, knowing the costs in Britain, or arrange for them to be cared for in their native country. New shorthold tenancies are now permitted, under the Housing Act of 1980. The whole question of women in lodgings is debated as an item on the agenda: one new feature is their feminine determination to cook their own meals, rebelling against the stodgy menus in Hall.

The undergraduate representatives mention what they see as a dislike of landladies for women lodgers and cases are discussed of turning away women on the doorstep when they come inquiring after rooms. On the other hand, Mrs Bishop, a Jesus landlady, is running a mixed house this year and reports how well it is working out, and a porter at Jesus is quoted as saying how the standard of behaviour and language has improved because of the presence of women and this goes both for college and for lodgings.

The office took an exciting initiative in the Spring of 1981 when Joshua Taylor's furniture store was persuaded to stage an exhibition. The Secretary had talked their merchandise manager into setting up a model bedsitting room, visible in the window of the shop in Bridge Street, with well-designed simple furniture from a range produced by Domino. Publicity material and handouts asked the customer what was he doing with unused space in his house and suggested he would do well to furnish it in the style shown and let it through the office to charming and grateful undergraduate lodgers. The show opened on 18 May with a sherry party of invited guests headed by the Mayoress and went on for six weeks. It was a light-hearted enterprise but went off very successfully, drawing much cheerful attention to the office and to the University's need, and had been helpful as a means of recruiting new addresses.

For 1981-82 an increase to rents of 12% was agreed, although the Secretary of State for Education had admitted that the rise in the level of the student grant for the same year was 30% less than it should be. Thus began the era of student hardship. A nice touch came from the undergraduate representatives who generously remarked what a valuable experience they had found serving on the Syndicate for their year and thanked the Syndics for being such a pleasant body to work with. Dr Bainbridge had largely helped to bring about this friendly concordance, drawing on a long experience as Tutor and Senior Tutor and with a benevolent interest in young people and a lovable disposition. To walk down King's Parade with Richard was an intriguing experience — it seemed as though he smiled and nodded at and greeted about 50% of the people one met or passed.

What was afoot in October 1981? The Tutorial Representatives were considering how to make the cuts demanded by the University Grants Committee. Robinson may be itself in the accommodation market by the following October, looking for perhaps 80 lodgings outside college: and where were they to be found, Newnham now having become such a sought-after and expensive area of town and no longer lodgings country? Some relief came in Sidney Sussex's news that it would have 60-80 new places in the spanking King Street building, whose opening the Secretary attended, much impressed by the flat-like provision of bathroom and kitchen to each group of four bedsitters. Trinity Hall, having built Bishop Bateman Court, were selling off all their large lodging-houses in Bateman Street.

The City Environmental Department were querying the letting of licensed rooms to summer visitors and at a seminar on tourism the Secretary had rushed to defend her landladies, for whom this had been a long-standing usage and an essential means of supplementing income. Students were beginning to realise that they were entitled to claim rent allowances, although at this stage they were refused to undergraduates. Again she reported fewer graduate families to house, which was just as well now that the cost of petrol ruled out accommodation in village houses beyond Coton or Impington. Another sign of the times is her mention of widowed landladies who traditionally (in the wake of two World Wars) offered space in their own homes in the hope of companionship as well as financial return. But modem-day students sheered away nervously from such propositions, as they also rejected any suggestion of a lower rent in return for small services, such as shopping, cleaning, baby-sitting and the like. Freedom and the absence of supervision were the ideals and at any price.

From January 1982, a much fuller record was being kept of individual postgraduate applications, and the degree to which each client was helped by the office. Thus it was now possible to track and quantify the efficiency and efficacy of help given. The Secretary had worked out the percentages of accommodation afforded by the colleges for 1981-82:

undergraduates housed in college   86.62%
postgraduates housed in college   58.55%

These proportions seemed to demonstrate a highly creditable degree of provision.

All University institutions were currently under review in the present financial recession and the Council of the Senate were vociferously calling for economies and staff reductions.

Under reserved business, an unusual and concerned discussion took place, regarding the conduct of a landlady. Mrs L. of Portugal Street was the object of an undergraduate complaint: she had phoned his parents after a dispute over the bill, and when he spoke to her critically about this, she attacked him shrieking and ordered him out of the house. The Secretary, called in, had visited and been subjected to an unpleasant display of deviousness and verbal abuse, culminating in Mrs L.'s hysterical breakdown. Her licence was not to be renewed at the end of the academic year, and this in turn involved the end of her tenancy of a Trinity house. An unexpected harkback to earlier times when the Syndicate's authority was more often exerted — as these pages have amply recorded.

A County Structure Plan had been drawn up by Cambridgeshire in 1980 and its tenets were now making themselves felt: planning policy led away from housing estates like the Arbury and from encouraging village expansion. The drive now was strongly in favour of keeping the centre of Cambridge in residential use. Planners did not want to see a ghost-town in summer when students go down. One result of this is that applications by Christ's and Jesus to convert lodging-houses into hostels were turned down. The planners made it clear they would oppose Emmanuel's intention to convert Park Terrace to student housing if the college was successful in purchasing it from Jesus.

By the autumn of 1982 the City had shot a further series of broadsides: for a start, it had a pilot scheme to register all houses in multiple occupation. It had published a draft report on language schools and secretarial and tutorial colleges operating in Cambridge. Already there were 57 such institutions with a student roll of 15,000, though these numbers were by no means present throughout the year. Short summer language courses, attracting vast numbers of very young foreign students bent on holiday-making, caused large-scale traffic and policing problems and cost the city dear in terms of litter, noise and the overcrowding of local facilities. No planning permission would be given for any new establishment. They also provided much competition for the available housing and the prices that landladies could charge for boarding and feeding foreign students far outweighed the kind of money University students could afford on a long term basis. And so the foreigners spoilt the market and made the Cambridge housewife greedy.

Thirdly, the City had published a policy guidance note on tourist accommodation and guest houses, and this was applied to anyone letting more than two bedrooms in their home. It imposed more stringent fire precautions and laid down rules about the provision of parking spaces. The lodging-houses felt directly threatened. To counter this, the colleges had not been impotent, and the Secretary reported her attendance at a public hearing at which Jesus had employed Counsel to argue that using lodging-houses in Jesus Lane as 'external staircases', (as if they were part of the college campus) did not constitute a change of use.

The sittings had gone on for several days, the barrister in question was an extremely senior and eminent figure and a procession of junior clerks seemed employed in bringing him pile after pile of learned law books from which he extracted the most telling precedents. The college wanted to operate the houses entirely under their own control, using bedders for cleaning and maintenance and dispensing with the presence of the landlady and her family below stairs. The City wished to retain the houses as year-round family homes, with the usual tidal flow of students during term not seriously interrupting the existence of the citizenry. The Syndicate, I think, felt itself divided, its collegiate and its civic interests being directly opposed over this question.

The difficulty over the shared ownership of the office was resolved by Land Economy's yielding-up of its rights on the fourth room which now became a useful part of the Lodgings Office.

The Secretary took to the air, broadcasting her appeals for more rooms, flats, houses, or houseboats, on Radio Cambridge and

Hereward Radio, on some occasions rising protestingly early in order to send out her message at 7.30 a.m. as commuters set off for work and turned on their car radios.

Cambridge took to paying more and more for its house-room — flats rented out at £30-£40 per week while rooms for postgraduates cost commonly £18-£20 per week or even, for the plummier pads, £25 inclusive of all costs. Those licensed lodgings that feel-free undergraduates rejected were filled up with Homerton women in the fourth year of their B.Ed. or by PGCE students of either sex, Homerton having given up its hitherto closely scrutinised approved lodgings scheme.

About this time the Secretary took the unexpected step of describing to Syndics a visit she had made with the owner at his request to a flat on Castle Hill occupied recently by three undergraduates. They had left it in chaos with upholstery torn, springs starting from the seats, chairs with legs and struts broken, outside walls with vomit stains below the windows, stained beds, ringed and spoilt tabletops, ripped and soiled carpets, odd belongings scattered about and not collected in spite of appeals: a charmless waste where the architect owner had supposed he was providing a central, well equipped and attractive shared house, likely to facilitate an harmonious life-style for the intelligent young. In the summer he let the house as a family holiday home. But in no way could he put on the market for adults a place that had been turned into such a pig-sty.

Another irate complaint came from a woman with several properties in one of which three undergraduates had repaired their motorbikes in the sitting room, stubbing their cigarettes out on the carpet as they did so. It was no surprise that landlords, hearing reports of such disastrous experiences, refused to let their properties to undergraduates. And this only spoiled the chances for the many who would have house-kept beautifully and caused no trouble. As an antidote it was good to hear that Fitzwilliam, having at the Secretary's instigation, taken over the tenancy of a block of flats and let them to undergraduate groups, were pleased and relieved when they found reasonable care had been taken of them.

To return to the controversial issue in Jesus Lane, a report was made in January 1983 on the favourable outcome of Jesus' appeal.

The Department of the Environment's Inspector had ruled that there was no material change of use in making the four properties into external staircases and that therefore no planning permission was called for. Jesus was automatically free to make what use it chose of its own properties. While it turned no landlady out of her home, it proceeded to march in wherever retirement, death or other opportunities offered, and before long their (major) part of the street — and of Malcolm Street also — became college-oriented hostels. This was a truly major decision, opening the door to many other college initiatives, pursued presumably because the college bowed before the expressed desire of its members for independence.

For the first time the Secretary did not attend the Spring Annual Conference of the Association of University Accommodation Officers. In 1983 it was being held at the University of Belfast and her husband refused to let her go. These meetings with colleagues were generally fun and useful and served as a training-ground for new methods of dealing with common problems and as a forum for discussing all the frequent changes in housing law. The Secretary wrote them up in some detail and Syndics liked to hear what was going on in the less privileged university world.

Callers at the office reached nearly 6,000 for the year 1982-3, breaking all previous records. But it was dismaying that property prices in Cambridge precluded the buying-up and letting of houses as a lucrative investment. There was no way of satisfying the demand by groups of three or four for a shared house in which to set up independent housekeeping, and those cheap terraced houses that were available often did not lend themselves to occupation by more than two or three. Cramped little houses with bedrooms leading out of one another or a downstairs room into which the front door opened allowed no proper privacy.

Staff in the office were frequently faced with emotional breakdowns, as when graduates from other universities confronted the particular difficulty here of finding the kind of accommodation they were used to. Colleges did not help by accepting graduate students well after the start of Term: such late arrivals inevitably found everything already booked and became quite desperate for any roof.

Thanks to the acquisition of an assistant with a talent for figures, it was now possible to collate more reliable statistics, and indeed it was imperative to collect accurate information in order to have evidence of the department's efficacy. The degree of help afforded to each college was now demonstrable.

The office was concerned to involve Rooms' Tutors more, and to brief them on changing student needs and the difficulty, mentioned above, in satisfying them. A seminar was proposed and all tutors invited to a meeting at the University Centre on 1 May 1984. Thirty-one people were present and entered on a most wide-ranging discussion on the sharing of houses by groups of undergraduates. Housing benefit was now payable to undergraduates during vacations and this facilitated the living by undergraduates all year round in Cambridge as was never the case before. This hit squarely at the old rhythms of term and vacation, and reflected social change in the family such as marital breakdown, so that many undergraduates had no settled home to go to or were no longer so welcome.

In October 1984 the Secretary's report on the previous summer revealed an office under enormous pressure and bedevilled by staff changes and the absences of staff on holiday. Shorthanded, they tried to cope with the endless queue and the intolerable phone. To quote her: 'It is essential to have back-up staff so that the interviewer doesn't continually have to interrupt the thread of her conversation in order to answer the 'phone. We have had the poor patient caller burst into tears at the third or fourth disruption of his tale. The effect of that inexorable 'phone on the line of waiting clients outside in the waiting room is pitiful. At each new ring they wilt a little more visibly into an apathy beyond hope'.

Now that the University Grants Committee frowned on undergraduate expansion in the universities, the recruitment of overseas students (mainly at graduate level) became increasingly important as a source of revenue, and several schemes were set up all over the world to enable people to be sent to Cambridge. This brought its own problems as many disguised their intention to bring wife and family with them until their actual arrival. The Syndicate urged the Board of Graduate Studies to tell applicants from abroad the realistic picture and warn them of the cost of living in England. To quote the Secretary again: 'If the University's policy of overseas recruitment is not to go hand in hand with provision by the colleges for their extra housing, it would simply be a problem heedlessly unloaded at the Lodgings Office's door'.

Dr Bainbridge himself went off to Hong Kong on University business involving recruitment overseas, as one of many such academic expeditions. In his absence Dr Alan Baker took the Chair at the New Year meeting where the graduate representative complained how much undergraduates were encroaching on accommodation formerly only available to graduate students, forcing the latter out to housing increasingly remote from the centre. This adversely affected their participation in social life and graduate affairs. The rent rebate scheme encourages students to book accommodation beyond their means and tempts landlords into demanding ever-higher rents (since they will be made up out of public funds). The poor overseas students, who are not eligible to apply for rebates, still have to match the spiralling prices out of their own pockets. The Syndicate was so concerned that in May 1985 it asked for fuller information to be published in the Graduate Studies Prospectus as to the amount of accommodation provided by each college for married and single graduate students.

Another interesting initiative was its proposal to the Registrary that accommodation previously used as the staff and nurses' homes on the old Addenbrooke's site (now bought by the University) should be made available to undergraduates, perhaps as an intercollegiate residence. The Lodgings Syndicate were quite prepared to undertake its administration if wished. But the Registrary's reply poured cold water on their hopes and said that the nurses' residence was to be offered on lease to one or more colleges.

Some modernising went on at the office: it was painted and carpeted, the staff washing facilities improved, a photocopier bought and installed — a great acquisition. The Secretary had been looking into the possibility of computerising office information and records with the help of the University Computer Service.

Her colleagues from universities in the Midland Region came to a day conference and a delicious lunch at Corpus in November 1985 and most of the Syndics joined them at table. On the Agenda would have been the Government's proposals on student entitlement to rent rebates, and early in 1986 Norman Fowler put his proposals before Parliament in the form of a Social Security green paper. Under this:

1. All housing benefit for those living in college would end by October 1986;
2. Supplementary benefit and housing benefit in vacations to end.,
3. Housing benefit to those living in the private sector to end in 18 months' time.

Some cheer was provided by the Secretary's calculation that for 1985-6 the proportion of undergraduates housed by their college was 88% and of postgraduates 59%. According to the Universities' Statistical Record, Cambridge accommodated the third highest proportion of students in the country, a record only bettered by Keele and St David's, Lampeter.

At the May Rents Meeting of 1986, a 6% increase in rents was awarded with a proviso that the landladies deserved more and that accommodation could not be acquired unless a fair price were offered. The Chairman was to write to the DHSS, the Department of Education and Science, all the local MPs and to all Heads of Houses, telling them of this decision, listing the reasons, with protesting against the proposed cuts in student financing and the withdrawal of benefit. The Syndicate recognised that it was the only formal University housing body and that it was necessary to assert itself as such. As a result of many similar pressures, the Government did make two concessions that October:

1. Those not in college accommodation would be allowed entitlement to housing benefit;
2. Those paying rent through the long vacation were given a year's grace and allowed to claim benefit, even if the housing they occupied were owned by an educational institution.

It is already apparent that the Secretary spent much of her time digesting government rulings, applying them and explaining them to appropriate bodies. This new climate contrasted strangely with the tradition of autonomy built up in the past — and so often illustrated earlier in this study. So now she explained to Syndics that claiming of housing benefit does not automatically lead to a referral to the Rent Officer — that new Gauleiter figure — but only where the rent seems abnormally high.

However, his decisions were bitterly received by the owners of property, and the rent set could not be changed for two years. Landlords hated losing control over their own possessions and the house where a Fair Rent was registered was almost inevitably put on the market the moment the tenants vacated it. It needed a lot of diplomacy to keep the relations between landlord and tenant sweet at this period and there were injustices on both sides of the table.

Where licensed lodgings were actually owned by a college, the benefit administrators wanted to apply the ruling making their occupants ineligible to claim: but the Secretary invited them to tea at the office and persuaded them that such a move would lead to shocking inegality as between the inhabitants of the house (owned by a college) and that next door in the keeping of a private householder.

The University Grants Committee budget for Cambridge was reduced which meant economies and cuts in every department. The Syndics felt the office was too small to admit of any pruning and was already operating on a very low and economical budget. Besides it was busier than ever as it plunged from one crisis to the next, ever seeking to act as buffer to the poor clientele. Now a new anomaly became apparent as the tenants of college flats realised they were not eligible for benefit and some even moved into privately-owned accommodation in order to qualify for help. Word came that the Observatory personnel (both staff and students) would be arriving from Hurstmonceux in 1990 and were looking for living space.

Christ's and Caius both raised a complaint that landladies were refusing rooms to women undergraduates, when their turn came to take a year out of college. This caused the Secretary to consult legal expert opinion on the working of the Sexual Discrimination Act, section 30.

Syndics themselves had for some time been convinced that computerisation would be an advantage to the office if it were affordable: various methods of raising money had been debated. They asked the Allocations Committee for half the sum involved (i.e.

£5,000) but the request was rejected out of hand so that it was pointless to go on discussing how to appeal for the other half.

Such minor setbacks dissolved as real tragedy struck. Richard Bainbridge died of a heart attack. Gordon Wright, as the most senior Syndic, took the Chair for the first Michaelmas meeting and Syndics, junior members and co-opted members stood in silence as a tribute to Richard's memory.

The Secretary appealed for accommodation on the Old Addenbrooke's site to be reserved for the University and pressure brought to bear on the Committee to offer interested colleges a long-enough lease at a low-enough rent to make the capital outlay on renovation worthwhile. She was exasperated beyond all patience at frequent reports that the site was to be used to solve CCAT's problems. Christ's had their new hostel in Hobson Street ready now for use and this would ease some of the strain.

The leaflet for landladies was to be amended so as to include a warning about offending against the regulations laid down under new legislation on both racial and sexual discrimination.

By December Dr David Kerridge of Fitzwilliam, a biochemist, had been chosen as Chairman-nominate and attended a meeting in Clare as an observer. The Secretary described a visit to her office of three quite intimidating officials from the Inland Revenue. They demanded the names of all landlords, or addresses at which accommodation was rented, and were vastly disconcerted at her refusal to divulge them, a line she was entitled to take under the provisions of the Taxes & Management Act 1970 (sections 14 and 19).

At several meetings previous to this, reports had come of trouble in a Caius lodging-house; the inmates complained of their landlady's dictatorial stance, putting up notices and restricting guest-hours, baths and so on. Warned by the college she at first co-operated, but as another year's intake moved into the house and started resenting her deprivations, they too complained *en masse* to the Senior Tutor. Regarding this as the culmination in a series of unsatisfactory dealings, he invoked the Secretary's help and she called at the house to remonstrate with Mrs R., only to be rebuffed rudely at the door. Finally the Bursar cancelled her lease under the Landlord & Tenant Act and announced his intention of converting the house into a college hostel.

The annual AUAO Conference in 1988 invited a crop of able speakers to bring accommodation officers up to date on the new Housing Bill, and fortified by this, the Secretary handed on the information to the Syndics. They asked her to send a full briefing to Bursars and Senior Tutors.

News came at last that CCAT were indeed to have the lease of the Nightingale Hostel at Addenbrooke's and the Shaftesbury Society hoped to house disabled students in the Peckover Hostel. The University had agreed now to offer 20-year leases, but none of the colleges had succeeded in picking up the opportunity, though Pembroke and Downing played with the idea. To spend money on a campus not their own was not to a Bursar's taste. CCAT was to achieve polytechnic status before long. They had fared ill at the hands of the Inland Revenue, losing 400 'bed-spaces' when tax officials took proceedings against householders who failed to declare income from lettings.

To reverse the damage, Queens' had acquired Owlstone Croft in Newnham, once used for CCAT students, and proposed to turn it into a hostel capable of housing 80 postgraduate students. St Edmund's, Lucy Cavendish and Pembroke all had building projects in hand.

By the Spring of 1989, the Allocations Committee relented so far as to say they were prepared to provide a sum of money for the computerisation project, £2,000 for a micro-computer plus £2,000 for software programming. On the other hand, they wanted the office to make a £5 consultation charge to every applicant: this was unanimously rejected.

Rents were set to go up by another 7% and a report justifying the award went out to the University. We hear the first mention of the Poll Tax as the Secretary describes the expected effects. There will be a city-wide census now in the Spring and again at Michaelmas when the new intake comes up. The charge will be payable from 1 April 1990 and each student will be billed for his 20% contribution. No liability whatever would fall on the landlord (of a shared house) or the landlady, in the case of a lodging-house. Syndics agreed to forbid the Secretary to give out addresses of students so that she could not be made an incriminating party to any check-up on whether students were complying with the payments demanded.

By Michaelmas a Viglen computer had been installed and the chosen program-writer was more than halfway towards compiling the customised database system. She was working in the office on the machine to set up the data files and train the staff in computer use. The Secretary hoped the machine would succeed in speeding-up access to data and provide total recall of what accommodation was currently available in contrast to fallible human memory.

The Allocations Committee returned to the charge with a new proposal that the parent college should pay £5 for each student using the office's services. This provoked a fiery and very hostile discussion and it was agreed that the unfeeling application of a 'market-related philosophy' would only worsen a situation already most difficult for today's students. Cambridge had seen a decade of rapid growth and high prosperity and property values had rocketed, though there were signs and portents that these ballooning prices had now peaked. The passing of the new Housing Act had visibly encouraged landlords to let their property more freely, on assured shorthold tenancies. Anglia Polytechnic's recent expansion was accompanied by shocking housing problems given much publicity in the Press. Mortgage interest rates reached a new high.

Against this background, the Syndicate at this time was much exercised about licensed lodgings and their continuing role and a report on their diminishing number had gone out, seeking the views of all interested parties. Several of the Syndics saw the licensed system as an anachronism and would prefer the office to concentrate on its welfare aspect and on building up a code of practice according to which lettings to students should be conducted. All agreed it was inequitable to compel the private landlady to accept rents for her rooms well below the market level.

Student representatives of course voted to maintain a system that benefited their members by keeping the costs low for at least a minority. The advantage to the undergraduate was also that he only paid rent for the 30 weeks of the year that he needed to be in Cambridge in order to keep terms. The landlady representatives valued the system for its protection and deprecated any move towards changing it: those who looked after a lodging-house as tenants of a college felt safer within the administration of the Syndicate than they would be as employees of the college.

Every meeting continued the debate on advantages and drawbacks and thrashed out the issues vigorously. The Rents Meeting in its old form was abandoned in favour of a meeting between the Secretary and the Bursars of colleges owning lodging-houses to agree on a level of increase appropriate to the times, and that level would be applied to college-owned lodging-houses. Privately owned lodgings were to be brought level with market prices as quickly as possible.

So it is clear that the Syndicate was very bent on self-analysis, and the Secretary continually fed it with facts and figures and the opinions of all whom its workings involved. Reform was in the air, and it was no surprise when a letter came from the Registrary announcing that a committee would be set up in the academic year 1990/1991 to review the licensed system and the future role of the Lodgings Syndicate. Dr Kerridge replied that they would happily contribute to that review, and the judgement of a dispassionate set of people was welcomed and had indeed been sought.

Meanwhile the Government was determined to end the drain on its resources entailed by financing an ever-growing student population. The student loan scheme they had invented was to go to the House of Lords in early February and if it were in operation by October (1990) housing benefit would almost certainly be withdrawn. The Secretary wanted the consequences faced: anyone taking open-market accommodation might be faced with finding the whole cost out of their own pocket. Some colleges were already devising schemes whereby those occupying college rooms should pay a supplement towards the costs of those obliged to live outside in private accommodation.

It was agreed that the Secretary should disseminate such modes of alleviating hardship to all Senior Tutors with a note asking each to bring the information to their Bursar's attention also. Senior members were equally ill-informed about the effect the imposition of the Poll Tax would have and again the Syndicate fulfilled an urgent need in protesting about anomalies to the local office and making its staff aware of factors affecting students that they had not taken into consideration.

For example, a postgraduate would only be liable to pay tax at 20% but if he came, perhaps from overseas with a wife in tow, she would be liable to tax at the full rate. Again, those who came on study leave for a period less than six months would not be liable to tax at all, but if they rented private accommodation their landlord could be made responsible and charged at the standard rate of tax, which might well be double the personal charge. The Chairman and Secretary went by appointment to see the director of the Poll Tax office and spent a session of almost two hours going over a set of controversial points.

The computer was now fully operational and assistant staff were proving clever and innovative in making use of it, but the software programme was an intricate one and proved very slow. The busy summer of 1990 overtaxed it. To speed up the programme and rectify faults, the Allocations Committee had granted £1,000, and the Computer Service was being consulted: a tie-up with the Society for Visiting Scholars was contemplated.

Another initiative was to propose to University officers that the new Business Expansion Scheme be made use of to finance the building on University land of accommodation for newly-appointed academic staff and post-doctoral research assistants. Thus in many areas we see the office exerting itself to inform the University fully and to meet the new challenges created by the changing environment.

The academic year 1990-91 saw the reviewing committee go into action. Its terms of reference were to review both the Lodgings Syndicate and the Society for Visiting Scholars, to consider their future role and function, whether to continue the system of licensing and whether those using the service should be charged. The student representatives made their own submission, proposing *inter alia* the setting up of a joint accommodation agency to serve the needs of the University, Anglia Higher Education College, the Cambridge Regional College and the language schools. As this seemed completely outside the Syndicate's remit, they advised the students to send in their proposals separately, but the ideas was not impossibly far-fetched and such a scheme did in fact exist already at Leeds.

The Syndicate proposed that one central accommodation body should be set up serving the needs of all sectors of the University, assistant staff, students, academics and visiting scholars: it thought the present system confusing, where students came to the Lodgings Office, visiting academics to the Society for Visiting Scholars, and a few newly appointed academic staff were housed by the Department of Estate Management who controlled such accommodation as the flats in Fen Causeway, for example.

At this date, the Secretary understood that her colleague, Brigadier Crosthwait, was in favour of such an eventual combination, his retirement being more or less timed to coincide with her own. But in fact the Society for Visiting Scholars made out a substantial case for its own survival, feeling quite justifiably that it served a most valuable purpose in offering hospitality and a welcome to visitors on sabbatical leave from abroad, and in arranging a social programme for them and their families. If such people were no longer to visit the Society for Visiting Scholars Office at 12 Mill Lane for the purpose of finding accommodation, they would fail to benefit from these other facilities offered by the Society. Both the President of the Society for Visiting Scholars and the Secretary to the Syndicate appeared in person to give evidence to the reviewing committee.

The figures for those consulting the office and for those actually housed by its help were both substantially higher, demonstrating the continuing need for an accommodation agency despite the expansion in college provision. About 6,500 interviews were conducted annually, with 700-800 people being seen each month from May to October.

By Michaelmas 1991 the property market had collapsed and this certainly improved the flow of housing for letting, as the owners failed to sell at the prices formerly obtainable. Students, particularly graduate students, tended to shun the readily available rooms in houses where the landlord was resident in favour of sharing a house with friends. It was difficult to explain to well-meaning houseowners why their offers of accommodation were not taken up.

Student representatives claimed that where there was a landlord in residence the student's legal rights as tenant were considerably reduced: but the supervisory presence and possible disturbance from the landlord's children were probably more instrumental in acting as deterrents.

In response to that earlier initiative, the Department of Estate Management had advised the office that a possible site for building accommodation for research workers existed on University land on Milton Road. The Chairman and Secretary took up the chance with excitement, and made many specific recommendations, the Secretary visiting the site which was capable of providing 60 units. The architect David Thurlow had been chosen, and there seemed real hope of progress. By January 1992 the projected building had been granted outline planning permission and funding was being arranged by the Financial Board.

The mechanism for appointing the Secretary's successor was now put in motion, her retirement becoming due that September. Advertisements were to appear in *Reporter* and the national press. The Syndics met at Christ's in April 1992, together with the Registrary, to interview the shortlist of five candidates: 81 had applied, 26 men and 55 women. They agreed to offer the post to Mrs Christine Tewson who had been a mature student of law at Lucy Cavendish. A final Syndicate meeting was arranged in May at Fitzwilliam by the Chairman's invitation. Meanwhile the Accommodation Syndicate had been established by Grace as a result of the reviewing committee's report to the University published in *Reporter*. Mrs Tewson had accepted the offer of the post of Secretary to the new Syndicate and would take office on 1 October 1992.

The Secretary gave her last report on the annual conference of the AUAO held at Warwick. It set a high intellectual tone and encouraged members to take a larger view of the whole field of university funding and the future, *vis-à-vis* the rapidly developing polytechnic sector. She described how the government intended a projected growth of forty-seven percent by the end of the decade, a move from an elite to a mass system. She herself had chaired a workshop on student hardship; debts of £2,000 at the end of the course were commonplace and the effect of the recession on parents' ability to make up grants was more and more apparent.

Her colleagues were appalled at the plight of mature students financing themselves, and of single parents struggling to obtain an education against overwhelming odds. Much tutorial time now had to be devoted to debt counselling. It had been a memorable last conference for the Secretary and she had enjoyed the gourmet food, the comfortable setting in a purpose-built conference building, and the kind tributes paid to her at High Table for the Conference Dinner. The AUAO had always acted as an admirable training-ground and every Accommodation Officer owed it a great debt for extending their vision and for constant support.

Formal permission was given by the Syndics for the Secretary to work in her retirement on appropriate records deposited in the archives of the University Library. The Chairman paid his final tributes to the Secretary for her long service and to the landlady representatives who had helped the Syndicate over the years with their valuable and experienced advice. He asked the Secretary to close the minute-book on this note, and all present dispersed to a celebratory luncheon in the Fellows' Parlour.

UNIVERSITY LODGING HOUSE ACCOUNT.

House _26 Earl St_

Easter Term, 19 _26_

Mr _Mr J. C. Allan_

College _Christs_

due to _E. Ayres_

When necessary details should be rendered weekly; totals only for the Term to be entered below.

	£	s.	
1. Rent of rooms			
2. Service	12	10	
3. Hire of plate, etc. _Linen_	1	.	
4. Hire of piano	–	–	
5. Hot baths	–	–	
6. Cooking	–	–	
7. Food supplied	–	–	
8. Coals and wood	–	15	
9. Electric light	–	–	
10. Gas (for lighting)	–	15	
11. Storing bicycle	–	5	
Cleaning Shoes		9	
wash up Curtains ek's		7	6
	£ 16	1	6

Received with thanks — E. Ayres

Landlady's account 1926

13

Reminiscences

In discussing a service of whatever nature, much can be learnt from asking the consumer what he thought of it in retrospect. Accordingly the writer put notices in *Cam* and in *Cambridge*, the organ of the Cambridge Society, and in several college magazines and newsletters circulated to alumni, appealing for reminiscences and views on any aspect of life in lodgings.

Their letters form the substance of this chapter and, allowing for some nostalgic softening influence of the intervening years, here is the authentic voice of the Cambridge undergraduate.

Let us first hear the most famous of them all, Lord Rutherford, writing at the end of the last century to describe life at Cambridge to May Newton, the daughter of his New Zealand landlady in Christchurch, where he boarded as a student and lived as one of the family.

3 October 1895. I have now been at Cambridge for three days and have worked two days in the laboratory. I cannot yet pass an opinion on Cambridge as I have not been about enough. The University term does not really begin till the tenth but there are lots of freshmen up for their 'little go'. They are mostly very young and innocent looking and a good many are attended by their papas and mammas the first few days and they knock about in cap and gown and one meets them everywhere.

Now for a few remarks on my temporary lodgings for I have not yet settled my future movements. The place is on a street full of houses and is inhabited by one old lady of about 55. She has two rooms to let for £7.10s a term — the regulation price for such type of lodgings. Everything is so different as regards arrangements that I will go into particulars. Rent of bedroom and sitting room 15s 6d a week and coal and firewood 1s 6d. Besides that I pay for oil and all my own tucker which she cooks. It is pretty expensive — the rent is so enormous but I believe I am in an extremely moderate show. I will know at the end of the week about how much things mount up to. Thomson [J.J. Thomson whose wife had arranged these digs] wants me to go into residence for the reason that by a new regulation Research degrees are offered to students (resident). At the end of the first year if the thesis is approved by the examiner, one gets a diploma. At the end of the second year a degree B.A. by research if the thesis is again approved.

Research students if they reside will be in the same position as the graduates of Cambridge and will dine with them. The expense will however be rather high I am afraid unless they can be cut down considerably. I will know for certain in a week or so at any rate. For the present I will stay in these lodgings till I see my way clear.

Rutherford was of course a Research student at Trinity and he and Townsend were to carry out experiments involving the transmission and reception of wireless waves between the Cavendish Laboratory and Townsend's lodgings at 23 Park Parade. Dr John Campbell of the Rutherford Biography Project (to whom I am indebted for this material) writes: 'Rutherford briefly held the world record for the distance over which a signal was transmitted and received before Marconi commercialised the field.'

With the help of the Trinity librarian I discovered that Rutherford was in lodgings at 49 Park Street from January 1896 till the summer of 1897. This was a licensed lodging house kept by Sarah Cracknell who let two sets at 16s and 12s a week. From October 1897 to the end of the Easter term 1898 he stayed in the house of Charles Levett, described as a tailor, at 16 St John's Road. Two sets were let here at 17s and 14s. Mr Levett was given a formal warning by the Syndicate after the Proctors found his front door unlocked at 10.10 p.m. on 23 October 1897, but as it was a first offence, they resolved to take no further action.

Dr Campbell came over from the University of Canterbury at Christchurch (New Zealand) after our several exchanges of letters and we spent a pleasant lunch-time walking round the streets where Rutherford and Townsend lodged.

The earliest memories written directly in response to my prompting record life in lodgings in the nineteen-twenties and 'thirties and have a real period flavour. Let us make a start with a very evocative letter from H.C. Dawson, now in Canada:

I was in lodgings for the whole of my period at Cambridge 1920–1923 when I was an undergraduate at Gonville and Caius College. They were on the North side of Market Square, now torn down for the extension to Caius and consisted of two buildings divided by a passage-way which had a gateway locked at night. The eastern one was over a jewellery and the western over a shop the business of which I cannot recall. (It was at or near the corner of Rose Crack).[1] As far as I can remember each section had three floors. I was on the first floor in the eastern section overlooking Market Square.

The lodgings were owned by Mrs Mason, a business woman who owned a cinema cum dance-hall called the 'Rendezvous' about a ten minute ride on an Ortona bus. She had a daughter who managed this business. The lodgings were looked after by a dear old lady, a Miss Mackenzie.

Because of the jewellery store, during the night a policeman every hour pressed a button to register his duty in the store.

My rooms, a large living room with small connected bedroom had a fine view of any goings-on in the square. In particular I remember the well-organised 'Rag' simulating Tutankhamun's Tomb. You can imagine the articles brought up from the underground lavatories. The following year was when Caius stole the gun from John's.

The already-mentioned Dance Hall was used by the University Dance Clubs, the C.U.D.C. on a Monday, and the Quinquaginta on the Wednesday.

I have some recollections of the two dramatic clubs. During May Week Jack Hulbert and Cecily Courtnedge visited Jacks brother who was studying law.

I remember the Gilbert & Sullivan Operas at the Theatre, which I best remember for the appearance of Paul Whiteman and his Orchestra with the signature tune 'Say it with music'.

I think I should mention S.P. Ora, a Syrian, who owned a tobacco store in the window of which was a woman making cigarettes by hand. Whenever you entered you were always offered a cup of Turkish coffee. He also owned a motor-boat. Once when a

---

1. Note this instance of the use of the slang word 'crack' for lane or, as in this case, Crescent. *Ed.*

friend of mine and I went by Rob Roy canoe to Ely, on the way back, much to my relief Ora came by and brought us home.

In a second letter in reply to mine, be noted:

> In addition to Jack Hulbert's son [brother in original letter: *Ed.*] George Robey's son was also up when I was there but I did not know him. However I knew quite well Dennis Arundell, the opera producer, because he was a colleague of my brother's at Tonbridge School and used to stay with us. While at Cambridge he wrote and produced a wonderful pantomime skit at the Cambridge Dramatic Society which normally did not enter the musical scene, which it left to the Footlights.

This fascination with music and dance, so illustrative of the 1920s and its cult of jazz and bright young things bobbing on the dance floor, is echoed by a near contemporary, H.D. Brown Kelly who went up to Emmanuel to start his medical career in 1924.

> For my freshman year I was lodged out in Mackenzie Road [off Mill Road] with a most kind and considerate landlady. Dear Mrs Harding, she had a lot to put up with. At the end of the war, I returned to Cambridge to take my M.D. and paid a visit to Mackenzie Road. I was still in Naval uniform and did not think that I would be recognised. 'Hello Mrs Harding', I said, 'I don't suppose you will recognise me.' She smiled. 'Oh yes, Mr Kelly', she replied, 'you used to take your motorbike in bits in my sitting room.'
>
> In 1924 everybody strummed ukuleles and thinking to go one better, I started to learn the banjo, and the noise of our 'musical' parties must have been distressing. Bless her, she never complained . . .

Here is a near-contemporary with an anecdote reminding us how rural Cambridge sometimes appeared in those days. Ralph Emery writes:

> I matriculated at Christ's in October 1926 and was allotted lodgings in Emery Street, way up the Mill Road from Parker's Piece. It seemed to me to be a long way out, even on a bicycle,

and I asked my Tutor if I could be found something nearer to the College. His reply was that he thought I should be very happy to inhabit a street named possibly after — who knows? — some distinguished ancestor. In any case the alternative would be just as far away, but on the other side of Cambridge uphill to Castle Hill whereas the Mill Road was flat. I didn't see any point in the argument. I am sure it was some whimsical idea that it would be amusing to have Emery of Emery Street in the College.

I don't remember anything about the Emery Street lodgings but in my second year I moved into New Square, where there were many Christ's men. I had rooms in a house on the north side of the Square (No.18 I think) with the sitting room facing into the Square so that whatever wintry sunshine there might be fell through the bare branches of the tall trees in to the window. But it cannot have been very often that winter, as I wrote a piece for *Granta* (which actually appeared in the January 18, 1929 issue, when I had moved in to rooms in College) from which the wintry scene seems to have impressed me more by its rather cheerless atmosphere. I must have been feeling very sorry for the cows.

Apart from that, one may have overlooked the rather pleasant architecture of the Square, the symmetrical lines of the small terraced houses on the north and south sides (were they Georgian?) and the green of Christ's Pieces which one crossed on the way to college. The houses had no bathroom facilities (at least not available to the lodgers) and in the summer we would walk across the green to the small back-door of the College in dressing-gowns, and thus to the college baths. We did this quite unmolested. Our landladies were indulgent, as long as we were not rowdy.

The Square had not been 'developed' into a parking-lot and the Drummer Street bus and coach terminal had not been dreamt of. Quiet peaceful days.

When I wrote to tell him about the re-turfing of New Square, he replied that he did know about that and offered some further memories:

. . . As far as I remember, the street doors of the houses on New Square were never locked during the day, up to 10 p.m. Certainly I never had a 'front door' key. Callers, who were usually friends, could walk in and knock on the door of one's room. I don't recall having a key of any sort in New Square. Whether this was the usual practice outside my circle of acquaintances I couldn't say but it was only after 10 p.m. that we had to knock on the front door, and latecomers had to be reported to the College for the appropriate fines to be levied, and warnings issued if too many late hours were recorded . . . After too many fines one was 'gated' and after midnight it was a visit to one's Tutor with a severe reprimand added to the fine . . . It is hard to imagine that security — against intruders, burglars, salesmen or anyone else — was a non-existent problem. That at least was my experience.

At this period 32 houses in New Square were licensed lodging-houses, that is, 32 out of a total 48 houses.

Thanks to Dr G.L. Robinson, at Trinity in the early 'twenties, we have a picture of Miss Ransome, his landlady at 22 Malcolm Street.

Malcolm Street racquet mender

I took this snap of Mr Cox, repairer of racquets, and Miss Ransome, Trinity landlady, at their door, 22 Malcolm Street in February 1923. The legend on Mr Cox's racquet reads: NEVER TOO LATE TO MEND. The luminous patch above Miss Ransome's head I believe to be, not some oriental head-dress, but the garden of Westcott House (parson factory) viewed through the open back door.

I can also remember that when confined to bed at 22 Malcolm Street I called through the door that I was ill and could not see my tutor.

I found out later that it was Mr Dykes himself who had taken the trouble to come and see me, and that he had gone away without entering.

Finally I was thrown out of these lodgings for breaking Miss Ransome's Law of the Medes and Persians: no baths on Sundays. Full of heroism — had I not jumped fully clothed into the Granta and thereafter applied artificial respiration to a friend extracted therefrom? — I took it on myself to suspend the Law of the M & P. It was a lesson in the ways of the world. For Mr Dykes only managed to delay, but not discountenance, the forces of destiny.

Beside myself, Miss Ransome harboured a married undergraduate who studied forestry after his demobilisation from the first World War. I then lived in the digs of the partially drowned friend (whose air way was by that time clear) at 161 Victoria Road. Of this I also have a snap. Here I was cherished by kind Miss White, while another friend, E.O. Symonds, lived with the Misses Allen,[3] and piano and the works of A.N. Whitehead, a few doors down. I regret Miss White is not in the snap. I called on her once, years later, when she had moved across into the square opposite.

Interestingly enough, I received contributions from two people about their time in lodgings with the same landlady: each has a very different recollection and they were not fellow-lodgers.

So first let us observe Miss E. Ayres of 26 Earl Street through the eyes of her more critical lodger, who prefers to remain anonymous.

For my first two years at Christ's from 1927, I lodged with a Miss Ayres, a somewhat dour lady from the North, in Earl Street — possibly No.10 — or was it 20? After dinner in Hall I would normally retire there to study for my Natural Sciences Tripos in a private old-fashioned front room with lace curtains and aspidistra, and in the winter a cosy warm fire. I never thought of entertaining anyone there, or whether even it would be allowed. My bedroom upstairs overlooked the back garden. It was all very quiet.

The only reproof I recall from Miss Ayres was on the occasion of my bringing some logs from our farm in Essex in the boot —

3. The Misses Allen kept a lodging-house at 147 Victoria Road. *Ed.*

or 'dicky' as it was called — of my mother's Standard car (10 H.P. Registration number F 80) to brighten up the fireplace, but Miss Ayres said, 'The billets waste the coals.' I had a feeling that the logs somehow put her out of pocket, but I never enquired how, and I was certainly charged for coal in the usual way on the college bill.

Most people would agree in thinking that putting wood on the fire makes the coal burn up faster and is therefore uneconomical. Miss Ayres was rightly considering her pocket. She comes over much more sympathetically in the letters written by James C. Allan who lodged with her as an undergraduate of Christ's from 1925 to 1927, thus immediately preceding the writer above.

Miss Ayres of Earl Street

I lodged at 26 Earl Street with Miss Ayres, a dear old lady. At least she seemed an old lady, and she probably was, for she died in 1940. Until 1925 I had lived at home, and Miss Ayres was like a mother. She was very kind and looked after me so very well. In my second year I had quite bad 'flu for a fortnight and I couldn't have been better in hospital. I have no particular memories. Miss Ayres was just kindness itself.

Years later, in 1959, I was motoring south with three of my children for a holiday in Tunbridge Wells, my wife having taken a younger child by train. I thought it would be nice to spend a night in Cambridge on the way, and I wrote to 26 Earl Street in the hope that it might still be a University lodging and empty during the vacation. All was well — and I was allocated my old bed.

Miss Ayres, as I have said, died in 1940 and was buried in the Borough Cemetery, Newmarket Road. I had kept in touch and sent her a present each Christmas. Since 1940 I have been in Cambridge by car two or three times, and each time, I took flowers to put on her grave. My only photographs are a few of Miss Ayres in her back garden and at the door of 26 Earl Street.

When I thanked Mr Allan for these and laughingly commented on the period flavour of his suit and her 'droopy frock', he wrote back:

> You also mention my three-piece suit, with turn ups at the foot of each trouser leg. I still wear, on special occasions, one pretty well exactly the same, but I don't think I would often wear a suit at Cambridge, except on a Sunday for going to church. The photos I sent were taken by my mother, when she, my father and my sister, came up for May week in June 1928. They stayed with Miss Ayres and as my sister had got off school, she and my father stayed only a few days, but my mother waited to go to my graduation. She had been, in 1898, the first woman to graduate at Edinburgh University with an Honours Degree in Modern Languages, so she was very interested to attend a Cambridge Graduation, which she found disappointingly informal. I expect I wore a suit for the occasion, so the photo may have been taken after the graduation.
>
> I probably told you that Miss Ayres had three sets of rooms, though in the two years I was there, she let only two. My sitting-room was on the left of the front door, my fellow lodger, now Sir William Harpham, was above. The third sitting room was behind mine and I think the third bedroom was above the front door. My bedroom was above the third sitting room.
>
> Half way upstairs I think the building may have jutted out a little to the back, and along a short corridor was the second bedroom and our only toilet. We had, of course, no bathroom and Miss Ayres brought me each morning a jug of hot water. About once a week I went to the baths in College, between the first Court and Christ's Crack.
>
> That, I think, describes the inside of 26 Earl Street, apart from Miss Ayres' 'quarters' on the ground floor to the back.

What she had I do not know, for I don't think I was ever there, and I don't remember how I communicated with her if I wanted to. Perhaps I had a pull bell in my sitting room, but she was so attentive I expect she was automatically there when I wanted her . . . Looking at the photographs there is, I think, just one other thing — the door to the left of my sitting room. I remember I put my bicycle through the door, which Miss Ayres may have locked at night when she put up the shutters at 10 p.m. to stop me breaking out.

Mr & Mrs Taylor
Gyp and Bedder, M staircase, Christ's College, 1928

Another of the photographs taken that week with his mother's new camera shows 'my 'gyp' and 'bedder' in Christ's, Taylor and his wife. I think they had a lodging in Christ's Lane — Christ's Crack[4] we called it.

---

4. Note the use of this word again for Christ's Lane, which no longer exists since the enlargement of Drummer Street and the creation of Bradwell's Court.

J. Taylor described as a college servant kept a lodging-house at 8 Christ's Lane with two sets. I think it is worth reproducing here for the sake of their clothes, their stance and Mrs. Taylor's hair-style, so evocative of the twenties.

Mr Allan would of course have been in College for his final year before graduation.

My jerking his memory sent him rooting about in a box of old letters and documents. Luckily among the survivors are these bills, his lodging-house accounts for two of the six terms he spent at Miss Ayres' (see p.211); a laundry bill with an arresting list of possible items; and a buttery and kitchen bill from his year in college. From this I have been able to construct the basic cost of living for an undergraduate of this date, assuming a year of twenty eight weeks at Cambridge. It would look something like:

	£	s	d
Lodgings:			
Michaelmas	17	12	0
Lent	17	12	0
Easter	16	1	6
	£51	5	6
Laundry: 28 weeks at 5s	7	0	0
Commons & dinners in hall roughly £2 10s a week while in college or £2 a week			
while in lodgings	56	0	0
	£114	5	6

Earl Street was of course very popular, extremely convenient lodgings country, commonly used by Christ's at this period. In a relatively short street, no less than nineteen houses were licensed. It is not surprising then, that we have another contributor recalling his days there at much the same date.

Let William C. Kerr, writing from Belfast, speak for himself:

I was so glad to read the article contributed by Mrs Weatheril to *CAM* about the lodgings system, for it was an element of my undergraduate life which after 65 years still remains vivid in my memory. It was on or about 6th October 1928 that I knocked on the door of 12 Earl Street where Christ's College had allotted me room for my first year. I was not a stranger to that street since in the previous December I had lodged there while I sat the

Scholarship Examination, but that was for only four days. I had been quite comfortable for that period but could not anticipate what it would be like to be in lodgings for a whole year. It was however very useful to have had an introduction to lodgings earlier on.

I felt at home immediately when Miss Agnes Dickerson brought me to meet her mother, who was officially the landlady, though owing to her age her daughter Agnes managed the house.[5] I was given the front sitting room on the ground floor and the front bedroom above, while my fellow lodger, John Prescot of Downing, had the corresponding back rooms. Mrs. Dickerson, her daughters Agnes and Ethel, and grand-daughter Connie, aged about five, lived in a semi-basement from which one could see the legs of passers-by. I never discovered what their sleeping arrangements were, except that they were somewhere upstairs in a part of the house which I never saw.

The limited facilities of the house were far outweighed by the unfailing kindness of the Dickersons. They had my breakfast, lunch and tea ready for me at the appropriate times and nothing was any trouble for them. When I got the 'flu' they brought my bed down to my sitting-room and did the same when my fellow lodger fell a victim a week later. When my father and mother came to see me Mrs Dickerson insisted on their lodging with her and was very reluctant to see them leave the house, chiefly I think because, like my father, she too was Irish, and she enjoyed 'the crack', as we say.

I didn't ask how they provided the extra sleeping space; they would just have smiled at me. There were no class distinctions in the eyes of the Dickerson family; my predecessors had come from all classes — the aristocracy and gentry as well as ordinary people like my family. I remember Mrs Dickerson telling me how the Countess of Denbigh had come down to the basement and begged her to give her the recipe for the scones which her son raved about when he came home.

5. See page 120 where the first part of this letter is quoted.

Though I was very happy in my second year to get rooms in College, I think that the year in lodgings was very valuable as a breaking-in period between the home life of a day-school boy and the independence of life in College, especially since I had had such fortune in my landlady and her family. I kept in touch with the Dickersons usually by letter, though on my rare visits to Cambridge I always called to see them until they were all dead except little Connie, who cared for her Aunts Agnes and Ethel in their last days. Of course, she is no longer 'little' Connie, being a grandmother herself, but I am in telephone touch with her and she will be sending me a photograph of Mrs Dickerson which I hope to enclose with this letter (*v.* p.120). I wonder how many men have kept in touch with their landlady's family for 65 years. I am very glad to have had this chance to pay my tribute to a system and to ladies whose existence did so much to make the entry to Cambridge so happy.

Little Connie duly came up with the photograph of her grandmother in the back garden of 12 Earl Street. Surely she and Miss Ayres, her neighbour up the road, must have known one another and it is amusing to put these two portraits together.

But let us turn now, before leaving the decade, to hear a very different voice, also speaking from Ireland but with a more patrician, certainly more ironic air. Two very amusing letters came from Norris Davidson, sometime Editor of *Granta*, and sent me scrabbling round old copies preserved in the University Library archives. Here is the first:

The St Catharine's Society magazine tells me that you are interested in memories of those who kept licensed lodgings; in my time I think they were banded together in a Syndicate. I heard much about them but never anything against them. When I came up [it would have been October 1927. *Ed.*] I kept in 56 Eltisley Avenue, Mr and Mrs Chapman. They were experienced, thoughtful and interested in one. Chapman worked in a tobacconist's called A. Colin Lunn, on the corner before going into Trinity.[6] The memorable thing about Chapman was his frequent comment on someone who had displeased him. I first heard it when someone failed to turn up to row in a Getting-On race: 'That man ought to be strung up and ostracised.' I felt that in saying 'ostracised' he meant something beyond its conventional meaning, possibly something surgical.

In the usual way, I went into college later on and then — because I was keeping a fourth year (for no disgraceful reason) I went into rooms in Trumpington Street, near the Porters' Lodge and I think the entrance was between a bicycle shop and G.P. Jones, the grocer, that was in 1930. Some time ago I was filming in Cambridge and went into G.P. Jones's successor. Someone there nearly cried when I mentioned Jones and the Wiltshire Bath Chaps he used to sell: a substantial lunch, to be rowed off shortly afterwards. 'You might get them in Sainsbury's, sir, but they wouldn't be the same, not the same.'

I can't remember the landlady's name because I used to write about her in the *Granta* as Mrs Wallaby and her daughter Gert, and Wallaby has driven out her real name. Once only I had trouble there. The house backed onto Sherlock Court, just a small garden space between. One warm summer night I opened the window while playing my gramophone. It was heard in college, after hours, and two distracted porters ran about trying to find it, the source of the music, and finally called the Dean, Dr Steers. Next day he found where it came from but could do nothing about it since I was playing it outside college. But he asked me to desist, and I did. Not good enough for Mrs Wallaby who took it as interference by 'them dirty old porters' and then repeated what she had often said (she said) to Challiss, the Head Porter: 'Mr. Challiss', I said, 'if you don't look dirt at me, then I won't look dirt at you, and we won't be looking dirt at each other.'

What I value most is the character she gave, of me, to a friend: 'He was a gentleman. He never threw up on my carpets, not like some I could mention.'

Michael Redgrave and I organised an exhibition of Landladies Art but thinking it might give offence we confined it to his descriptions of pictures to be found in lodgings. I recall his

---

6. Colin Lunn had a tobacconist's on King's Parade until the 'eighties. *Ed.*

sad *Granta* comment on the unseen shooter in 'The Stricken Hind', 'who wots not what he has shot or shotten.'

I proposed the names of several landladies of this date as the original Mrs Wallaby but missed my target. Norris Davidson wrote again on ancient brown paper that provided the answer we sought, since it had on it the address of his lodging, 68 Trumpington Street, kept at the date in question by W.J. Hunt, who is described in the official lodgings list as a Dairy Manager.

> I am writing on this dirty piece of paper because it fell out of one of my *Grantas* when I was on a Wallaby hunt, and finding I wasn't as funny as I once thought I was, I handed Editorship on to Alistair Cooke. The paper is a slip that used to be put into the copy of a (*Granta*) staff member and delivered to his door which, as you see, was No 68 in 1930–31. Mrs Wallaby was not any of the names you gave me. Her husband Wallaby did a milk-round with a horse; he left the house very early and slept for the rest of the day. I rarely saw him. The house had no front windows on the ground floor; where a front room would have given on to the street was the bicycle shop sliced out of No. 68.[7]

I had asked him whether the garden at the back of Cat's that he mentioned was the one with a water-tank in it that I had read about elsewhere:

> You mention the 'swimming pool — probably in the garden you call Sherlock Court'. The garden had a sundial in the middle, a tortoise called Albert and a building of two sets of rooms each opening on it by two doors. I slept there on a camp-bed for a short time in a hot summer. In the end it rained on me. With one's back to the street-facing buildings (G.P. Jones, Mrs Wallaby etc.) that had small gardens abutting on the small Court, one faced these two-story sets . . . four sets and to the right of them, and squeezed behind was *The Tank*. This was a sort of swimming pool but I am not sure if it was meant to be one or had another purpose . . . maybe a water re-

---

7. There was until quite recently a bicycle shop at this site, with at Christmas a bicycling Father Christmas in the window. *Ed.*

8. Bull-dog or University Constable. *Ed.*

servoir in case of fire. Certainly a Master of long ago, Dr Johns the Botanist, would not have thought of it as being a necessary swimming-place because in my day, we learned of his views on baths. 'You have one before you come up, you have one in mid-term and one as soon as you get home.'

In my time we had baths or showers every day in the basement of Old Lodge, the then J.C.R. Heat was maintained by Johnson . . . also a gyp and a night-time buller.[8]

Sara Payne has a note of the Tank in the first volume of her series *Down your Street* — speaking of St. Catharine's she writes:

One of the college's more unusual building schemes involved the construction of a swimming bath, one of the first in Cambridge. It was built at the back of 70 Trumpington Street, G.P. Jones, the wine merchants. No.70 was acquired by the college in 1871. The wages of the bath-keeper W. Sell are first noted in the account for 1872-3. Mr John Poole of Holbrook Road, Cambridge remembers swimming in the pool when he visited the college with his father, who had been a student there at the turn of the century.

She recalls that skeletons of horses were found by builders digging foundations for the Porters' Lodge in the thirties, which takes us back to Thomas Hobson who lived and kept his stables on this site and to whom we owe the Spinning-House (*v*. ch. 2.)

Although I exhaustively researched the *Granta*, following Norris Davidson's detailed references, I was forced to agree with his honest verdict that they weren't as funny as he had thought at the time of writing them. The Wallaby anecdotes we would nowadays find long-winded and a touch patronising in tone, and the dead-pan descriptions of 'art-works' in lodging houses have lost what edge they had. But I am grateful to Mr Davidson for the two items reproduced in this book; the cartoon of a henpecked lodger and a caricature of the Lodging House Syndicate that must have seemed a hoot to the undergraduates of its day; though to those of us who have seen landlady representatives serving usefully on the Syndicate for years it fails to strike so comically unthinkable. For their period value, they are reproduced on pages 52 and 183.

While on the subject of *Granta*, here is a poem printed in January 1933 and sent to me by its author, J.C. Andrews, who adds the note:

At that time as I am sure you are well aware, the average undergraduate spent two out of his three years in digs. Mine were in Newmarket Road, not far from the old Festival Theatre: but this verse had no reference to my own landlady, who was a very decent person indeed.

Ode to a former Landlady

Good Madam, every little while
I meet you in the town
I pass you with a nod and smile
— You pass me with a frown.

That frown of yours recalls to mind
The many terms I spent
Beneath your roof, landlady kind,
In one long argument.

You overcharged me for my coal:
You robbed me of my tea:
You never swept or cleaned the hole
My room appeared to me.

You gave me breakfast — at a price
Unequalled, as I know:
The coffee — with a film of ice:
The eggs — so much *de trop*.

My carpet, stained with many tints
Of coffees, teas and beers:
My walls adorned with finger-prints
Amassed throughout the years

The pictures you refused to move
Of all your ancient aunts:
The cat I never might reprove:
The aspidistra plants.

And yet your rooms — I say it now —
Were really not so bad:
— Did not, I'm sure, deserve the row
We very often had.

Good Madam, stand you not amazed
If now I praise in verse
What formerly I never praised
But often used to curse.

At least you made me decent toast,
And spared me coffee-dregs,
And had more art or skill than most
At cooking hard-boiled eggs.

I cursed your rotten memory, when
You let me sleep unknocked:
But it was useful, after ten,
To find the door unlocked.

Yes, on the whole I wished I'd stayed
In those old rooms I knew:
You swindled me, of course, but made
Me feel at home with you.

But since I left you I have had
A sorry tale to nurse:
Your rooms, indeed, were very bad:
My present digs are worse.

Here is a Magdalene man, H. Ramsay Cox, 1931–34, mentioning some of the perils of lodgings as he remembers the two landladies with whom he stayed:

My first was a dear elderly lady Miss Hills at 29 Bridge Street. It was a ricketty old house next to the river, and the other lodger was a chap called Maurice Doorman who later became Sir Maurice — I think a bigwig in Australia. Miss Hills used to bring us bacon and egg for breakfast but the egg was always underdone — she called it 'flollops'. She lived in a funny little room downstairs full of old bric-à-brac, and after a night out in the pubs we would creep up the narrow creaky stairs trying not to disturb her. My room at Miss Hills' was a real fire hazard and there was a peculiar rope affair at the window in case of emergency. The bedroom above it was terribly cold and the bed most uncomfortable.

My next stay was with Mrs Golding at 10 Castle Street (or Hill). Mrs Golding's husband Fred was a porter at Magdalene and was a very good friend to the three of us who lodged at No. 10. I remember entertaining a girl friend at No.10 one day, which would have been frowned on by the authorities in those days, but although I am sure Mrs Golding knew I had got female company she did not tell me off about it . . .

Norman D. Ingle writing from Durban, South Africa, is still delighted to read in the Downing College Association's News Letter of his old college's activities, academic and sporting. He says: 'At ninety years of age I am glad that my memory of those happy days has not gone.' He graduated in 1934.

Mr Berry admitted me to work for the Natural Science Tripos and I was told that I could find digs on Leinster Road (Have I got the name right?).[9] That road ran westward towards the Leys School from the Catholic Church. The digs were quite close to the West entrance of the college. I already had a degree from the University of Natal so I had a pile of books. My brain-wave had been to have a large wooden box to hold them and the box opened out on hinges to become a book-case. Alas, that box would not go up the stairs to my digs but with great effort the porters hoisted it up outside and through a door into one of my rooms. (Sea travel only in those days permitted such an obstacle to travel with me.) I discarded that cursed box-bookshelf later. I had very pleasant companions in those digs who in their second year gave me good advice.

After Christmas vacation I moved to Warkworth Street — across the Green. Here again I had pleasant upstairs rooms. I became very friendly with Hedley Crabtree — an engineering student who was an expert on gliding. He came from Ilkley, Yorkshire and I stayed with his parents one week-end. I had relatives in Harrogate.

9. He means Lensfield Road. *Ed.*

I imported from Germany — the rage then — a FOLBOAT or folding canoe. With wooden rods one fitted them into a large rubberised bag to produce a good two-seater canoe. For land transport it all went into two bags. I assembled it in my digs but had to lower it into the street through the window. I took it to the Granta and greatly enjoyed paddling in it. With various students I sampled many English rivers but the most enjoyable holiday of my life was to join Austrian students and travel down the Danube from Regensberg to Vienna. It all started in my digs where the owners looked after us well.

The following year I moved into the excellent rooms in the new buildings close to where the chapel is now. To go to dinner 'in Hall' was only a few yards walk then, and also to the Science laboratories, but digs had a special characteristic . . .

Another Downing man writes from much the same period: the Reverend Neville Brazier was in licensed lodgings twice during his three years at Downing (1931–34)

Firstly in rooms belonging I believe to a Mrs Waddington overlooking Parker's Piece. I was on the ground floor with a quite large sitting-room and a bedroom on the first floor adjoining the bathroom. The landlady was very discreet — she occupied the basement and I remember served me tea the afternoon of my arrival. We were about five undergraduates in the house and we were never any trouble. I cannot remember any of their names but one was a member of a famous Cornish family who made porcelain, and I am sure still do.

We were not served any meals — we were served these in the College hall. When we ate out it was usually at the Dorothy Cafe in the street behind Heffer's bookshop. I remember attending a meeting on its top floor. Meals were served on all the floors. It must have been a very prosperous enterprise.

My second year I had rooms in the College and in my third year I had more Spartan accommodation in a house in the street behind the huge Roman Catholic church at the corner of Lensfield and Hills Roads. My sitting-room was under a staircase and I remember distinctly that in the house next door all the muffins that were sold in Cambridge must have been made. I watched with keen interest the creamy liquid being poured into moulds and then slid into ovens. The house bore no resemblance to the Dorothy or other cafes. It was just a house turned into a bakery.

My accommodation served only to make breakfast and tea — all other meals were taken in the College dining-hall. I remember well the bedroom adjoining my sitting-room in College cleaned by a college servant. My brother and our partners changed in them before attending the May Week Ball on the Backs of Trinity and a splendid supper in the Great Hall. Dancing was in a huge tent where we danced round the band from the London Mayfair Hotel. We drove to Huntingdon for breakfast, still in evening dress. . . .

Dr Colin Bertram, Senior Tutor at St. John's for many years and at one point a member of the Lodging House Syndicate, sends me this reminiscence from his undergraduate days:

> You ask for memoirs. Here are two from 1929, on my first arrival at No. 3 Round Church Street — only lavatory through her kitchen and in the yard. Two of her remarks: — 'Sir, there ain't now no more mahogany backs: the College has done me up'. [This enigmatic utterance translates as: 'My landlord the College has repainted the house and there are now no more bugs, i.e. cockroaches'.] One day when a bit dishevelled, she said, 'Sir, excuse my dishabille'.

He may be talking of Mrs A. Cherry of whom he adds: 'a fine person who died after being with St. John's over 50 years'.

The plumbing crops up in many letters: here is Canon W.W. Tymms on the pre-war scene:

> Certainly, one of the more bizarre aspects was the way in which the front door was locked at 10 p.m. to coincide with the locking of the College gates and then the procession of landladies next morning to report the time their charges came in the night before. (Fines were levied accordingly).
>
> In New Square where many Christ's men were housed and where I spent two years, the 'loo' was at the bottom of the garden, and the approach was through the living room / kitchen

— not always very convenient for either party and certainly not for guests.

My landlady's husband had an important role to play, especially in winter — he used to keep the path clear of leaves, and very often of snow and ice. The actual 'loo' was mighty cold at all times.

It is true that many landladies took on a 'motherly' role, but the master/servant relationship was part of life. All undergraduates were addressed as 'Sir' and although it was rumoured that one such in the locality used Christian name familiarity, he was regarded as extremely 'odd'.

Times have changed as the years have passed — my son followed me at Christ's and my grandson has just gone up this term. I notice that he starts off in College which is far better.

The remark 'not very convenient for either party' brings to my mind a letter with a rather sad and pathetic anecdote which I will give here although it belongs to another era altogether. Michael Luton writes from the United States about the lodging he shared with John Humble while they were undergraduates at Downing in the late 'forties.

I lived on Mill Road, just before the railway bridge, and the landlady was a Mrs Paige . . . it was a narrow house, rather old and shabby. She had two student lodgers; we each had a bedroom upstairs and shared a living-room downstairs for our studying . . . I don't think she was very well off, in spite of sons who seemed to be doing well, judging by the general shabbiness of the house and of herself. I recall the house being cold, although she did let us have a fire in the dead of winter. The most inconvenient feature was the lack of an inside toilet. We had to go through the kitchen and out the back door. One memorable winter morning, on getting out of bed, John had to use the facility rather urgently.

He grabbed a coat or dressing-gown, dashed down the stairs, barged into the kitchen — and there found Mrs Paige, with her lower limbs partially clad but nothing on above the waist, in the process of dressing in front of the stove. (The only way to warm up in early morning in such houses was to go in the kitchen, light the oven and open the oven door.) Anyway, she screamed, John withdrew and had to wait another painful minute behind the door while she covered herself, murmuring and whimpering in acute embarrassment. When it was over, and John had achieved his much-needed relief, there were of course apologies on both sides and no harm was done. Afterwards, when the confusion and embarrassment were over, she said to him: 'Never mind, dear, you've got a mother, haven't you?'

Before leaving this lavatorial subject, I must quote a most amusing confession made to me by a Canon of St Patrick's Cathedral, Dublin — ('shades of Dean Swift') he adds.

Dare I tell you of my very first Cambridge lodging? I came up to sit for a Scholarship (to Emmanuel) in October 1939. The 'digs' were somewhere off Drummer Street, near the Unitarian Church. I was a shy schoolboy. It was a cold spell. On my last night I was too cold, or too nervous, to go to a W.C. I used a brass vase on the mantelpiece and completely forgot to empty it in the morning. When I came back in October 1940 I gave the place a wide berth, and never dared confess what I had done as a schoolboy.

A postscript adds: 'This is the first time I have 'confessed' in over half a century. It is 'good for the soul'. The poor man's conscience was troubling him so much I took pity and wrote awarding him the remission of sins. In answer he says, 'Many thanks for your Absolution after Confession (53 years later.) for the

---

10. Maybe within the single-sex colleges, men were not so uptight and inhibited about bodily functions. I spotted a note in the Christ's College magazine about the Original Christian Minstrels, the oldest social club in the Varsity, founded in 1867; it describes its fortnightly meetings thus: they met in a room in the Second Court of Christ's at 8.30 p.m.

The Minutes were read and then each member in turn performed on his instruments, or sang, interspersed by the whole of the assembled company singing one of the many 'Club songs' washed down with Dale's Audit Ale . . . Our principal Patron Member was Dr T.B. Marshall (Tibby) the Dean, who always entered into the spirit of the occasion, and who was well loved by all of us . . . There was a bucket between the door of the room and the Oak, provided for the relief of members, of which the dear old Dean Tibby made regular use.

The writer is remembering 1932.

'Drink Offering' (sic)'.[10] He also recalls being at 55 Warkworth Terrace in 1940-41 and at 1 Warkworth Street in 1945–46:

> On my demobilisation from H M Forces . . . my relations with my landladies and their husbands were 'correct' not cordial — never very close. I was closer to the bedders in college . . . I think I felt rather guilty as my first landlady and her husband had lost their son in the first year of the war — and my second landlady rather 'mothered' the two 'schoolboys' who shared the house.

This last remark mirrors the slightly impatient view a mature returned serviceman took of fellow-undergraduates who came up straight from school. And it also echoes this question of mothering, the really close relationship that sometimes developed between landlady and lodger. We have already seen something of this in the letters of William Kerr and James Allan (*q.v.* pp. 121 and 120) written in the pre-war period when men were perhaps less sophisticated and self-determining. But the next few examples I shall quote are all post-war experiences. First, another churchman, Canon A.C. Phelps:

> I went up to St Catharine's in October 1948 at a time when the University was full to overflowing. There was not only the usual intake of students straight from school, but also a backlog of ex-service people like myself. As a result of this bulge in the student population an advertisement was placed in the local newspaper asking for additional lodgings. Looking for more new accommodation inevitably meant that it would be further away from the city centre than normal.
>
> A couple who offered and received a licence were Mr and Mrs A.J. Barrett of 113 Coleridge Road, a corner house almost opposite the park. I can remember that there was a Plymouth Brethren Gospel Hall at the bottom of their garden. I was their first student. At that time the College kept students straight from school in college for at least their first year, whereas older ex-servicemen were placed in digs for the first year. In fact I was one of the few who, because of the bulge in the college population, spent two years in digs with Mr and Mrs Barrett, as opposed to the normal two years in college. I had the use of their dining room as a study as well as a bedroom.

Mr and Mrs Barrett had no children and treated me almost as a son. Food rationing was slowly being phased out but I remember collecting my ration of butter, egg and bacon each week from the college buttery and presenting it to Mr Barrett to cook for my breakfasts. In spite of all that I was very well fed. That continued during my last year at St Catharine's when I moved into college, and during the following two years when I was at Ridley Hall. Mr Barrett was a book-seller at Heffer's in what was then their main book-shop in Petty Cury. Every Saturday in term-time (including the Long Vac term) during those three years, I collected a food parcel which Mrs Barrett had cooked and he brought into town by bicycle. It usually contained a fruit pie and some cakes. I doubt if many (or indeed any) students were so well treated. [11]

I recall that they continued to have students at least during the following three years whilst I was still in Cambridge. I remained in touch with them, at least every Christmas, until they died. I call on them several times after I was ordained when I visited Cambridge, by which time the demand for lodgings had decreased and they had given up having students. When they died, having no family, they left their house to St Martin's Church in Suez Road to provide accommodation for an assistant curate.

Having been an audit clerk before I went to University and familiar with accounting, I kept a record of every penny that I spent. Receiving grants for my training from various bodies I thought that I should be able to account to them if necessary how those grants had been spent. In fact I have continued the practice for the last 45 years. I see that I paid the Barretts £17 a term rising to £24 depending on the number of weeks in a term. [12]

Canon Phelps' record of kindness received is much tied up with food, a theme we shall return to in detail later. But as to the relations between landlady and lodger, let us hear the extraordinary anecdote that Dr A.P. Joseph recounts:

11. The previous Canon (letter *q.v.*) wrote, 'We were never 'students': always 'undergraduates' or 'gentlemen'.. *Ed.*

My acceptance as a medical student at Trinity College at the commencement of the academic year 1955-56 had been delayed until the publication of the 'A' Level results for that year.

Accordingly, although my attainment was satisfactory to enter the course, by the time the formalities had been completed, the question of accommodation was still unresolved and it was now getting quite near the start of term. The college finally persuaded Mr and Mrs Wallman to rescind their decision no longer to accept lodging students (they had been giving notice of this intention for two or three years) and I found myself in 35 Jesus Lane, duly subject to the usual conditions of undergraduate lodging.

However, there was perhaps one important difference. Mr and Mrs Wallman's wish to relinquish their role as landlord/landlady on numerous occasions expressed to the college by giving notice to quit and then acquiescing to college pressure that they should continue with lettings, had this time progressed to the stage that they had arranged an alteration in the electricity tariff. The new charging structure favoured low-consuming customers but inflated the bills for heavier users much more than would otherwise have been the case. I did not discover this 'fact of life' until the end of my first term and I thus faced the winter term with an urgent need to make severe economies of fuel consumption — achieved at a price of endless foot stamping and cold extremities.[13]

My landlord and landlady were in their early seventies and Mr Wallman had suffered during the First World War, which left him with a permanent and, by now, considerably handi-capping limp. Mrs Wallman was clearly somewhat burdened by looking after him and had come to regard the presence of students lodging in her house as an additional chore that she no longer really required.

Nevertheless she was a good landlady and I was mostly comfortable enough, albeit on somewhat formal terms with her.

---

12. In the list of lodging-house licences granted for the year ending September 1949, the maximum rent for a room in the Barretts' house is £17. *Ed.*

13. The reader in his centrally-heated sitting-room will note with surprise how often a man complains of his cold conditions — almost reminiscent of the mediaeval student and the one brazier of burning coals in the Hall. *Ed.*

Everything changed dramatically on the 1st of March 1956 when Mr Wallman suffered a heart attack in the middle of the afternoon of that day. My medical studies, by then towards the end of their second (and so far only pre-clinical term) had not adequately prepared me for this situation. The general practitioner attended, pronounced the case as likely to be serious, administered a morphine injection for the pain and departed. Mrs Wallman and I found ourselves mutually bewildered for different reasons and we sat with her dying husband for several hours. Luckily the morphine injection had at least controlled his pain and his physical distress gradually subsided into semi-consciousness.

Over the next few hours this progressed to unconsciousness and he slipped away peacefully at about two o'clock in the morning. As he breathed his last, Mrs Wallman looked at me and said, 'Oh, Mr Joseph, I think he has gone.' Indeed this seemed to me to be the case and I was unsure of what the correct proceedings should be. I decided that perhaps I should tell the doctor and I wandered out onto the streets of Cambridge searching for a public telephone box. In due course I negotiated the system and spoke to an irate, very sleepy doctor who berated me for having troubled him to let him know what he had already predicted was the likely outcome of the case.

He made no allowances for the inexperience of an eighteen-year-old faced with an unprecedented crisis, somewhat earlier in his medical career than the course usually recommended. To this day I learned the lesson that if somebody telephones you to report a death, it is not an appropriate response to lambast them for doing so, however much you may feel that the call was 'unnecessary'.

When I returned to the recently-widowed Mrs Wallman I did not report to her verbatim the doctor's reaction but merely said he would attend in the morning for the appropriate formalities. Neither of us felt like sleeping and the rest of the night was spent with Mrs Wallman reminiscing about her time spent in Cambridge and in particular with her late husband and in their capacities as retainers of student lodgings.

The funeral was at Cambridge Crematorium a few days later, and I declined Mrs Wallman's offer that I came with her and the others of her family (she had no children, only nephews and nieces) in the cortége. I elected to make my journey on bicycle and as ill-luck would have it, I developed a puncture and arrived late, breathless and flustered.

Nevertheless the experience of the previous few days had been cathartic and the bond between us remained for the rest of her life. She was prevailed upon by the college to accept students for one more year after myself and then she did carry out her long-uttered threat to retire and relinquished the lodgings.

She moved out to suitable accommodation for elderly people in Bottisham, and remained there until her death at the age of ninety-three. I visited her on every occasion that I was in East Anglia and I sent her something each year for Christmas.

She, in her turn, wrote regularly and always enquired about my then expanding family, which from time to time she also had the mixed pleasure of meeting, if we were passing through Bottisham on the way to a family holiday destination. They were normal healthy, high-spirited youngsters, and she was by this time very elderly and somewhat frail.

Her death marked the end of an unusual relationship forged between two people of very different age-groups, backgrounds and temperaments, linked by one of the most basic of human eventualities, contending with the inevitability of death. I doubt (indeed I hope) that most student contact with their landladies was not governed by this type of experience.

A milder, more jog-trot co-existence is recorded by C.R. Berridge of which he has 'the clearest and happiest memories', 33 years later. The interest of his long letter, reproduced here, is mainly in its stress on the amount of bicycling a man had to do if he was unlucky enough to be allocated a distant lodging. Like Dr Joseph, he too kept up the acquaintance long after leaving Cambridge and made a point of introducing his family to his old landlady.

In 1958-61, Selwyn College practice included the allocation of rooms by the College. Nearly everyone in the first year was allocated a room in College, but in the second and third years, rooms there were normally only allocated to scholars, exhibitioners, and those with some position in a University or College organisation. So nearly everyone was in lodgings for at least their second year, and quite a lot for their third year as well. Rooms in hostels, which were large houses near the college and divided into rooms for undergraduates (there was also at least one for graduate students), were mostly allocated to third year men, or to office-holders, and were highly prized.

It had been verbally agreed that I would share a large room which had separate tiny bedrooms with a friend who was going to be college representative of a large organisation. It could have its meetings in the room. Unfortunately, everyone slipped up and assumed someone else was applying for it, with the result that no-one did, and the meetings had to be held in an inconveniently small room, and I was allocated lodgings at 34 Shelford Road, Trumpington, nearly three miles from the college, and only just within the limits then imposed on residence.

No. 34 Shelford Road was (and is) a semi-detached house of conventional layout. The landlady was Mrs W. Shanks who had lodgers partly because she liked having younger people around, as her daughter had emigrated. A further reason was tradition — her mother had been a full-time landlady before 1939, when they were already becoming rather rare. I used the front downstairs room as a sitting-room, and my bedroom was the third bedroom, over the hall. Mr Shanks worked for one of the big building firms in Cambridge, I think Rattee and Kett, and I did not see much of him, as he left the house at about 07.30.

In those days, central heating was rare, and the heating in the front room was provided by an electric fire, which cost 6d an hour for two bars and 3d an hour for one, and I recorded this as I used it. I soon realised that I could be comfortably warm with one bar at 3d an hour if I moved it from the fireplace and pointed it at my chair. The room was very well-furnished, with a bureau-desk, an armchair, a dining-table, and dining-chairs. The only thing missing was a bookcase; it seemed that my predecessor had kept his books in the desk, but I had too many. A rush job at home at the end of September was the construction of a bookcase, which came with me at the start of term. I still use it.

The bedroom had a bed, a chair, a hanging space in one corner, and a four-drawer filing-cabinet which made good storage for clothes and shoes. It was unheated, but I do not remember being unduly cold. I had no qualms about using a hot-water bottle, which my predecessor in the rooms had not had. Fortunately the winter of 1959-60 was not very cold, and I think the only snow fell just before the start of the January term, and melted within a few days.

The room over my sitting-room was a bed-sitting room occupied by a freshman who was allocated it for some reason I did not know, but he was only there for the first term, and he was not replaced. I somehow never got to know him very well; breakfast was not his strong point, and inevitably we had very little in common.

Breakfast was charged at 2s 4d a day. This was splendid value, for I got a bowl of cereal, a plate of cooked food (bacon, fried egg, fried bread and so on), a large pot of tea, and as much toast and marmalade as I liked. I never had much lunch, as I did not need it after Mrs. Shanks' generous portions.

I do not recall any difficulties about the use of the bathroom, but I think Mr and Mrs Shanks got up early. It had a huge gas-operated geyser of a type I had seen but never experienced. Although it was rather noisy, it is only fair to state that it always worked without problems.

The main problems of lodgings so far from everything were the time taken to get to and from them and the amount of cycling. If I played hockey in the afternoon, it was almost impossible to avoid three return trips, to lectures in the morning, to hockey in the afternoon, and to the evening meal and possibly a society meeting. I cycled well over a hundred miles a week regularly, and it was quite often nearer 130.

One of the amenities was the use of the garage next door for my bicycle, which was therefore under cover at night. I do not remember much problem with getting wet while cycling, but I was probably lucky that there were no particularly wet spells of weather that year — it was certainly a lot wetter the following autumn.

On one occasion, I saw the 'gate bill' which would be sent to the college once a week. While the overall record was not one to cause any awkward questions, I was quite sure that the times of my return on the Friday and Saturday were reversed, as I remembered that I had got in about 7 p.m. on the Friday, and nearer 10.45 p.m. on the Saturday, as I was almost always out till then on Saturday.

The only limit on my activities was a ban on major cooking operations on the gas-stove in the kitchen, where I was limited to boiling a kettle, which I did from time to time in the afternoons. Naturally, very few of my friends called by chance, but a number came by invitation. One friend of particular long-standing and wisdom said that I needed a visitors' book, which I got at Christmas. I still have this, and soon established a tradition that callers who have not been to the house previously sign it, so some friends have signed it several times, and the record gap is over 18 years.

Most of my friends were provided with crumpets, which were quite easy to cook with a toasting-fork and the electric fire. One friend insisted on spreading his crumpets with Marmite. Although I have always been very fond of it, I drew the line at putting it on crumpets. Two heroines came from Girton in the course of the year; one found me cleaning a brass nameplate from a railway locomotive, while I sat in the front garden, as she arrived.

Towards the end of the first term at 34 Shelford Road, a friend who was occupying a very small room in a house in a road just off Barton Road and therefore very close to the college told me he was moving out, and he asked me if I would like it. He knew I was finding the distance a bit of a restriction, so I asked Dr David Harrison, later Vice-Chancellor of Keele and Exeter Universities, and the Tutor who allocated lodgings and hostel places, if I could move. While he did not refuse the request, he told me that he always gave people who had been in Trumpington priority when he allocated hostel rooms. I therefore took his advice — and got a splendid room in my first-choice hostel for my third year.

I do not think many people had lodgings as far out of the city after 1959-1960, and I think Selwyn found rooms which were closer for everyone the next year. I did not see much of the other Selwyn people who were in Trumpington, but I recall that one did get permission to have some sort of small motor-cycle, on the grounds of distance. One exasperating episode involving my bicycle occurred when the lights failed on the way back to the lodgings, and I was stopped by the police who caught up with me, so I decided that discretion was needed and I walked the rest of the way. My friends regarded this with amusement, but at the time, I did not find it at all funny. In those days, the police were a great deal more zealous about cyclists' lights than I gather they are now.

I am glad to report that Christmas cards have been exchanged with Mrs Shanks ever since, so it has been possible, year by year, to tell her of my movements, marriage, and the births of our children. I have been back to Cambridge from time to time since 1961 and have had time to call in at 34 Shelford Road. In 1980, we stayed at the Camping and Caravan Club's site a short distance away, and I had the great pleasure of inviting Mr and Mrs Shanks to meet my family. I was sad to hear a year or so later that Mr Shanks had died, and shortly afterwards Mrs Shanks moved to 28 Crossways Gardens.

But by far the most lighthearted and affectionate recollections centre on the celebrated Agnes, about whom I heard from several sources. The first is a letter from a woman, Stephanie Holmans, my correspondents so far having been male. Mrs Holmans explains that she herself was at Girton and never lived in lodgings but she must have been a frequent caller in St Clement's Gardens. She writes:

I hope you will consider including something about the late Mrs Agnes Smith who was a landlady in St Clement's Gardens, Thompson's Lane (No.3 I think) for very many years (from the First World War to around the early 1970s — others may be able to fill you in on dates). She was very well known and a marvellous 'character'. She knew Rupert Brooke and was a childhood friend of Sir Dennis Robertson, the famous economist and contemporary of J.M. Keynes. (She inherited Robertson's personal possessions when he died and I have some of them.) Her students included Lord Annan,[14] the Earl of Harewood and very many others, mainly (but not entirely) from Caius and Trinity. She was always full of stories about them. Sir Christopher Mallaby, the UK Ambassador to Bonn was also one of Aggie's students. He was present at her 80th birthday party.

I am probably not the person to give you more detailed information about Aggie (as we called her), as I can't remember her many fascinating stories as well as my friends can . . .

She goes on to give me the names of possible contacts and as a result I came one evening to meet Jean Currie and hear her reminisce at first hand about her old friend. This is what I wrote after that fascinating *rencontre*.[15]

Jean Currie read economics at Girton from 1955-58 and lived in college. She had two fellow student friends, Stephanie Edge, now Holmans (who first wrote to me) and Shanti Wickram-singh (now Redcliffe) whose father had been one of Aggie's lodgers so she stayed there in the vacations. All three women became friends and devotees of Aggie and J.C. occasionally stayed as a lodger in vacations, paying £3 10s a week ('Are you sure that's not too much?' Aggie used to ask anxiously.)

Mrs Smith let four sets to men undergraduates at King's and Caius but her lodgers were not the only attraction. It was Aggie herself who kept open house. People gathered there, the door was always open, except on Wednesdays when she often went back to her home village of Whittlesford, but even then she left the key under the mat and the house was a home for anybody associated with her. J.C. would call three or four times a week. Aggie made lots of cakes and loved people to

---

14. No. I wrote to him with high hopes of an amusing portrait but though he remembers her he was not her lodger. *Ed.*
15. Interview with Jean Currie, Girton, 1955–58, 8 November 1993:

call in for coffee and to help themselves to thick slices of chocolate cake or Victoria sponge. On Sundays she held open
house for lunch and always made enough food for whoever
turned up: perhaps five to eight people would assemble to eat
her roast joints and caramel custard. Afterwards they would
sing Edwardian songs. J.C. quoted one that went

> 'After the ball was over
> See me take out my false teeth. . . '

J.C.'s face lit up and her eyes glittered with affection as she
talked about Aggie. 'She is alive in my heart for ever', she said.
'To me she epitomised Cambridge. She had a wonderful
philosophy of life, was very devout and completely unpomp-
ous, and thought the best of everyone. Aggie coloured Cambridge for me'. It was thanks to J.C.'s director of studies, Mrs
Holland, and Aggie Smith, that she formed the right attitudes
to life.

J.C. got the impression that she had lost a fiancé in the first
world war. Then she married Mr Smith (still alive in the reminiscences of Dr C.D. Lacey in the 'forties) but Aggie in
J.C.'s time had long been a widow. She used to show J.C. the
letters her husband wrote her on her birthday, to thank her
for the lovely year he'd had with her.

Aggie had a fund of stories about her lodgers, past and
present. Jack Hulbert used to tap-dance on top of the piano in
her sitting room. A friend of Peter Scott's lodged with her,
and Peter Scott would come and tap on her basement window
as a signal to her to rouse the friend to go duck-shooting. J.C.
remembers her in tears at the time of Suez, aghast at the
thought of her dear young men being called up to sacrifice
themselves in yet a third war. The Earl of Harewood had been
one of her men and Aggie knew him and his first wife. When
the scandal broke over his divorce in the sixties, Aggie wrote
him a letter saying she didn't at all approve. He wrote back to
say alas her advice came too late — he was reputed to have
two children by his mistress.

Sir Dennis Robertson, famous economist and contemporary
of J.M. Keynes, was another ex-lodger whom she had known
as a boy since his father had been Rector of Whittlesford

where she grew up. He left her a bequest of personal possessions when he died. As Professor of Economics he headed a
school of thought in opposition to that under the leadership of
Joan Robinson.

One of her men — who shall be nameless — became in the
course of time Senior Proctor, and one of his duties would
have been, of course, to check on the locking of lodging house
doors at the proper time. He made a visit to Aggie and promised, 'I'll never test your back door'. She always went to bed at
9.30 and could therefore protest her innocence of openings
and closings downstairs. But it was quite against all the rules.

Sir Christopher Mallaby, later the U.K. Ambassador to
Bonn and then to France, invited Aggie, as one of her old
boys, to his wedding and J.C. drove her to it at Hampton
Court, his parents' grace and favour home, in about 1961-2.

Aggie's men adored the way she would feed them up and
her breakfasts were proverbial, always fresh grapefruit and
never less on each plate than 3 eggs, 3 rashers of bacon and a
sausage. How well set-up they must have been to go off to lecture or laboratory. To be so liberal, she must have been quite
well-off. She had no children and her property in her will
went to a niece and nephew. (A note on one of the office record-cards implies that she was the owner of both 2 and 3 St
Clement's Gardens and they were sold to Trinity Hall in 1969
for £17,000 after her death.)

Members of the Bulmer family made a point of reserving
lodgings with her. Aggie's soft spot was champagne which she
adored, and one of the Bulmers donated the champagne for
her 80th birthday party, organised as a surprise by Jean Currie in June 1966 or 67. She was sent out to tea first with one of
her whist-playing cronies and returned to find 30 or so people
gathered in her house to welcome her, with a special cake lit
with 80 candles. A good few of her old boys were there to tell
her how much loved she had been, among them Mallaby and
David and Shanti Radcliffe. J.C. has a photo album full of
snaps taken at the occasion, showing a beaming and well-
preserved Mrs Smith in her best floral frock surrounded by
genial and affectionate faces.

Aggie was dead within a year or two, carried off by pneumonia, the traditional old man's friend as J.C. smilingly put it,
and so spared the indignities of old age.

Could there be a better tribute to the Cambridge landlady at her
most generous, revelling in the young she housed and lovingly
remembered by them in frank return?

It was all the more exciting to receive an earlier account of Aggie's reign from yet another devotee, Dr C.D. Lacey, at King's
from 1944-47 at the end of the war. He wrote the following piece
for his local parish magazine in Sussex.

The world is full of uncrowned — or uncanonised — saints.
They 'go about doing good', and behave so very differently
from 'do-gooders'. Sometimes we recognise them immediately; sometimes only years after, in retrospect, do we realise
that we have kept company with one. Such a one was Agnes
Smith, my landlady.

She kept a lodging-house for four students, and had no
doubts that the Lord had put her on earth to be the best landlady that hard work and loving care could make her. He reputation was such that in 1945 released prisoners of war,
awaiting repatriation and continuation of their interrupted
university studies, wrote to their college tutors from Germany,
Burma and Japan asking them to arrange lodgings for them
at 3 St Clements Gardens with Mrs Smith.

Like many saints Agnes did not follow the orthodox path of
the established church. Indeed she took a mischievous delight
in being 'naughty', as she called it, particularly if this enhanced her mission of providing for her 'young men'. At the
time I was lucky enough to be one of them, the war was
drawing to its close, rationing was severe and food scarce.
Agnes dealt unashamedly in the black market and we flour-
ished on her illicit provender.

Under the terms of her contract she was only obliged to
supply bed and breakfast, but she loved to catch you in at tea
time, or before you went to bed, and urge you to have 'a little
something'. If you weakened, then a monstrous plate of hot-
buttered toast, piled high, six layers of it, dripping with butter,

would be brought to your room. Sometimes a knock at the door at eleven o'clock at night would herald the arrival of one of her famous cheese and chutney sandwiches and a mug of cocoa. But those breakfasts!

While our contemporaries in college were having to survive on lumpy porridge and toast and scrape, we would be confronted each morning with a bowl of fruit; another of cereal; bacon; eggs, fried, poached or scrambled, and a rack full of toast. It was almost a hardship to struggle through it. I once appealed to Agnes to give me a little less. She was very upset. Her face crumpled at the suggestion that six pieces of toast were more than I could manage, but reluctantly she reduced the number to four for about a week. Then, as the half-filled rack offended her she reverted to the original number, 'in case you might be needin' it, Sir', as she explained, restored to cheerfulness.

While Agnes prepared these Lucullan feasts each morning in the steamy kitchen Timothy, her husband, circulated them. It was his duty to take the laden tray to each one of us in our own rooms every morning. The ceremony was formal and unvarying. Three sharp knocks on the door, a cautious entry, and then, expertly holding the tray aloft in his left hand, he would say, with just a suggestion of a bow: 'Your breakfast, Sir', an announcement which was a glimpse of the supremely obvious.

The rooms above me were occupied by a real live peer of the realm. This confused Timothy at first, but having done some studying, he changed his formula, when taking the earl his breakfast, to 'Your breakfast, m'lord'. He was obviously not happy with this variation in routine, and after a week or two, having delivered his lordship's breakfast one morning, he paused and asked, 'Excuse me, m'lord, but I needn't say 'M'lord' every morning, need I m'lord?' Having given a gracious dispensation from this burden the peer was relegated to 'Sir' like the rest of us.

Agnes' black market sources were a constant marvel and mystery to us. She had various friends and relatives in the surrounding villages, and she would go away for a whole day into the countryside for pillage and rapine, returning laden with eggs, butter, and bacon in immoderate and illicit quantities, far exceeding the ration allowance. There was a shortage of paper as well as food at that time and Agnes used to return from one of her plundering excursions with enormous rolls of lavatory paper, two or three times the conventional size. One of my fellow lodgers, an economics student with a face like a hatchet and a very dry sense of humour, was brave enough to ask her where she obtained them. 'Well, its my cousin, sir' she said. 'He works in the paper-mills over at Coton, you see. I find them very useful.' 'I find them essential, Mrs Smith,' he replied.

Agnes' religious worship was truly catholic. Her favourite place of worship was a chapel in a small village, where the services were conducted by a pastor of a fundamentalist persuasion. His sermons, which seldom lasted less than forty minutes, were concerned principally with warning his flock of the inevitable consequences of their undoubted sinfulness, unless repentance was complete and immediate. Assuming that neither of these conditions was likely to be fulfilled, he proceeded to elaborate in imaginative detail on the tortures of hell fire. 'A lovely man', Agnes used to say on returning from one of his exhortations. His other great reputation was for extempore prayer. He was reputed to have started one prayer: 'Paradoxical as it may seem unto thee, O Lord . . . ' I can't vouch for that, but his prayer in times of drought was undoubtedly genuine:

'O Lord we pray for rain. Not the tearin'
drivin' rain such as 'arries up the face
of Nature, but a sizzlin', sozzlin' rain
such as rains all day and most of night. Amen'

Agnes' other excursions into religion took the form of Anglicanism, Methodism, Roman Catholicism, and the Salvation Army, all of which she sampled and all their services she affirmed as being: 'Lovely' with the exception of Spiritualism. It was her friend May, next door, who persuaded Agnes and Timothy to accompany her to séances, where the medium was trying to make contact with May's late husband, Fred. After three or four sessions I could see that Agnes was uneasy, and Timothy frankly derisive about the whole idea.

'You see,' Timothy told me one evening, 'This ol' woman sits there with her eyes closed and pretends to be ol' Fred. She says: 'Are you there my darling? Is my darling May there?' Now I knew straight away it was all a load of rubbish, 'cos Fred never called May anything except his bloody ol' woman'.

If one came back to one's college or lodgings after ten o'clock at night, the time had to be entered by the college porter or landlady. Each week these times were sent to the Dean, which gave that gentleman some idea as to whether you were studying diligently in the evening, or whether you were consistently out and presumably enjoying yourself. Should you return after midnight, which was strictly forbidden, the Dean was informed next morning. Agnes interpreted these regulations with commendable licence. If I were out on some amorous or alcoholic business, and expected to be back after midnight, I suggested to her that this might be the case.

The front door was locked, as regulations demanded, punctually at ten o'clock, but the back door was left open to admit me at any hour, and, as often as not, beside a written note requesting me to lock the door behind me, reposed a large cheese and chutney sandwich to restore my expended energies. When I happened one day to examine the returns of the lodgers' times of re-entry to the house, kept scrupulously and tidily by Timothy, I noticed that the time of my return after these nocturnal excursions was always entered as 11.59 p.m. I suggested that it might be simpler to leave it blank, as if I had not been out at all. Timothy looked at me in shocked horror. 'But that wouldn't be right, sir. Not right at all, it wouldn't,' he said.

To my shame I only went back to see her once after I left. I found her, characteristically, on hands and knees polishing the hall floor. Delighted to see me she at once offered me a 'bite of something', and in no time at all I was confronted with the familiar mountain of hot-buttered toast. If there is a Heaven, Agnes is there now. But she won't be sitting on a cloud playing a harp. She'll be making cheese and chutney sandwiches for St Peter — 'In case you might be needin' it, sir'.

I have abandoned a strict chronological sequence in order to show how this affectionate regard for one's landlady remained a common feature over several decades and certainly did not just exist in the sentimental and nostalgic imagination of very old men. I do want the reader to have a strong impression of what, pre-war, a lodging looked and smelt and felt like, and for this purpose I propose to quote Professor J.R. Lander's evocative contribution:

> I was awarded a minor scholarship in history by Pembroke College in December 1939. Normally I should have come into residence the following October but to get ahead before possible call-up for military service, like a number of others I came into residence in January 1940. 'Bye-termists' such people were called and we were faced with the task of cramming three terms work into two. Normally as a Pembroke freshman I should have had rooms in college, but arrival in January meant lodgings.
>
> Arrival was a depressing experience. My father was dying of cancer at home. It was the worst winter within living memory, extremely cold, with snow on and off for weeks. I arrived by train from Leicester, a slow cross-country journey, with stops at heaven knows how many stations between Kettering and Cambridge.
> I went immediately to College to see my tutor (the Rev. H.E. Wynn, afterwards Bishop of Ely) who gave me the address of my lodgings — in a narrow street off Petty Cury (the Pembroke side of it). Alas, I now forget the name of the street.[16] It was a house with a basement and four storeys above — the basement being the habitation of my landlady, her aged mother and their servant, the ground floor was offices and 'the lodgings' occupied the upper floors.

16. His digs were at 12 Alexandra Street, an area that totally disappeared in the vast post-war redevelopment of Petty Cury and Lion Yard in 1970. *Ed.* Plates 10a and 10b show Red Hart Yard as it was in 1868 and Alexandra Street shortly before its demolition.

Red Hart Yard

Alexandra Street

The front door was opened by Miss Harvey, the landlady, a pleasant elderly woman. On the wall of the narrow passage I noticed an enormous steel engraving of Frank Dicksee's 'La Belle Dame sans Merci' — a tremendous piece of late Victorian sentimentality.

Then followed the dangerous ascent of a staircase covered with highly-polished linoleum, lit by a gas-jet turned economically low at each turning, to my sitting-room and bedroom on the second floor. There was a bright fire burning in the sitting room and Miss Harvey said that she would send up a simple supper in about three-quarters of an hour. Having washed my hands in ice-cold water in the bedroom I sat down and took stock of the sitting-room — a decent, if rather worn carpet, bright floor-length curtains on the two windows, a large Victorian mahogany sideboard, a large table covered with a plush cloth between the windows, with a gas fixture over it and another at one side of the fireplace, a plain but attractive mahogany bureau, all shining with polish, a comfortable brown leather sofa and two easy chairs. The bedroom was bleaker, linoleum on the floor, a chest of drawers, a wash handstand with jug, basin and chamber-pot, an iron bedstead with a feather bed — the last feather bed I ever slept on. The rent was £13.10.0 a term plus coal at 9d [between 3 and 4p. Ed.] a scuttle and an estimated amount for gas. The supper duly arrived — scrambled eggs, sausages, a slice of tart and coffee.

After supper the landlady's old servant, Miss Clements, gave me the low-down on the house. Miss Clements was a very small woman in an almost ankle-length dress of some mysteriously drab material and a bizarre kind of cap of the same stuff on her head. Poor woman, I later discovered that she was never without it because she was almost bald.

A very instructive speech followed which began: 'Now, Mr Lander, Miss Harvey and me have kept lodgings for gentlemen for nigh on forty yeer and we knows what gentlemen like'. I drew the implication — that if I didn't fit in with the customs of the house I was obviously no gentleman. The most depressing piece of information was 'Now, about baths, Mr

Lander. There's no bathroom, Corpus being the landlord and too mean to put one in — not that there's anywhere to put it. So you can have your bath, when it's your turn for the hot water' — there were two other students in the house — 'either in your bedroom or in front of the kitchen fire, but it bein' cold and snowing you won't want a bath more than once a month, will you?'

I elected for the kitchen fire once a fortnight. I did once try the communal baths in College but they were disgusting — generally filthy with the mud of a succession of rugger-players.

Miss Harvey and Miss Clement 'knew their place' as the saying went in those days, but you were also expected to know yours — and displeasure was manifest if you stepped out of line. Occasional drunkenness after a party was viewed with sympathy to the extent of an offer to help you upstairs, but questionable women were viewed with very obvious distaste. They followed the careers of 'our men' with great interest. After you had left the University they expected you to send them a Christmas card, and if you returned to Cambridge on a visit they would have been deeply hurt if you failed to look in for a cup of tea. They were respectful but far from servile: they treated you with courtesy and expected an equal courtesy in return.

The lives of those women seemed to me to be lives of unremitting toil. The sitting-rooms were cleaned and the fires lighted before the students got up. Hot water for washing and shaving was carried up from the basement in brass cans. In a corner of the landing on the second floor, concealed by a curtain was a cold water-tap and beneath it an outlet for slops. There was a speaking-tube on the wall. You took a kind of cork out of it, blew vigorously into it, a voice answered and then Miss Clements toiled up from the basement with a tray of tea or whatever else you might demand. To earn a little extra money Miss Clements also cleaned the offices on the ground floor in the early evening.

The greatest (and to me their only obvious) pleasure was to be taken for a Sunday drive during the vacations in the car of

Miss Harvey's prosperous brother.

One thing I have forgotten in my description of their work: at first Miss Clements seemed genuinely surprised that I could light the gas and put coal on the fire myself instead of summoning her to do it. She regarded books almost with a veneration beyond her understanding, dividing them into 'reading books' and 'writing books'. Both women regarded themselves as somewhat superior in the social hierarchy, pitying those who 'went into college', i.e. bed-makers.

I look back to those two long-dead women with gratitude and affection.

In writing to thank Professor Lander, I expressed surprise that his room was lit only by gas. He answered:

Yes, there really was gas lighting in my room. This in fact was by no means unusual in 1940. The houses of both my sets of grandparents still had only gas, like many small shops in provincial towns. I also remember in Leicester the lamplighter going round on his bicycle with a long pole to light the street lamps. About two years ago I read that in 1940 almost half the dwellings in London still had only gas . . . 1940 was the last year in which Miss Harvey kept lodgings. Then she and Miss Clements retired to a little house in one of the side-streets off the road leading out to Girton. Alas. I now forget the names of both. [He means the Huntingdon Road. Ed.] I used to call on Miss Harvey and Miss Clements in their new home with a bunch of flowers and stayed for a cup of tea. They seemed very happy in their well-earned retirement.

Contrast this positively Dickensian account with the three post-war examples that follow. The first forms a bridge as Dr Patrick Wayman himself acknowledges. He came up to Emmanuel in October 1945 from the City of London School to read Mathematics and Physics and stayed four terms in the house of Mr B.J. Darkin at 13 Warkworth Street.

The Warkworth Street houses were (are) built on four floors with, generally, only two rooms on each floor. At No.13 the basement was used by Mr and Mrs Darkin, the ground floor had two student sitting rooms, the first floor had one very large student sitting-room and one bedroom, and there were two student bedrooms on the second floor, plus a third room. There was no proper bathroom, but on one landing, as well as a separate W.C., there was a partitioned enclosure containing just a bath, with a water supply from a turn-of-the-century gas 'geyser' that took about 30 minutes to provide enough hot water. Actually, I never used that bath, taking frequent showers at the Boathouse after rowing, and the occasional bath in the College bath-houses near to the Library, where a very conscientious and genial bath-attendant seemed always to be on duty.

Mrs Darkin was of the 'grande dame' variety of Cambridge landlady and her husband was correspondingly of slight stature, a dispensing chemist by trade. They would have made a good seaside-postcard pair. They had very high standards of propriety and their furnishings had clearly lasted for many years, not by any means uncomfortable but a little depressing in style, which was Edwardian, or late Victorian, as was the dark wallpaper in the large first floor sitting-room, which I occupied together with the front top-floor bedroom. My friend, the late Max Colebrooke, told me the Darkins had a car, a 1939 Morris Ten, a valuable asset in post-war Britain, but I only saw it outside the house about twice. It had probably covered less than 10,000 miles in its six-year life.

There was, of course, no central heating, and we washed, country-house style, at washstands in the bedrooms with hot water brought in a jug by Mr Darkin at waking-up time. I broke a water jug once and had to replace it, being lucky enough to find one at a reasonable price, probably about 12s or 60p. (One would be £18, now, at least).

Dr Wayman's living-costs are put in terms of a useful comparison:

We had breakfast in college, due to food rationing, and paid less than 25p for the three meals served each day. The rent was £16 10s per term so that my 24 weeks' basic costs at Cambridge came to about £90 out of my State Scholarship of £180 p.a., soon raised to £240, plus a School Scholarship of £50.

This compares with present day finances when a £3,000 grant has to cover basic accommodation and food costs of around £2,000. I hardly ever had to have money from my parents, although after my first term I had run up a books bill at Heffers that had to be notified to my father, and he, much to my surprise, said he would pay it.

When I was ill in early 1947, and could not leave my bed, Mrs Darkin ministered to me in very kindly fashion, but on the whole we did not enjoy a close relationship. There was a telephone in the basement that I never used, and I recall her coming up late one Saturday night, puffing and grumbling, saying there was someone asking for me on the telephone. With surprise I went down, but it was an inebriated gentleman looking for someone called Patsy, not Patrick or Paddy (we never used first names anyway). Understanding it to be a wrong number, she was mollified, I was glad to find.

On another occasion, just as I was leaving for breakfast I stopped to tie my shoe lace on a chair near to the door of my room, finding Mr Darkin passing the open door just at that moment. The next day, and for about six weeks afterwards, a duster was carefully placed on that chair, as if I was in the habit of misusing that particular piece of furniture; not a word was said about it.

Another embarrassing moment came due to my undignified habit of occasionally helping myself to a spoonful of Drinking Chocolate powder straight from the tin. I was in the process of doing this just as she knocked at the door and came in. The chocolate was in my mouth, but I could not speak, only nod or shake my head in reply to whatever she came in about. Again, nothing was said in the matter of explanation or enquiry, then or subsequently.

Mrs Darkin prided herself, probably with some justification, in having a good rapport with Mr Welbourne, the redoubtable Senior Tutor, and later Master, of Emmanuel. When relating past demeanours of earlier students, she would often say, 'I got straight on to Mr Welbourne, and he came round at once to see me about it'. Reputedly, one such occasion was when she found a condom, which we used to call a 'French letter', in the double bed of the best student bedroom. My astonishment was that any student should have had the temerity to try to smuggle a young lady into his bedroom because of the high risk involved with Mrs Darkin around nearly all the time (and Mr Darkin sometimes).

In retrospect, it is clear that Mr Welbourne, or someone acting for him, took care that troublesome students were not allocated to 13 Warkworth Street. The Darkins were, even in 1945, a remnant of an earlier era, perhaps the 1920s without the glitter.

At 18 years old and away from home for the first time, I was fairly 'green', but those first two years at Cambridge were so memorable that all the experiences of that time are remembered clearly, including the severe winter of 1947, when we had 5 p.m. supervisions by candlelight even though the electricity was connected (it being illegal to use it domestically).

Here is a picture actually from the wartime years from J.A. Robinson who came up to Gonville & Caius and lodged at 12 Park Street in 1944-45. He had forgotten his landlady's name but I was able to trace her from the licensed lists and told him it was Mrs Holmes.

The house was, and probably still is — on three floors plus a basement where the landlord, landlady and their 12-year-old grandson lived. I occupied the top floor and when I last saw the house a few years ago, my living room now saw eye-to-eye with a multi-storey car park. The price of the top floor rooms was £13 per term, including breakfast, coal and shared use of bathroom. My friend and colleague David Daniels had the ground floor rooms; a man in the middle set has only one claim on my memory — that he carpeted his room with a large German flag liberated by his brother from Gestapo headquarters in Belgium.

During the course of the year, I recall two major happenings. Very sadly the 12-year-old grandson killed himself one afternoon with an aspirin overdose. What impressed me most was how this very great tragedy was not allowed to affect the lives of their 'young gentlemen' in any way that I can recall.

The other event concerns the very rigid rule which allowed us to enter the house up to midnight but under no circumstances to leave between 10 p.m. and midnight. On one night about 11 p.m. I partially witnessed a knife fight in Park Street which left one man injured and groaning on the pavement. In no way would the landlord allow me out to see what might be done. Nor did the police really want to get me involved in giving evidence, and were very glad when I had nothing useful to offer.

My actual rooms were typical of the period — and much later I suppose, with no running water, only the customary jug, ewer and chamber-pot, plus a can of hot water brought up in the mornings. The mattress on the bed was about 9" thick goose feather, and very warm and comfortable. I was allowed visitors of either sex, but strictly only in the living room. The rigorous daily fitting of the wartime blackouts was a problem, as I remember it. Breakfast was taken jointly in David's room and was substantial. There was one bathroom/loo on the ground floor with hot water from a gas geyser. This was very slow to fill a bath and we were expected only to take about one per week. Thus I used mostly to bathe in the splendid baths in the College basement — a fairly short bicycle-ride away.

It is amusing to see how opinions on the College baths differ, and how much the facilities varied from one college to another.

Colin Walters judges there was nothing particularly special about his experience for the time at which it happened, but since that was nearly 40 years ago, it will probably sound positively antediluvian to the modern generation. He writes:

I went up to Cath's in 1953 to read English, having completed my National Service. I was thus 21 and more mature than some 50% of my contemporaries. In truth, I think that most of us, even at that age, although we had lived away from home and, in some cases, seen military action (a particular friend of mine had fought the Mau Mau in Kenya) and were thus mature and self-sufficient in many ways, were thoroughly innocent in others in comparison with even our 18-year-old successors today. We would not otherwise have accepted without question the restrictions which were imposed upon us.

Because my surname is at the end of the alphabet, the regular lodgings had all been allocated by the time that they came to me, and I was therefore placed with a landlady who took students only occasionally. She was Mrs Chapman, a lovely elderly widow, who lived in a little terraced council house at 6 David Street, definitely on the wrong side of the tracks way down Mill Road, with goods trains letting off steam just outside the back door. The house was spotless; I had the best bedroom upstairs, and the front room downstairs as my lounge, breakfast-room and study.

There was no running water upstairs. Every morning Mrs Chapman brought up a jug of piping hot water for me to wash and shave in the washstand in my bedroom, and she then gave me a cooked breakfast before I cycled into College. The toilet was at the back downstairs, through Mrs Chapman's kitchen/parlour; having experienced communal living in the Army, I never suffered any embarrassment in marching through her quarters to the loo at any time of the day or night. The only heating in my living-room was a single-bar electric fire; in what was, as I recall, a fairly cold winter, I remember lying full-length on the floor beside the fire with my books to try to keep warm.

Mrs Chapman owned a television set, a rare luxury in those days, although the reception was diabolical. I remember overhearing a conversation between Mrs Chapman and a somewhat outspoken college friend who was visiting me, and who had gone off to the loo through her room. I heard him say, 'Good Heavens. What on earth is the matter with your television set?' I did not hear her reply, but I then heard Alastair say, in a very different tone of voice, 'Oh, it's always like that, is it?'

Because she was used only occasionally and was well out of reach of prying proctors, Mrs Chapman could afford to be very relaxed about interpreting the college rules. She had to report weekly on my comings and goings; at the end of each week she would ask me how she should fill in her return, and I, being a law-abiding young man, told her the truth about the time of my return to the lodgings, whether she was still up or not.

She would certainly have been drummed out of the club if the College authorities had learned how she had given accommodation (in the spare bedroom, of course.) to my girl-friend for the night of the Cardinal's Ball (an annual Cath's function at the time): it was all entirely innocent (at least, that is what I tell my wife.)

About halfway through the year she progressed cautiously from calling me 'Mr Walters' to 'Colin', but it cost her an effort. I do not know that I was an especially thoughtful lodger, but it was highly embarrassing that, when my parents came to collect me at the end of the summer term, she burst into tears. I called to see her once or twice during my second year, and indeed she again provided accommodation for my partner (a different one, and still not my wife.) for the next year's Cardinal's Ball. Regrettably I failed to keep in touch thereafter.

When I moved into College for my second year, I found my movements more restricted. Whereas I could come and go to and from 6 David Street as I chose, I could not leave College after 10 p.m. Since you could have ladies in your room until 11 p.m. the effect was — ridiculous and indeed, unsafe as it now sounds — that you took them to the gate at 10.30 or whenever and waved them 'bye bye' (or climbed through the window with the loose bars on 'C' staircase).

Fortunately my last year was the first when the college gates were left open until midnight. It was during that year that I met a young student midwife from Mill Road at the University square dance club (such was the imbalance of the sexes among the undergraduates that we sought women for the club from wherever we could find them.) Three children and four grandchildren later, we recently celebrated our 35th wedding anniversary . . . it has certainly been fun writing (these reminiscences) down and sharing them with my wife.

Two things strike me forcibly about this letter. I suddenly saw the age-old connexion of bringing up the hot water for the morning wash and then serving a large and satisfying breakfast as smacking decidedly of *Nanny*. I wonder whether some men, particularly public-school men, became aware of this unconscious projection of their nanny-figure onto their landlady? The admixture of authority with class subservience must in some cases have seemed comfortingly familiar.

Mr Walters also enters the vexed question of women visitors in lodgings, about which some landladies felt very strongly. A critical letter from an anonymous correspondent starts:

> Arranging accommodation for my second year went as smoothly as can be expected. On arriving at Mrs H's house I expected the usual exchange of mutual greetings. Rather, my salutation was returned by 'No girls in your bed.'

But John Massingham met with much more understanding from his landlady, whom he wishes to be referred to as 'Mrs C'.

> I matriculated at Magdalene in 1950 and spent my first year in lodgings at Priory Close at the top of Castle Hill. My landlady, though a trifle reserved, epitomised much that was best in the landladies of Cambridge. I remembered her with affection.
>
> She became very excited to learn that my fiancée (whom I was to marry at the Shire Hall at the end of my second year) was planning to come to Cambridge for the weekend. But she also showed some signs of discomfiture. Finally, she blurted out apologetically that, although there were no locks on my sitting-room door: 'I always knocks and gives yer time.'
>
> It seems that one of my recent predecessors had been something of a libertine, so she had not only had the door locks removed but she had also had to warn him that 'my cushions were not made for that sort of thing, Sir.' That final 'Sir' reveals how long ago that was and adds a delicious touch. Forty years on, my wife and I still chuckle at her kindly if earthy concern for the privacy of our courting.
>
> Am I permitted a story from Oxford? After graduation I was privileged to translate to Magdalen Oxford for a post-graduate academic year. There I had no kindly Syndicate to guide my search for lodgings. Eventually I found some suitable cheap accommodation of a remarkable nature in a sprawling decayed house at the top of Headington Hill. The gates leading into its

acres of grounds bore the legend: 'Cats and Dogs Boarded Here'

Having decided to take the rooms, I explained to the aged landlady that my wife and I would be accompanied by our young baby; did she mind? In the booming tones so characteristic of a class that ruled the Empire she responded, 'Not at all; I love all animals.' . . . Landladies could and did teach us so much more about real life than most of our academic tutors. Coping with them, too, was a valuable lesson in itself.

Even a man whom I shall quote later as one of those making strong criticisms of the landladies had to admit: 'There were indeed some lovely landladies — those in Portugal Place — 'will there be an extra pillow required Sir?' to those bringing up partners for the Pitt Ball. There was the famous Mrs Dench of Green Street. But don't forget the nasties. . . '.

The Oxford anecdote above reminds me of the plight of the married undergraduate, much more frequent a phenomenon at the end of the war but one for whom Cambridge most inadequately catered. Listen to T.W. Tinsley:

> I enlisted in 1939, joining up as a cadet in a training scheme for potential young officers. I had six months as an undergraduate of Christ's College, living on 'R' staircase.
>
> After the war having obtained a regular commission in India and having got married, I was suddenly posted back to England to complete a degree course (Mechanical Sciences Tripos) in two years. We had been married for six months by then, and my wife managed to get a passage to England, arriving just before the Michaelmas Term began. I had received 'joining instructions' which informed me that lodgings had been arranged.
>
> My wife and I duly arrived on the day suggested and we rang the bell of the small terraced house, somewhere between the back of Christ's College and Christ's Pieces. I do not know who suffered from the greater shock — the landlord (when he discovered that we were expecting a double room) or ourselves (when we learned that the licence for official lodgings forbade the presence of ladies in digs).
>
> An undergraduate who was married? Impossible. The only

solution I could find was to book my wife into a hotel. It was not easy. Rationing was in force and hotels were only allowed to book in guests for five days at a time, so I spent most of my first year going round Cambridge on my bicycle prospecting for a hotel with a room vacant for the next period of five days.

Eventually I found a landlady in Chesterton Road who could take us both in, and in my second year I managed to buy a house in Arbury Road. The story simply points to the absence of females still (in 1946) within the walls of licensed lodgings.

Let us hear a few more pre-war voices before going on to study actual wartime condition in more details. First, another soldier, my namesake, Brigadier D.E. Holbrook (no relation), inspired by the article in *CAM*, 'to write a few reminiscences about the two splendid landladies who looked after me many years ago, when I was an undergraduate'.

Let me first set the scene. On leaving Wellington in 1928 I went to the Royal Military Academy, Woolwich, for 18 months and was then commissioned into the Royal Engineers in 1930. In those days all R.E. officers went to Chatham on leaving Woolwich, for further military training. We then went on to Cambridge for two years, to take the Mechanical Sciences Tripos. About thirty of us arrived in Cambridge each year and we were allotted to Colleges in pairs, all of us living in digs. We were well disciplined by then and I do not believe that we caused our landladies much trouble.

I was sent to Trinity Hall with a great friend of mine, Jack McKendrick, who was gifted with one of the best brains that I ever met in my life. Our digs were at 11 Jordan's Yard, with a very kindly Mrs Sharpe as our landlady.[17] The house was quite small and has now disappeared underneath a car park. There Mrs Sharpe took great care to make sure that we were warm and comfortable, and that every morning we had a good breakfast before setting off on our bicycles for the Engineering School. We came home for lunch on most days, having bought some bread and chicken roll for lunch. It cost us about 1*s*

17. There were seven licensed lodging houses at this date in Jordan's Yard, off Bridge Street, where the Park Street multi-storey car park is now built.

each. Games or rowing filled the afternoons and we bought our supper at a café, when not dining in Hall. Our evenings were mostly spent in writing up our day's lecture-notes, or at the cinema.

We held no parties. We were both determined to put our backs into our University course and to obtain the best degrees that we could. The only hiccup in this routine was caused by the fact that Jack McKendrick was Scottish to the backbone and had brought his bagpipes with him. His practising, almost every day, took place in his bedroom at 11 Jordan's Yard. I was mobile enough to go out for a walk when this happened, but unfortunately Mrs Sharpe was not. The consequence of this was that she told us at the end of the first year that we should look for digs somewhere else. Apart from the noise of the bagpipes, she thought that he had a foot-pump in his room to blow them up. In fact, of course, he was beating time on the floor with his foot as he played.

We found other digs for our second year with another kindly landlady — Mrs Wilton Kahl, who lived at 1 Mount Pleasant at the top of Castle Hill.[18] She had a rather large house and kept a living-in maid, who used to bring us a tea-tray when we were in at week-ends and a hot bedtime drink every evening to keep us going over our books. I well remember that the striking of a nearby church clock at 11.0 p.m. was the daily signal for me to put my books away.

There was a garden attached to these digs, which solved the problem of the bagpipes. Mrs Kahl kept hens there. I don't know how much they appreciated the bagpipes, but one day Jack McKendrick and I decided to enlist one of them to try out the theory that a hen can be mesmerised by drawing a chalk line on the ground in front of it. Two people are needed for the experiment, one to hold the chicken and one to draw the line. It worked. When the line had been drawn, the hen remained squatting for a little while and then rose to its feet and walked away, after a dignified look around. (Unhappily Jack McKendrick was killed in the war when crossing the Rhine in 1945).

18. Listed as 105 Castle Street and as having six sets to let

Wray's Court

These little yards, packed with small houses, and built at right angles to the main town streets, were a feature of Cambridge and dated from the 18th and 19th centuries. Our next contributor, Dr E.J.T. Prettejohn (Sidney Sussex, 1937-40), sent me a photograph of his lodging, 5 Wray's Court, in a little cul-de-sac that has also disappeared, this time into the maw of Sainsbury's. He writes:

> I was fortunate to have lodgings in a quaint little cobbled courtyard entered by a narrow passage just across the road opposite the main entrance and porters' lodge of my college — Sidney Sussex. I believe it may now have been destroyed or 'developed'? I enclose a copy of an old photograph which you may care to use. Mine was the attic bedroom one window of which is seen in the roof of the little house at the far end. I had a downstairs sitting-room, and another undergraduate occupied the first floor. My splendid landlady Mrs Cooper lived in the basement.

There was gaslight only and an outside lavatory, but we were most comfortable. Mrs Cooper also owned the ancient cottages seen on the right of the picture, which were occupied by postgraduates. The small flat-roofed block at the end of the path just outside the garden gate was a tiny bakery which supplied the college with bread. This was 1938–39.

My attic window on the opposite side of the roof gave extensive views over the rooftops and dreaming spires in the direction of the Backs colleges.

And the next letter is from a contemporary of his, Dr Harry Butler writing to me from Saskatchewan.

I went up to Queens' in January 1936 as a bye-termist (I had failed Little-go.) and lodged in a small house in Newnham Road (now gone). I don't remember much about my landlady except that she was a retired midwife. But I certainly have vivid memories of my second landlady, 'Peggy' Paine, who lived in Newnham Street (No. 10 if I remember correctly).[19]

'Peggy' referred to her wooden peg-leg, not her Christian name. She was a most delightful person who looked after me very well. It was said that if her gentleman overslept, she would take off her peg leg and beat the ceiling under his bedroom to wake him up. It is sad that the tradition of landladies has gone — bless 'em all.

I wrote to tell Dr Butler that in 1937 he would have paid Mrs Paine £10 15s 0d a term for his lodging (A. Paine is listed as a tailor though he doesn't figure in this account.) and I must have queried the term bye-termist; this elicited a flood of new memories.

Of course I never knew how much my set at Mrs Paine's cost. In those days in Queens' I paid £80 each term, which included:

1. Tuition fees. 2. Cost of set. 3. Hall dinner
4. Commons — small loaf and 1 pint of milk
Monday-Friday, 1lb of butter each week.

---

19. In fact the address is 10 Derby Street, the home of Mrs A. Paine.

Breakfast and lunch you could have in Hall — if you could afford their prices. Most of us would use our commons plus marmalade for breakfast. For lunch we would go to one of the cafés and get cold meat and salads — the Dot was particularly good and quite cheap.

Now Queens' did not put first years into lodgings except under certain circumstances. The normal was — years one and two in college and year three in lodgings.[20] Scholars, of which I was one, had all three years in college.

A bye-termist was a first year student who, for various reasons could not come up at the normal time. In those days, Latin was a requirement for entry into Cambridge and if you had not taken Latin at the appropriate standard in school, you had to take a University examination in Latin commonly known as Little-Go (don't ask me why.) At this time students were beginning to come from State Schools which did not teach Latin. I was one of these and was in fact the first member of my school (Birmingham Central Secondary School) to win an open scholarship to Cambridge.

In the summer I had to take special classes in Latin, and then take the Little-Go, which I failed. However I did not know this until the day after I went up to Queens' for the first term. As a Scholar I was allowed to have another shot at Little-Go, but I had to go home the day after I had arrived in Cambridge. Fortunately I managed to pass and that is how I became a bye-termist[21] and spent two terms in lodging in Newnham across the road from the grocer's shop. He used to visit all Queens' men at the very beginning of term, to sell you marmalade, coffee and a tin of biscuits.

I was last in Cambridge in 1980 for a conference and my old friend, Max Bull, then Senior Tutor, allowed me to have the guest-room in the latest building for my wife and myself — a far cry from the days of all ladies out at 10.00p.m., a fine of sixpence if you came in after 11.00 p.m. — the time being geared

20. This was certainly not the case in the sixties and early seventies when first years were sent into lodgings. *Ed.*

21. This means that he was allowed to return to Cambridge and start his course in the Lent Term of 1935-36. *Ed.*

to the arrival of the last train from London. Terrible trouble if you came in after midnight without prior permission. Oddly enough we all accepted these regulations, including wearing your gown after dark in the Town 'so beware of the Proctor and the Bullers if you didn't.'

Captain Sir John Leslie was up at much the same time and sent me an odd little anecdote about his fellow undergraduates. In fact, the Mrs Edwards mentioned in the *CAM* article is not Mrs Edwards of Neville House. I went to call on my Mrs Edwards in Thompson's Lane imagining she'd be delighted to have news of one of her old 'boys' but she knew him not. A pity, because she is notorious for having a tale to tell and has a very pithy, witty way of describing people and the past.

After reading the article 'The Last of the Cambridge Landladies' in the *CAM* of Michaelmas Term 1992, I noticed reference to Mr and Mrs Edwards at Magdalene College. I was at Magdalene from 19351938 and spent the first two years in Neville House which was run by Mr and Mrs Edwards.[22] They ran it very well and Edwards would come around to each room and say, 'have you any requirements sir?' In the winter we nearly always needed more coal for the fire, and so he would fill the coal scuttle and bring it up to your room. They had a nice little baby who I suppose will be aged about fifty-five now.

One evening I brought back John Straker and another undergraduate whose name I forget, to have a drink. We had been drinking much too much before, and for no apparent reason they suddenly pushed me on the floor and tied my hands together with string. I struggled violently and then they squeezed my gown over my head. Fortunately Edwards appeared at the door and gazed incredulously at what he saw, as normally I led a very quiet life. Straker and the other fellow deemed it wise to depart and depart they did. I was very grateful that he arrived at that moment.

22. In fact, Neville House was a hostel, approved for college use by the Lodging-House Syndicate, but not a licensed lodging-house. The hostel-keepers would be employees of the college and paid a salary. *Ed.*

23. Now Basing House really is a lodging-house, a big one with rooms for nine men. It was kept at this date by Mrs. A.E. Eaton. *Ed.*

In my third year I moved to Basing House[23] on the quay and had the top room in the gable looking down on the river. The gyp was called Till a very nice and obliging person. He polished my shoes beautifully. The house was run by Mr & Mrs ? I forget their names and there was a young man who made the beds, etc.

When I went back to see these rooms some years ago I found them all closed with Yale locks. We never thought of locking our doors and I remember leaving a gold watch and diamond cuff-links in a drawer in my bedroom and never thinking anyone might steal them.

It might be appropriate to pause here and listen for a change to some reminiscences from one of a long line of lodging-house keepers. They came to me in a most interesting pair of letters from the granddaughter Mrs June Jessop (née Thurston), niece of the Mrs Thurston whom I remembered well at No. 2 Mortimer Road, running a large Caius house. I was particularly glad to have this record because it illustrates how the occupation passed from one generation to the next and how other family-members got drawn in. Here is Mrs Jessop:

> Several members of my family have kept lodging-houses. My grandfather, Frederick Thurston and his wife Minnie, kept No.3a Bridge Street during the 1920s and '30s. Frederick was also a porter at Trinity College; my uncle (also Frederick) a porter at Gonville & Caius, and his wife Ivy kept 4a Bridge Street and she subsequently kept 2 Mortimer Road. Their daughter (my cousin) Mrs Doreen Pearson and her husband Roy lived at 9 Pretoria Road where they also took in students for a number of years. Another uncle, Reginald Thurston and his wife Nella kept 65 Chesterton Road until their retirement in the 1970s — sadly both they and their two sons have also passed away so I am unable to obtain any reminiscences from them.
>
> I do recall from my own memory however, that they kept in touch with many of their 'boys' over the years and would receive Christmas cards from all over the world from former student lodgers.

My own father was the youngest of the family of six children and he (now 81) and his sister (now 84) were both at home during their formative years when they were able to absorb something of the character and personalities of the students living in their upstairs rooms during the 1920s and early 30s. I have asked both of them for any particular memories they have and I have given them on the enclosed sheet.

The names of some of the undergraduates lodging with landlord Mr Frederick A, Thurston and his wife Minnie at 3a Bridge Street during the 1920s and '30s are remembered by their youngest son, Maurice, and daughter, Mrs Minnie Robinson.

'Charlie' Cavendish was son of the Duke of Devonshire. The Duke himself came to the house on Charles' 21st birthday to take him out to Newmarket Races.

Nelson Dixon was a racehorse owner. He gave Minnie a solid silver tea service as a wedding present in 1935. He became a Commander in the Royal Navy. Dick Seaman was the only British man who drove racing cars for the Mercedes company.

George Easton, who became a top racing motorist was always in a hurry and used to hurtle up to the back gate of the house from Jesus Lane and frequently trod in dog-dirt which had been deposited by the family black dog. He was often heard to utter, 'B***** dog, s***, s*** everywhere.'

Lord Glenconner and his brother the Hon. David Tennant. My aunt's cousin was a tailoress, Winnie Harding, and she made my aunt a pale blue Harris tweed costume. Lord Glenconner wanted to see my aunt in the suit and asked her to model it for him. When she did he gave her 2s 6d. This happened in the No.1 sitting room. These two young men used to eat bread and dripping at night before they went to bed. They had valets come in to the house in the morning to get them up and to lay out their clothes.

Frederick Thurston made a 21st birthday cake for Lord Glenconner, which apparently did not please the family cook. Lord Glenconner subsequently offered Frederick a job on his Scottish estate of Gleneagles, and work for the family, but his wife Minnie did not wish to leave Cambridge and they did not accept the offer.

Frederick was an excellent cook and the undergraduates would often bring in game, etc., for him to cook for their private dinner-parties. He was a dab hand at making fancy fruit jellies and also a skilled cake decorator.

Hoping to dig out some more anecdotes about these Champagne Charlies I sent back a list of questions, which elicited the following reply from Mrs Jessop:

> When I asked my father (Maurice) about the points you raised in your letter he came up with the following:
>
> Who cleaned the shoes? Dad's reply — he laughed and said 'I did.' and received a few pence for doing so. Shoes were left outside the rooms at night as in hotels. The more well-to-do students, such as Charles Cavendish and Lord Glenconner, had their own valets who would come in and tend to their masters' requirements, clean shoes, lay out clothes, etc.
>
> Women visitors: not allowed.
>
> Boisterousness: no comment made about this and I suspect it did not happen. The college authorities seemed to have much more control over the undergraduates then.
>
> Letting in after hours: if the students returned to the lodging-house after 10 p.m. (at which time the gate was locked) they had to ring a bell and be let in by my grandfather or one of the family. The time of their return was noted and the information was returned (weekly, I think) to the College Proctors who would take any further action. This procedure was known as 'gating'.
>
> How did they (i.e. the lodging-house keepers) regard the lodgers? Again, no specific comment forthcoming but from the way they talk about them I would suggest they took a maternal/paternal interest in their lodgers — they certainly weren't envious of them.

Naturally the wartime reminiscences take on a very different flavour. First listen to two short-course men. Here is John Grant, writing from Madeira:

In 1943 at the age of 16 I volunteered for the Royal Navy under what was known as the 'Y' scheme. I was then at Bancroft's School, Woodford Green, and later changed to Earls Colne Grammar School. I was accepted for a University short course to read Law and Geography after an interview in Cambridge by the Royal Navy and went up to Downing in October 1944.

My headmaster at Earls Colne was J. Gordon Sykes, a Downing man. Under wartime dispensations, I was able to matriculate without ever having learnt Latin.

I spent six months, less a short Christmas leave, in digs with two fellow-members of the University Naval Division, which was based in Downing's West Lodge. The then Master was Admiral Sir Herbert Richmond. The college was largely occupied by 52 Maintenance Unit R.A.F. I cannot remember how our time was divided — two or three days a week were given to naval training and the balance to academic work. One of the outstanding members of the UND was a man named Methven, who after war service became a solicitor, a director of ICI, and one of the first Ombudsmen. My law tutor was a Mr Ziegler of Pembroke, who had been expected to attain the Bench, but for deafness. Among the demonstrators in the Geography Department was, I think, Dudley Pound. One also had time for sport: I chose rowing.

The two I shared with were Lawrie Hawthorn and George Betts from St Dunstan's School, Catford.

I think our digs were in Earl Street, between Christ's Pieces and Parker's Piece. The landlady was Mrs Skinner.[24] Her terraced house had a front door which opened onto the street and the three of us had separate bedrooms and a common study. There was an outside toilet. One of my colleagues earned the landlady's oppobrium for using his chamberpot in the night. Mrs S. used to record our late returns to digs and report them to the college. We took all our meals in College, which meant much walking to and fro. Undergraduates took turns as waiters in Hall. We wore mufti on academic days, and

---

24. No Mrs Skinner in the licensed list but there was a Mrs A. Souter at 18 Earl Street. *Ed.*

uniform on UND days. We short-course men did not wear gowns.

Downing allowed all those short-course students who wished to do so to return after war service, and I went back in 1948. Hawthorn returned at the same time. I spent a year in college and started 1949 in digs. I had found digs before I went down for the summer vacation, but they were no longer available when I returned. The College found remote digs for me in, I believe, Girton Road. The place was dismally gas-lit and not at all conducive to work, my landlady quite elderly, and I was not at all happy there.

I was business manager of *Varsity*, and one morning I found that there had been a fire at possibly the Wellbrook Laundry in Girton Road, in which the linen of some members of various colleges had been destroyed. Reporting this won me a welcome £1 prize. Downing found a room for me for the remaining two terms of that year.

Geoffrey Haworth echoes much of this experience in what has become one of my favourite contributions:

I came to Downing on an R.A.F. short course in October 1944 returning four years later for a degree and Cert.Ed. course, leaving in 1952.

Cambridge was so crowded in those post-war years that I spent but one year in college and nearly four in digs, in fact the same digs at 13 Mill Road with Mrs Pursey. Mrs P. was a formidable lady who became over the years a sort of second mother. So scarce were licensed lodgings that ex-servicemen were encouraged to take their degrees as soon as possible (using 'credits' earned by war service) and then to vacate licensed lodgings for unlicensed ones. It was, then, a common sight to see candidates sitting their Part I Tripos examinations in long B.A. gowns. When I took my degree Mrs P. promptly relinquished her licence and I stayed put.

Looking back it astonishes me how readily older ex-servicemen acquiesced to petty rules intended for 18 year-olds. Perhaps we had been brain-washed into obeying orders. The 10 o'clock rule was patently absurd yet we knew that landladies

were expected to report our after-10 returns to the college. I
doubt if, in practice, they did. Nevertheless we did hurry back
for 10. I well recall hurrying back across Parker's Piece at
about 9.50 p.m. with another undergraduate whom I knew
slightly. 'It's a bit of a bugger', he said, 'six months ago I was a
Colonel.'

Cambridge was very different. At first we had blackout and
frugal fare indeed — as it remained after the war. Undergraduate ages ranged from 17+ to nearly 30. Many of us were
surprised to be there at all (and would not gain entry now),
having by-passed normal entry requirements. So we worked
extremely hard. Nearly half a century on I retain fond memories of Mrs Pursey and 13 Mill Road.

J.V.G. Williams comes up with some 'odd thoughts of a remarkable landlady', as he puts it, remembering his time at Clare from
1942–44.

With regard to the note in *CAM*, no record of Cambridge
landladies can be complete without a reference to Mrs Edna
Gare, 33 Thompson's Lane. I lodged there in 1942.

She was a kind, caring person, but was very definitely in
complete charge of her lodgers.

There was a brass plate on the door so I imagine that her
father-in-law had perhaps lived there. In later years her husband Sydney was a barman at the 'Blue Boar'. Her son was in
the Royal Marines — and sadly killed.

We always had a large cooked breakfast, and cocoa before
we went to bed. I always addressed her as 'Mrs Gare', and she,
me as 'Mr Williams'. Christian names were not the thing.

Behaviour was important. You might not be thrown out,
but life would be very uncomfortable if you transgressed.

Mrs Gare used to 'help out' at the Synagogue across the
road, for whom, though a Christian, she had some affinity and
friendship.

With regard to the 'after 10 gate-fine', Mrs Gare was very
strict. However, the dodge was to find out when her elderly
mother-in-law was on duty. You then rang the front door and
entered through the back door.

I expect, with intelligent and high-spirited young men, there always was a dodge of one sort or another.

My next contributor re-introduces the complex subject of food, one of enormous importance to still-growing and ever-hungry young men. Rationing meant such complications that at some colleges, junior members took all their meals in Hall and landladies lost their culinary function. But as Professor O.L. Wade explains, he went up before that era began:

I have recently been looking back at old diaries and writing something for my grandchildren. I found it was difficult to start, but once started has been rather fun. . . . I was a medical student and on the outbreak of war we all received telegrams telling us to report immediately at Cambridge as the University intended to compress our course from three to two years.

So I arrived in Cambridge at the beginning of September 1939. At first I was in rooms in Emmanuel College. But when full term started in October I was put in lodgings in Warkworth Street. I think it was No.54 but I can not be sure. However I remember Mrs Scammons well.[26] She was wonderful. She made great efforts to feed us well; rationing did not start until sometime in 1940. The episode described below must have happened about December 1939 or January 1940 . . .

I had a room with Mrs Scammons in Warkworth Street with two other undergraduates from Emmanuel. Ken was a medical student and Peter an engineering student. Ken had an *Encyclopaedia of Sexual Knowledge* on his bookshelf. In those prim days such books were not usually left on bookshelves, and it enhanced the drawing power of Ken's room. I was amazed how many people dropped in to see him and how dog-eared the encyclopaedia became over the next few months. Ken had a firm belief that exercise wore out the human frame and he avoided it carefully.

Peter was athletic and a member of the college rugby team. The main consequence of this seemed to be that Peter was frequently ill; he got colds and 'flu' much more frequently than Ken

---

26. There was a Mrs L. Scamans at No. 13 in 1939 and 1940 but her name was replaced by Mrs Darkin in 1941.

or me. He also suffered terrible hangovers from the rugby club dinners.

I remember one morning well. I had got up at my usual time and had been given the usual splendid breakfast by Mrs Scammons. Ken had come down looking, as usual at that hour, a little jaded. He never had a proper breakfast, much to Mrs Scammons' distress, just a banana and toast. Peter usually came down just as we were leaving to go to our lecture to gobble a king-size version of Mrs Scammons' breakfast and then run to the Engineering School where he was invariably late for his lectures.

That morning however he did not appear before we left. As we knew there had been a rugby club dinner the night before this occasioned no surprise. What was surprising was that when I slipped out of the dissecting room to get a cup of coffee at the Copper Kettle in King's Parade in the middle of the morning, I saw Peter sitting pale and poorly in a corner trying to drink coffee. When he saw me he called me over, 'Owen', he said, 'something dreadful has happened'.

There was a long pause during which I ran over in my mind a wide spectrum of potential disasters. Then in a hoarse whisper, because it was so embarrassing, he explained that when he had eventually got down to Mrs Scammons' breakfast he had felt unable to eat it. He thought this would upset Mrs Scammons so he had gone up to his room to get a paper bag, and had pushed the bacon, sausages, eggs, kidneys, tomatoes, mushrooms and fried bread into the bag. He had drunk some coffee but then realising that he was dreadfully late for his lecture he had rushed out of the house leaving the paper bag on the table. He was distraught.

'What will Mrs Scammons say? What ought I to do? Oh, my God, I am a fool' and so on. He was in no state to see things in their proper perspective and he needed comforting. 'Mrs Scammons has been a landlady for fifty years', I suggested tentatively. 'She must be used to this sort of thing'. Poor Peter, he did not believe me. He was upset all day. When he got back to the 'digs' in the evening he was prepared for the worst as indeed so was I despite my brave words. But to our amazement and relief Mrs S. never said a word about it. She just went on worrying about the inadequate banana and toast meal she had to get for Ken.

At the other end of the war, David Harrap found himself just such another landlady, anxious to nourish her young gentlemen, after a terrifying experience in a Blackpool boarding-house while serving in the R.A.F.

I found Mr and Mrs Bromell of 20 Selwyn Road to be quite different. I went to live with them in October 1949 and they were kindness itself. For the small sum I was charged they were not supposed to give me breakfast, but Mrs Bromell refused to see a young lad (I was 23 by this time) go to work on an empty tummy, and for some ludicrous payment (I think it was fourpence a day) she served me a daily breakfast of bacon and egg and fried bread, toast, marmalade and tea. She and Mr Bromell both declared that neither of them ate bacon or eggs — rationed in those days[27] — so I ate three people's ration every week. I was not averse from telling this to friends who were in college, and had had to fight for the last piece of rock-hard toast and the last drop of stone-cold coffee.

Mrs Bromell used to worry that I might feel a bit peckish first thing, and having been a housemaid in her younger days, always woke me with two slices of thin bread and butter and a cup of tea. (How different from my awakenings in my first year, when I often found a thin film of ice on the shaving water in my wash-hand basin.) When I came in at night, Mr Bromell would be waiting in the kitchen with cocoa and ham or cheese sandwiches. He — Mr Bromell — was a very intelligent man. He had been with the University Press all his working life, and took a keen interest in his work. He had spent several years in Greece before the First World War and whilst there had taught himself Classical Greek. He told me of an occasion when he had been visiting the Porters' Lodge at Selwyn and had been able to assist a young Don to explain to a young female audience the translation of the motto carved over the door, and then to suggest an explanation of why there was an

27. Rationing went on till May 1953. *Ed.*

iota too few in *te* or an *iota* too many, in *pistei*. 'He didn't seem very pleased,' said Mr Bromell with a twinkle in his eye.

Mrs Bromell, although most wonderfully kind, was not a very practical person. I remember how, on one occasion, I triumphantly brought back half a pound of mushrooms which I had bought under the flaring gas-jets in the Market Square one darkling February evening. (What with the War and having spent two fairly miserable years in the Far East, these were the first mushrooms I had seen since the summer of 1939.) She cooked them all for breakfast on Saturday morning. She had carefully scraped away all the insides and fried the skins. I hadn't the heart to tell her.

Normally I used to send my laundry home — which I think was probably just as well. There came a day when Mrs Bromell volunteered to wash all my socks for me. Happily I did not hand over the pair I was wearing at the time. When she proudly handed them back — about half a dozen pairs I suppose — they would have fitted perfectly on six Victorian dolls. 'I gave them a good half hour boil', she said.

I remember them both with great affection. I spent my third year with a Mr and Mrs Woods in Marlowe Road. Having by this time forged an alliance with a young lady from Newnham, I tended to spend rather less time actually in my digs, but my memories of them are equally of their great kindness. However, it was a wrench going back to a single egg and bacon ration. Other people may have had other experiences — as for me, my memories of Cambridge landladies are one hundred per cent kindly, and I view their disappearance with great sorrow.

The reader will remember Michael Luton's story about surprising the landlady at her dressing.[28] He told me other anecdotes about Mrs Paige on this same food and drink theme:

Her family occasionally visited her on a Sunday morning, crowding into her kitchen, where she baked some very tasty buns or scones. Her tenants enjoyed these Sundays because she always made some extras for us.

---

28. Page 234

We occasionally had guests in for tea — I can't remember whether Mrs Paige made us tea; she did from time to time, but I think we usually got it ourselves — we would treat ourselves to crumpets and sometimes bought a bottle of gin. (I recall our telling people our favourite snack was 'gin and crumpets'.) Whenever we had a drink, we would take one in to Mrs Paige and that seemed to make her happy. (We may have been cynically buying insurance against any objection to possible noise from festivities). She would say 'I think you put a drop of gin in that drink didn't you?'

You see, Mrs Paige had terrible adenoids — I think that was the only major health problem she had. The adenoids affected not only her speech, we suspect it severely affected her ability to taste anything. So a drink would have to be rather heavily laced before she would notice.

Now we must have drawn the conclusion about her taste ability from the fact that she so heavily seasoned everything she cooked. But how did we know? Her scones were very spicy, come to think of it, but perhaps there were other instances of her cooking things for us that I just don't remember.

It is quite extraordinary how long this habit of feeding the young went on. Listen to the experience of Derek Franklin, up at Christ's and in lodgings at 8 Downing Street in 1957.

The house was not that big — into the hall, stairs straight up on left, two rooms 12 feet square on right and one room entered under the stairs 16 x 10 where the Hopkins lived (foldaway bed) with a minute kitchen and the only toilet built out behind. We went to College to bath in the bathhouse lovingly tended by Jock: enormous Victorian baths and loads of steaming hot water.

We were all at Christ's. Full cooked breakfast was served in the Hopkins' room for the four bed-sit occupants. The two other rooms on the ground floor were sitting-rooms for chaps who slept in an attic. Three bedsits on the first floor and one other in the attic about 8' by 8'. I think that it was £17 10s (a term) including breakfast.

Mrs Hopkins was a formidable landlady who didn't like her young gentlemen to take her for granted, and so, in all but four cases that I am aware of, refused them a second year in her house. Further than that, she vetted all the young ladies who visited and made her opinion very clear in all but words; she wouldn't go that far, but only a bare handful in all her years were honoured with the offer of a cup of tea. She offered a very good breakfast, but a truly wonderful Sunday lunch. Typically six courses, it went roughly thus:

> Grapefruit
> Home made soup
> Roast beef, covering the plate and then covered
> over with Yorkshire pudding, roast potatoes,
> three veg. and gravy
> Choice of trifle
> and/or
> Home-made lemon meringue pie
> Cheese and biscuits
> Coffee

This took from one o'clock to three fifteen and cost in 1957 4s 6d [$22\frac{1}{2}p$]. If that wasn't enough, any left-over desserts were put in our rooms to eat on Monday.

Her husband Jim was for many years retired from the Post Office where he had worked as an engineer and serviced the very first broadcast of the Boat Race. He made the beds and I have never met a comparable bedmaker: never a crease or a wrinkle and everything so tight it was a struggle to get in.

She must have been in her mid-seventies but when her house was pulled down, she moved to Thompsons Lane and continued for another few years.

Food and drink are the main components of a scurrilous (and maybe much-embroidered) account sent to me in a book published in America. It is called *The First Book of Attorney Abuse and Bench Bashing*, a series of facetious sketches by Howard L Meyer who was in Cambridge as a post-graduate law student in the late 'fifties. I accept no responsibility for this vignette of his landlady . . . I believe an American describes a ground-floor room as a 'first-floor'.

We graduate students did not sit at high table, were required to wear gowns to class, and lived in colleges or licensed college digs which kept the same rules. But we were obviously older and more experienced than undergraduates. We were therefore dealt with in typical English fashion; the form was kept but the substance removed.

I had a tutor, but at our first meeting he told me that I need not ask his permission to go to London (or for anything else for that matter), but to look in on him if I would like a glass of sherry and let him know how I was getting on. I was given a room at digs with a first-floor unlocked window and a tolerant landlady. In fact, she was generally juiced, was my 'Annie Laurie'.

My rooms were Clare digs, although I was at Sidney. It was not unheard of to go to another college's digs if they were available, and these were splendid rooms. One room actually, the living room of a Victorian castle built by two eccentric Scots ladies and named Castle Brae. I figured that it must have been built in the late 1890's.

The pubs were open between ten and two and from five until ten; a taxi picked up Annie and she got drunk twice a day.

In 1939 the army had taken over Castle Brae and broken the central heating which had never been repaired. Annie spent much of her time complaining about this. The electric system was appalling and the lights kept going off. When a fuse blew it had to be replaced in a box over Annie's bed in Annie's room.

Here is where the trick came in. The 'fuse' was a large ceramic device with a handle on it. You had to pull it out, wind copper wire around it (which made the fuse), and shove it back in. This had to be accomplished while balancing on Annie's bed while she was snoring away in a happy alcoholic daze. At night, forget it; wait until morning.

Annie would regale me with tales of the past when heroes had my room. An American millionaire named Libby (I gather from the glass family) had allowed Annie quite free play with his liquor supply. Annie mentioned him and his generosity quite often.

Another famous tenant was McClean [sic] of Burgess and McClean fame of whom she exclaimed, 'Broke 'is mother's 'art when 'e went off to Russia like that'. I replied, 'It didn't help the western alliance any either.' Annie said, 'I don't know about that but it broke 'is mother's 'art. What a gentleman 'e was; you should 'ave seen the bottles come out of there of a Monday. Now these boys' idear of 'ospitality is a cup of tea.' That was my cue to offer Annie a drink of sherry.

Then there was 'Brownie' who cleaned my room, more or less. She was very short and very old, and you could see her arthritis advance in a rather archeological study of the depth of the dirt on the wall. As she got older she was able to reach less high, so my walls shaded from almost a burnt sienna near the high ceiling grading down to fairly nearly white for the bottom three and a half feet which she was still able to reach.

George was Castle Brae's general factotum, handyman and carrier who was the descendant of the previous generation's 'man', now much diminished. However, George, dressed in an ancient tail coat, did serve dinner for me when I gave a small dinner party (black tie) in my rooms for a few friends.

At that time with your tuition you got a weekly 'commons' which I think I remember as being a twice weekly delivery of a pint of milk, two small loaves of bread, a quarter pound of butter and a small firkin of marmalade. This I donated to the kitchen at Castle Brae (the dollar to the pound being somewhat different then), but to many of the lads it was a substantial part of their diet and calorie supply.

Breakfast I still remember with horror as being the one cereal the English ever discovered, Corn Flakes, along with some blue milk (I think my commons milk, much watered), followed by a hot breakfast of bacon and eggs (there known as 'egg and bacon'), but with quite a difference. The bread was very heavy and cut thin (again I think my commons), it was then fried in bacon fat on both sides, the eggs were fried hard, and this together with the bacon (we would call it fat ham) was presented as breakfast. Additional toast, carefully chilled, came in a metal holder. Then there was strong tea; the 'strong' did not relate to the essence of the tea, but rather to the amount of sugar in it.

Annie, because I was an American and she was fond of me (probably because of the sherry), made coffee for me on occasion. This she did by boiling the coffee grounds for a while, adding hot milk and a great deal of sugar (presumably to make it 'strong' coffee), and triumphantly and with great flourish served it to me. I finally persuaded her that I had become Englishized and preferred tea.

Before leaving the food-and-drink topic, let me quote a very special case where a young law student found a particularly happy ambience in accord with his religious scruples and practice. Murray Cohen writes:

> I went up to Downing in 1950 after my National Service. The first year was spent in College and the next two years in Chesterton Hall Crescent. This was the home of the late Rabbi and Mrs Margolies. Rabbi Margolies had died and I never met him. Mrs Margolies took in graduates as well as undergraduates.[29] The men like myself who experienced her kindness and motherly affection were all Jews who wished as far as possible, while at Cambridge, to follow the faith and in particular to be in a position to eat Kosher food. Mrs Margolies was therefore the perfect lodging hostess for this purpose. If my memory serves me correctly, there were with us in the house at the same time from Downing, Gerald Goodhardt (now Professor at City University) Phillip Chody (now a Solicitor) John Rau of Jesus College and Sigbert Prais (a graduate at the time and who is now a professor of something or other, I believe, in the Midlands).
>
> We were all fairly grown-up young men since National Service had a tendency to make you grow-up rather quickly, and Mrs Margolies treated us as such. We all had keys to come and go as we wished, although we all took care not to abuse her generosity with the keys.
>
> However, what particularly stands out in my mind were the Saturday (Sabbath) luncheons which took place in the house.

---

29. She was not a licensed landlady. Maybe Mr Cohen obtained special permission to live in an unlicensed lodging on the grounds of his faith; or perhaps she counted as an M.A. lodging. *Ed.*

Not only did Mrs Margolies cater for her own boys, but in addition senior members of the University as well as other undergraduates, both men and women, came to join in the Sabbath lunch. So far as the senior members of the University are concerned, I particularly remember lunching with the late Dr. David Diringer of Alphabet Research fame, and Dr Teicher who was in the Hebrew Department. These were always fun occasions filled with banter and to a certain extent intellectual argument. I believe that Mrs Margolies died in Cambridge sometime in 1991 or 1992.

In passing, although they were not concerned with the lodging of undergraduates, except when they invigilated students who did not wish to sit an examination on the Sabbath, or on a Holy day, may I mention the late Dr Erwin Rosenthal and his wife who still lives at 199 Chesterton Road.

When I came up to Cambridge to take the entrance examination I found that one of the exams was on the Saturday. The University arranged for me to stay with Dr and Mrs Rosenthal on Friday and Saturday and take the examination in Dr Rosenthal's study on the Sunday morning, and that was the first occasion that I experienced their hospitality but not the last.

When I eventually went up to Downing I discovered that they kept open house to Jewish students on a Saturday afternoon, and I spent many such Saturday afternoons having tea in their house and engaging in invigorating discussion. I am sure that they are both remembered by many generations of Cambridge Jewish graduates.

I myself remember desperately searching for appropriate lodgings for orthodox Jewish students where they could have their own cooking space. It was particularly desirable to find them a house from which they could attend the Synagogue in Thompson's Lane without exceeding the permitted distance. Many times I deplored the absence of a Hillel House in Cambridge, such as exists in most University towns, and fulfils all the requirements of this strict faith. But after the war, the main concern of everyone was to find sufficient space to accommodate the hordes of returning servicemen. I wrote to Lord Annan originally because someone listed him as one of 'Aggie's' men: this was incorrect, but he nevertheless summoned up some interesting memories.

Shortly after I returned to Cambridge in 1946 I was appointed Assistant Tutor at King's and one of my duties in those days, when the undergraduate population was swollen by ex-servicemen, was to find lodgings for them and deal with any problems which arose. So I have memories of cycling into what were regarded as the wilds of Cambridge, e.g. Grantchester Meadows and the Newmarket Road, in search of landladies. On the whole we were very lucky at King's and had good landladies and by about 1950 we had built a new hostel west of the Fellows' Garden and had converted a house in Peas Hill into lodgings.

I was lucky as an Exhibitioner in 1935 never to have to go into lodgings as my first year was spent in the Peas Hill hostel over the newly constructed Arts Theatre, though I know how much a good landlady mattered and conversely how much a bad landlady could blight one's time. The trouble is I cannot remember any good stories about Agnes Smith except that she was a marvellous landlady whereas an appalling couple, mother and daughter, who lived a few doors down in St Clement's Garden, were intolerable: and I remember one morning having to go and remonstrate personally with them about the way they were treating their lodgers.

One of the undergraduates lodging there subsequently said that my words had been so earth shaking that they went around saying that I must have been drunk — which as it was 10.30 in the morning seemed a trifle unlikely. What of course is odd looking back is that young dons should have spent their time doing such work when they ought to have been, according to modern practice, researching fourteen hours a day.

The only other landlady I can remember from my undergraduate days lived in 22 or 24 Grange Road. She was a thoroughly modern landlady and my friends who lodged there wisely invited her up from time to time for a slug of gin after which they could usually get into the lodging-house at any hour.

The two following contributions came from Canada. First is David H. Scholes, at St Catharine's from 1944-47

> I have just shown the current issue of *CAM* to my wife saying that she might find the article on 'The Last of the Cambridge Landladies' interesting. She read it and said 'Are you going to write to Mrs Holbrook?' My reply was that I had no photos and no anecdotes worthy of interest. Her reply was that 'You took me to see Mrs Undrill on our honeymoon trip to the U.K. — surely that meant something important?'
>
> Well, she's right of course. I had spent just one year with Mrs Undrill and her husband and that was my last year in Cambridge (1946–47) and the said trip visiting my homeland was in January 1955. (My wife is Canadian-born). We continued exchanging Christmas cards always with more on them that the legal 'five hand-written words or less.' until she died (in the 1960's I think). She was a very wonderful lady and obviously there was a great feeling of affection between us . . .

He went on to mention the escalating costs of student-living nowadays, so in my reply I reminded him that Mrs Undrill's address was 41 Owlstone Road and that he would have paid either £15 or £14 per term for his set. The present-day cost of such accommodation, I added, would be about £400. He wrote back:

> The rates which you quote completely astound me. Mine would probably have been the £14 per term rate because I had the back living-room rather than the front — but I seem to remember that I thought at the time that the size of my bedroom rather made up for that fact. But the £400 present day cost for a bedsitter (I presume you mean per year in this case?)[30] is absolutely unbelievable. Especially when I think of the kindness and loving care which Mrs Undrill so generously lavished upon us (let alone the breakfasts and afternoon teas, etc.) compared with the coldness and messiness of communal accommodation. We certainly didn't think of ourselves as prisoners of an overly zealous regime. But that was a different world and we were still in the pre-Second World War world. We were so fortunate (and we knew it).

---

30. No. I stated the cost per term as a direct comparison. (*Ed.*)

The second Canadian, a friend and near-contemporary of David Scholes, sent a cooler but still admiring appraisal of his landlady. Here is Joseph MacDowall, O.B.E., Hon.Sec. of the Cambridge Society Ottawa and up at St John's 1948-51. I was able to tell him that he lodged with Mrs Martin at 33a Halifax Road and that in 1948-49 he paid £16 a term for his set.

My friend David Scholes sent me a copy of your letter and it set me to thinking of my first year up in lodgings. I didn't think I had much of interest to say but on reflection I guess every little bit of information could help you, so here goes.

My first year up at St John's in 1948 was in lodgings off the road to Girton, on the left hand side of a road to the right of the Girton road. I have forgotten both the name of the road and of my landlady. However, both are forever engraved on my mind a major experience of life at Cambridge.

My landlady was a perfectly trained professional but I have no idea where she learnt her trade. As a result, my lodgings were a good example of a superbly-run establishment. A veritable oasis of calm and order with style where I could relax and concentrate my mind on the challenges of the Mathematics Tripos.

I never learnt anything at all about my landlady as a person or of her family; she was rather remote. But she was a perfectionist as a lodging-house keeper. Never before or after have I experienced anyone who came near her standards of unobtrusive, efficient service. There was no telephone in the house. My rooms had neither radio nor television. I'm sure the landlady had a radio but I never once heard it.

I had the front room of the house equipped with table, sofa and easy chairs. My bedroom was upstairs and it had a feather double bed, wash-stand, mirrored dressing-table and wardrobe. The tables were covered with pristine white, starched linen cloths. There was no running water upstairs, or at any rate I never saw any.

The W.C. was just outside the back door downstairs and rather primitive but impeccably clean. I had a chamber-pot in my room and it was understood that I should use that after retiring rather than go downstairs. I took my baths and showers in College or at the Lady Margaret Boat House.

My day would start at about 7.30 to 8.00 a.m. when she brought up to me the hot water in a large china jug for my shaving and washing. Downstairs there was a full cooked breakfast laid out for me on crisp white tablecloth and a full white napkin neatly folded on a plate. In my second term I brought back from home my silver napkin ring and that was always used from then on, and kept brightly polished. I kept my bike in the diminutive front garden and took off for my lectures, gown flying behind me, at about 8.30 a.m.

When I returned tea would be set out on the table and a fire laid but not lit. I clearly remember that she would place an opened box of matches alongside the carefully laid fire so that I could light it for myself. It was so well laid that one match always worked perfectly.

At the end of the first term I was somewhat surprised to find that a small extra charge was made every time I lit that fire. In the winter the bedroom was freezing cold, that I do remember. She would always put a hot water bottle in the bed but I can still remember shivering with cold for the first few minutes in that bedroom.

My normal routine was: lectures in the morning, lunch in hall, rowing in the afternoon, tea usually in lodgings but sometimes with friends in college, followed by study, dinner in hall, then work again till bedtime. I took lunch in hall and stayed in College until I went to the river and then usually went back to the lodgings for tea. As the year progressed, and I made more friends, I would have tea with them in College, but I don't think I ever brought any of them back to my lodgings. I do remember being rather careful to let her know if and when I would be back from the river each day.

I was never at all conscious of my landlady keeping the gate book but then I didn't go out at night all that much in my first year. I knew the rules and was quite happy to abide by them. After a full day of study and rowing I was quite happy to retire at a normal time.

A propos the discipline and conduct of a lodging-house, Bernard Burton has sent me a photocopy of two communications from his landlady.

When I went up to Emmanuel in 1950 I lodged with a Miss Canham at 15 Warkworth Street. She was registered with the college for many years and was a rigorous upholder of the regulations — I think she was genuinely afraid of losing her licence.

I enclose two photocopies; one of a welcoming letter which she wrote some time in September 1950 which I think shows her concern for the well-being of her young men, and the other her 'orders' which awaited me on the mantlepiece in my room. I was not beguiled by her 'what's on your plate' for a 1s 9d breakfast and instead cycled into college each morning. However I gratefully used the basin and jug of hot water for shaving, placed outside the room with her morning call.

She lived with her father and I particularly remember on the occasion of his sudden illness in the house, she invited me to see him in bed. I declined politely and hastened off to my first floor front room as quickly as possible. He died shortly afterwards and I was sorry I had not been more supportive, although the immediate sealing-up of the room's doorway with tape was to a 20 year-old rather alarming.

Undergraduates generally remember and enthuse about their landlady, around whom everything revolved, but the mention of Miss Canham's father in the last letter reminds me of two other anecdotes featuring other members of a lodging-house family. Here is Frank Butler

I had to seek lodgings for the year 1942-43 after having rooms in Caius the previous year. At the time I was not aware of the Lodgings Syndicate. However I had a friend with lodgings in Maid's Causeway who was occupying one of two sets of rooms. I took the ground floor rooms and he the upper floor. The family, landlady, husband and daughter, occupied some concealed territory in a basement — garden flat.

Our contact was minimal, but on occasion the daughter would ask me whether I would be in on a Saturday evening and then if I would mind if she and her boy-friend used my sitting room. I suspect this may be a unique request.

And the other comes from William Stanley in South Africa, who entered Trinity in 1958:

CAM says you want snippets on lodgings. I lodged with Mr and Mrs Lacy at 26 Jesus Lane in 1959-60. He was always rather morose and had a pet blame for all the things that were wrong with the world in general and life in particular. It was the early days of satellites and sputniks and he blamed them for all the problems that anyone could mention. He would say 'They're up there now — goin' round and round'.

When I moved into rooms in College the next year, I missed the excellent breakfast Mrs Lacy gave us each day.

The *CAM* article reproduced, at my suggestion, several photographs of outstanding landladies who had been the subject of a presentation, years earlier in the *Cambridge Evening News* by the reporter Jon Hibbs [7 May 1982]. Chief among these is the arresting portrait of Mrs Evans, late of 5 Mortimer Road. Two of her old boys were so delighted at the sight of her and the memories it evoked that they wrote to me, one, R.J. Wyber saying how he had 'greatly enjoyed her generous hospitality in 1967–68' and asking if she were still alive.

I had to reply that she died in the eighties and that I had visited her in the Tower Hospital at Ely in her last years and found her sadly confused and exhausted and quite unable to understand who I was or why I was bringing her flowers. Mr Wyber mentioned some connexion with the Freke-Evans family and Lord Carbery but with no details.

A friend of his, Christopher Deacer, also enjoyed the 'happy photograph' and volunteered to talk to me on the telephone about what he could recall. I made the following notes of our conversation, which conjured up my own remembrance of her eccentric wittiness and originality.

Mr Deacer stressed how she vetted people on the doorstep and would only take a man if she thought him right for her house. She only took Caius men, of course, since Caius was her landlord. She was the widow of an Army officer and had spent many years in India. Now she was living on an Army pension and it suited her to take Caius men of her own choosing as a sort of extended family. She had an only son, the apple of her eye, also in the Army, who visited occasionally.

Mrs Cecil Freke-Evans
Photograph courtesy *Cambridge Evening News*

Her undergraduates ate in the basement kitchen, off a table laid exactly as in the photograph, using crested family silver. Breakfast was a five-course meal — juice, fruit and/or porridge, cooked bacon and eggs, mushrooms, toast and marmalade, coffee and tea, quantity unlimited, cost 1s 6d per day.

There was always a bowl of home-made soup and bread on the go if men wanted a lunchtime snack, or to avoid the bother of cycling into College. Mrs Evans dashed about the kitchen, cooking and talking, small, bony, her hair screwed back, woollen socks rolled down around her ankles, her accent determinedly upper-crust.

There were nice pieces of furniture round the house and plenty of books. Men were free to watch T.V. in her sitting-room, and to have girl friends to stay in their rooms — with prior notice

— they, of course, making do with a camp-bed put in her study.

When Christopher Deacer left she gave him a nineteenth-century satirical political tract (he being an economist) and he and another lodger took her out to dinner at the Garden House Hotel. He invited her to his wedding in Essex, to which she came, and they exchanged Christmas cards for about five years after he had left Cambridge.

Another fellow-lodger was Gavin Stamp, now Professor of Architecture at Glasgow and appearing often on T.V. as an 'old fogey'.

She had five cats (Phoebe, Christopher . . .). She would put a bottle of whisky beside the bed of a man who was poorly with a cold. Men made their own beds. Gas fires were, he thought, unmetered. She must have subsidised Caius men heavily. Her crony was Lettice Ramsay the photographer and sister of the then Archbishop of Canterbury, who also lived in Mortimer Road. She was clearly not matey with other Caius landladies.

If Mrs Evans represents the upper echelons of the class-system, here is another 'character' with a more down-market air, though, one must note, equally pernickety about the choice of her inmates. The Senior Bursar of Caius sent me a rather cruel portrait of Sadie Barnett; cruel because it is an obituary notice in the *Daily Telegraph* for 15 August 1991. (Reproduced in the Appendix).

I also remember well another of the landladies featured in that *Cambridge Evening News* article (and copied again for *CAM*), Mrs Olive Mansfield. She got her daughter to write the following account to send me from her residential home in Waterbeach: as a landlady she let rooms in her own house at Hardwick Street, and always took students from St Catharine's.

I was very pleased to read the article on Cambridge landladies and surprised to see the photograph of me and my students. I was in hospital recovering from a hip operation and some of my students had come to visit me. I didn't know they were coming and asked the nurse to do my hair for me. The students had arranged for the *Cambridge Daily News* to take the photograph.

I remember you saying that you would make sure that the students would be just right for me and they were all very friendly and I enjoyed having them in my home. I remember some of the students particularly well and I have still got the book on smocking that Brian gave me.

Inside the book he wrote: 'To Mrs Mansfield, with many thanks for making my year out of college seem just like being at home. I hope you find this book of use although from what I've seen of your smocking and toy-making you'll soon be writing your own book. . . . love Brian'.

I remember one student, Richard, had the same birthday as mine. He took me out for a meal on 'our' birthday and he had booked a table for eight of us at The Mill, by the river. He asked me if I knew everybody — they were all my past students except for one and he was the student who was to come the following year.

I was very fond of my two lady students and I am still in touch with them. Karen was married in St Catharine's Chapel this September and I enjoyed going to the wedding. Charlotte is coming to visit me here next month. I have a lot of happy memories of my landlady days.

In a different key but equally enjoying both the experience and the memory is this letter from someone in a separate category, what the office called 'an M.A. landlady' meaning a senior member of the University who took lodgers but was exempt, on the grounds of status, from any necessity of observing regulations. They were not required to hold a licence, nor were their room-rents assessed. Residence in such a house qualified an undergraduate as far as 'keeping terms' was concerned, but had to be reported to the Syndicate by his parent college.

Mrs T. Garnett-Jones writes:

My father (b.1873) was a Clare man, and I was given my first taste of Cambridge at a very early age, including his room in Clare and the deer in a little garth behind Peterhouse.

After leaving Girton in 1931 I married my curate (Westcott, 1926) and we settled into our native county, Yorkshire. To make ends meet, I filled our big vicarages with foreigners, mostly Scandinavian girls, and we managed several visits to Cambridge with them.

In 1950 my husband was appointed Church of England full-time Chaplain to the Cambridge hospitals. No house was provided, so we bought a (dilapidated, therefore cheap) Victorian house in Harvey Road; Mrs Keynes was a good next-door neighbour. I turned two floors into self-contained flats, which left us with two, and a guest room.

I cannot remember why Clare asked me to take in an ex-naval man, but nor do I remember any rules or regulations. Peter was a charming and rather wild fellow. Apart from breakfasts in his bed-sitting room we saw little of him; but he sometimes joined my two daughters at tea-times for 'Mrs Dale's Diary'. He led a social life and was astonished to appear in the *Tatler* as 'Mr Peter —— enjoying the rigours of the Lent term' — with some lovely ladies. In a couple of days his angry father appeared and attacked me for being an inefficient landlady. Peter landed an important job in Kenya, married and we kept in touch till he became a London stockbroker.

Next year I took in Bill, a quiet athlete who wanted to be near Fenner's. He took his baths there, which helped the family. He stayed for six years and left no particular imprint; but every Monday he brought me an egg, two rashers of bacon and a sliver of butter from College (still Clare); so I hope he remembers me as making him happy.

When my daughter left the Perse and was teaching in Cambridge she searched for a flat to share with friends. Luckily a family trust was available, to buy a house, and we were lucky to find one in Panton Street. I cannot tell you the number, but it is the one before the Lord's Day Adventist Hall. [The Panton Arms] was the last pub in the town to brew its own ale.

In 1964 my very aged father came to live with us. When he asked to visit Panton Street I shepherded him across Hills Road — and off he strode, into the house and up the stairs. My daughter's bedroom had been his lodging in 1893 and he was young again.

Two further thoughts: my uncle/godfather was Master of Clare, a bachelor,[31] and I lived with him in the Lodge for a term after leaving Girton. Perhaps this was why I was linked with the college as a landlady. N.B. I was then the only female there, apart from his housekeeper.

Lest my readers should become surfeited with so much eulogy of landladies, I now propose an antidote — some hostile comments from those who suffered at her hands during their time in lodgings. I had stressed in my canvassing that I hoped to receive critical accounts as well as sweet-talking; no-one knew better than I that there were mean and penny-pinching lodging-house keepers as well as generous ones. So I was delighted to get that first letter from Robin Carver, he whom I have already quoted, fair-mindedly noting the 'lovely landladies in Portugal Place' ('will there be an extra pillow required, Sir?', as the May Balls loomed near). The bulk of his letter, however, went like this:

> When you write your book please do not give the impression that life in lodgings was always rosy; it often was the opposite.
>
> I went to Trinity in 1952. My lodgings were in the Chesterton Road opposite Jesus Weir (now forming part of the hotel). They were very cold. My room facing north over (appropriately enough) Frost's Garage was dark. The landlady did not offer breakfast and was 'unsmiley' at best and positively cold in reality most of the time. I never even met the other occupants of the building. I was miserable.
>
> I was no shrinking violet and used to hardships after post-war public school life and two years in BAOR as an army officer. I did complain to Trinity and was able to move in college for the Summer term and life thereafter was very different.
>
> In those days everyone boarded out in Year 1 and Year 2. Later the colleges realised this could lead to much loneliness and the custom changed so that you lived in for the first year.[32]

And here is a thought-provoking letter from Professor M.J. Col-

---

31 She must mean G.H.A. Wilson, a mathematician and Vice-Chancellor from 1935–37. My thanks to the Clare archivist for this information.
32. I thoroughly agree on this point: given a first year in college you have the opportunity to make friends and form part of a group and thus going into lodgings later becomes less of an ordeal. *Ed.*

lie, expressing the exasperated sentiments that many of the more mature men must have felt:

When I went up to St Catharine's in 1949, I discovered to my great surprise that the older dons had opinions about what was good for a person. At my country grammar school my teachers had been rather scathing about mere opinions, especially moralistic ones. But now I learnt that being confined to quarters at an early hour was good for me, as was sharing accommodation with people whom I didn't necessarily want to know.

The Senior Tutor had decided that a bed-sitter in a remote part of Cambridge would be salutary in my case. It measured 6 x 9 feet. Falling down after a party was a hazardous business. Horizontal love-making was a possibility since the bed occupied most of the available space but in 1949 lovemaking was not good for one. A physical relationship with a woman was reported to the Head Porter but fooling about with naked rugger players in the College's communal bath was all right.

At Christmas I fled to King's Road which a good friend argued couldn't be worse than what I had. He was right, but new problems were encountered. Having lived on a farm in the Vale of Beauvoir I knew about livestock, but I found I didn't enjoy either the cock perching on my window sill at an early hour or one of the ducks having precedence in the outside lavatory merely because she had laid a clutch of eggs behind the toilet bowl. Had I jumped from the frying pan into the fire?

In the kitchen Mrs Hayward's cats had precedence and often was the time that one got that part of a sausage for breakfast that a cat had failed to polish off. Mrs Hayward, the landlady, maybe knowing her Hume, considered, and would argue the point, that there was no clear evidence to indicate that World War Three wouldn't start during my freshman year. There were sacks of rice in the chest of drawers where I thought I might stow some of my clothes and tins of corned beef and evaporated milk in the wardrobe. What did I care about most, she once asked in a hostile tone: my appearance or the nation's survival? Besides, her husband might return from the dead; therefore leave his razor, shaving brush, toothpaste, toothbrush, clothes and fireside chair exactly where they were.

The dons at that time had no knowledge of and apparently no concern about the student living conditions for which they were responsible. In my opinion, the Senior Tutor of those years was mistaken in believing that a first year out of College would be 'good for one'. It wasn't. Having been conscripted into the army against my will at a time when no war was being fought, I'd luckily ended up in Greece where I'd had a flat of my own overlooking the Gulf of Salonika, where I could have books around me and a table to write on. What was provided in Cambridge, and paid for out of a scholarship, was absurd by contrast. This note isn't about comfort and amenity. I wasn't brought up to expect or need either. It has to do with the extreme inappropriateness of the College lodgings I happened to know for anyone who wished to take his academic career seriously.

The next contributor must have spent his year in lodgings in a state of suppressed fury from the tone of the letter, the first paragraph of which I have already quoted earlier in this chapter: he does not want his name published.

On arriving at Mrs H's house I expected the usual exchange of mutual greetings. Rather, my salutation was returned by 'NO girls in your bed.'

Not long into my stay I was transiently in a state of undress first thing in the morning, having just got out of bed. Without warning Mrs H. entered. Rather than making a discreet exit, she said 'Don't worry, I've seen it all before.' The worrying thing was if her statement were true, did it apply in general or specifically? . . . At the beginning of the second term I acquired on loan a small microwave oven. Not wishing to make an issue out of its presence I just unpacked it and left it on the table, using it occasionally. Eight weeks later I encountered, let me say, an irate landlady. Apparently she thought it was something to do with my computer — open the door and watch BBC2?

The Rev. T.F.D. Bravington takes a more lighthearted view but his letter from S. Africa distinctly enough conveys the discomfort of his stay with Miss Darnell.

In my first year (1953-4) at Trinity I had lodgings at 19 Chesterton Road on the top floor, looking across the road to the Cam and beyond. The problem was that my landlady had a wonky elbow. She was knocked down the stairs by the blast during the war.

This meant two things to me:

1. The bath hadn't been cleaned since the war.
2. The mattress hadn't been turned since the war.

I tackled the first with *Vim* and elbow grease and I thought it was a good deal cleaner. The second was more complicated. When I turned the mattress it still sank into a hole in the middle of the springs of the metal frame bed. Using my pliers I was able to remove some links from the chains between the springs. This left the springs level but the mattress still had something resembling Table Mountain in the middle. I duly turned the mattress every week and by the end of the year it was quite comfortable. The elbow remained wonky.

Michael Crouch writes from Australia a reminiscence with a rather wry taste in the mouth:

> I was up at Downing 1954-7: I spent my first year in College and was in digs for the last two years. I cannot now remember my landlady's name: I occupied a modest room that — while convenient to Downing being on the main road to the station — was immediately opposite the top deck of the bus that stopped outside the door, whose passengers had a habit of eyeing one's deshabille from close range, as it were.
>
> Being conveniently close to college, was important for one main reason. There was no bath in the house. Mrs X used to bathe weekly at her married sister's on 'the estate' ('Ever so naice, you knaow, Michael', [we were on first-name terms at least in the beginning, see below] 'though my sister's neighbours — they don't like to bathe, they keep the coal in theirs').[33] My landlady's husband, a ponderous hen-pecked man, bathed once a fortnight at least, in a tin tub drawn up in front of the kitchen stove when Mrs X would attend to him

---

33. This was an unpleasant sneer, usually unjustified, always being thrown at the working-class in the better-equipped new council houses. *Ed.*

herself. The lavatory was in an outhouse and deadly cold most of the year. It was a small house but the front room was usually only used at Christmas, when the plastic-like covers on the acutely uncomfortable chairs and sofa ('the leounge') were swept off and everything was minutely dusted.

Mrs X had favourites who were always the undergraduates who were the latest to board — she only took two. My predecessor was a boozy Welshman who very much fell out of favour as soon as I crossed the doormat. His crime apparently — apart from a dissolute life-style based on being drunk most nights of the week (we were all ex-national servicemen who tended to think we held our liquor) — had a fondness for Benny Goodman which he played loudly in his room, causing Mrs X to put on her 'refained' look and to sigh deeply. But, at the beginning for me, she couldn't do enough. Apart from pressing my own key on me (strictly against the rules really, because we were meant to be in by ?10 p.m. I can't remember), it was cups of tea and portions of those slices that look like squashed flies — and the purgatory of Mrs X's photographs taken on some very ordinary outing to the south coast. But it was worth bearing because while Ted got snapped at, I was smiled at fondly.

I had thought in retrospect that I was once going to be thrown out when — having attended a bottle party earlier in the evening at which I had mixed my drinks — I had staggered back to my digs across Parker's Piece, with my bottle of cheap wine still in my overcoat pocket. I had entered Mrs X's kitchen and she as usual greeted me warmly.

I was determined to have her and her husband join me in a little drink. With some difficulty (so I was informed, later) I managed to get the cork out and seizing what I thought was a glass from the dresser, I poured into it with a flourish, offering it in an expansive way to Mrs X. She declined and I insisted, pouring the while and pursuing her round the kitchen, still pouring. The problem was that I was pouring into one of those glass funnels and I emptied almost the whole bottle through it, before it was taken off me and I was shown my bed — where I was most dreadfully sick . . . I should have been thrown out for that but Mrs X just shrieked with laughter, 'Your fyce, Michael — I could've died.' Came the day when — during my last year — a friend moved in — and immediately became the flavour of the month. Mrs X became cold, formal and really quite unpleasant. I was glad to leave.

Another unhappy lodger was Jim Davies of Merthyr Tydfil who came up to Cats too young as he says himself, and never got fully involved in his studies. But being stuck out in a grim-sounding Chesterton lodging hardly helped; we have barely discussed home-sickness before.

Quite unknown to me then, in October 1954, I had arrived in the great open fields of a settlement of our ancient enemy the Saxon (or 'sais' as we Welsh say). And the spoiled and young Welsh undergraduate for the first time actually missed the adulation of his family, missed those excitable and voluble voices, missed his exceedingly beautiful land. Almost certainly the phlegmatic Mrs C. was shown some disinterest and disdain, as was her invalid husband.

They lived in a grey, semi-detached pre-war council house on an estate where everyone spoke in a cockney accent — that is, when they spoke at all. It was a tight, muted, highly respectable sort of place where 'the grads' were bracketed and handled in a subservient, almost sullen style clearly borne of centuries of knowing one's place.

Part of the duties Mrs C. and her ancestors were well aware of was to provide a quiet room for studying with a bookcase, a good firm table, a reading lamp, and a gas fire. Never was I to be offered better facilities for such a modest lodging fee. And the dutifully delivered breakfast was always ample and well-cooked.

Occasionally, as was the custom in 1954, I held a tea session: — half a dozen hearties out to —— field on their bikes, for crumpets and chocolate cake. No girls. They did exist, but for an immature seventeen year old, out of reach. (I was in fact practically the youngest undergraduate in Cantab at 17 years 9 months.) Indeed, the nearest I came to sex was the rhythmic clamour that nightly came through my bedroom wall from next door. My digs-mate, an anthropology student and generally my mentor in these matters, was just as amazed as I was, but I always felt let down by the quite unpretty and rather mean looks of the late-middle-aged man and woman seen in the cold light of day over the privet hedge, shaking the ashes out.

We cycled three miles each way, each day in all weathers, meeting the stream of red-cheeked Girton girls after two miles. Sometimes we met up with Sidney K. who had neighbouring digs. By extraordinary coincidence he was engaged to a star of my old Sunday School, well known as a young evangelist. And before long I became targetted by the student Christian radicals as a soul badly in need of salvation, but somehow, despite attending two Billy Graham services at Great St Mary's, I emerged unscathed, keeping Jesus at arm's length.

I did no study at Mrs C's; her attentions and her house pride were casually trodden on and I remained restless and unhappy. After two terms only I left (that address) for the flimsiest of reasons and shortly afterwards ended my brief period as a medical student to take up Botany. And indeed plants remain my life-work — back among the shales and the peats of *Cymru annwyl*.

News that I was a fellow countrywoman elicited a further letter about his third term in a vastly different lodging:

It was another wretched term; I was totally failing to study for my Prelims; I had had no release by giving up medical studies for Botany. But I do remember the beautiful sun that summer term (1955). My bedroom in M.'s attic faced south; and Mrs M did laugh — even when I burned a hole through all my bedclothes and mattress through smoking late whilst trying in vain to study . . . I think Dickie James probably prayed for me; alas to no avail. I had the most appalling exam result and left Mrs M.'s rather messy place in a far more serious personal mess of my own.

The next extraordinary reminiscence takes us way back in time: Bernard Gooch sent this to me from Portugal.

How many of those Cambridge landladies I wonder, allowed
their lodgers to keep dangerous animals? At 8 Park Parade between the years 1925 and 1928 I kept from time to time
poisonous snakes, albeit only the small English Adder or
Viper, some spiders, a black and yellow Salamander and a
white Rat. I was at Trinity College reading Zoology. The animals I kept, therefore, were all chosen for a specific purpose,
especially the Vipers.

In the Zoological Laboratory there was a large working
model of a Viper and its poison fangs.[34] I was told that the
fangs automatically erected when the snake opened its mouth
and folded when the mouth closed. Nobody believed me when
I said that, on the contrary, when a Viper opens its mouth, it
can erect and fold its fangs at will and often does so when it
yawns. My Vipers demonstrated this in my lodgings but not
unexpectedly refused to yawn when taken in their glass cage
to the Zoo Lab, being too much distracted by a crowd of
human onlookers.

The spiders were Water Spiders making their webs under
water and filling them with air, safe from my landlady's broom
or duster. These I was watching because of my interest in
fresh-water invertebrates. The Salamander was odd man out.
With the help of the late Miss Joan Proctor, first curator of the
present Reptile House at the London Zoo, I was trying to cure
an open sore brought about by the insanitary conditions
under which the poor animal was kept by the collector before
being put on sale to the public. This took eleven months.

The Rat alone I believe my landlady secretly admired. It
was so beautifully marked and always came out of its nesting
box when anyone approached its cage, hoping for food. Perhaps she fed it. The Rat I kept to study the development of
play, deprived of which no Rat, apparently, can take its
proper place in adult Rat society. Having only me to play with,
play it did and so I was able to watch everything.

---

34. I wrote to get an update on the model viper from the present Professor of
Zoology, Gabriel Horn, who asked the expert Dr Adrian Friday to let Mr Gooch
know the present state of knowledge on this subject. The model is still there but
it is now conceded that the snake can also erect or lower its fangs at will. *Ed.*

To thank my landlady for her forbearance — and her husband, no doubt — I gave them (characteristically I now think) a large dead Hare, apparently unblemished. It had killed itself against the wheel of my motor bicycle. It went straight into their kitchen.

His landlady's name was Brett, I was able to report. He replied:

Directly I read the word Brett I remembered this as the name of my Cambridge landlady. I am so glad you are going to pay tribute to such a woman, fantastically forbearing, as you say. I was also allowed to keep live adders in my study when I was a small boy at Greshams School, Holt . . . When I complained to the Zoo. Professor that I had come up to Cambridge to read Zoology but found myself studying Comparative Anatomy he replied, 'But they are the same thing'.

No wonder Peter Scott, renowned for his interest in animals, did not find comparative anatomy quite up his street and threw it up.

What with tracing the distance from the old Cavendish lab. to Park Parade in the interests of Rutherford research, and checking up on viper models in the Zoo lab. I plume myself on having turned out quite a useful correspondent all round. Any other gaps of knowledge to be cleared up?

Patrick Harrison sent me this account of his lodgings which he took in the fifties when he was up at Downing:

The college suggested I try a Mrs Mingay at 37 Bateman Street which was slightly set back over a basement with a narrow area bridged by steps up to the front door.

Mrs Mingay was more like a proper landlady than the woman in Trumpington although, as I quickly guessed, she too was new to the job. She was a countrywoman 'from out Waterbeach way'. I suppose she was in her early fifties and indoors she invariably wore a pale overall.

On the rare occasions I saw her go out, she wore a coat and hat whatever the weather. She was slimmish with a pale square bony face, a thin wide mouth, grey hair and pale blue eyes with a very direct, enigmatic and faintly provocative stare. Her talk was direct too, pithy and amusing; and her letters were good: straight onto the page, just as she spoke. There were no children and she was not a motherly character. Mr. Mingay, Robert, was a van driver for Matthews, the grocers in Trinity Street. He was very dark, altogether rougher than Mrs. Mingay, but very nice.

I was offered a choice: a sitting room on the ground floor back with a bedroom on the first floor above it at £16 5s 0d a term; or the sitting room and adjacent tiny bedroom on the first floor front at £17 5s 0d. I took the latter.

My sitting room possessed one of the square bays with a window seat. If I leant well out I could see up and down the street. Both rooms overlooked a girls' school and the side entrance to the Botanic Garden, an amenity of which I made frequent use. The only serious drawback, with which I soon learned to live, was the crash of the girls' breaktime milk being delivered in its metal crates at five in the morning.

The empty cast iron fireplace was embellished by a fan of orange crepe paper. On the tiles in front of it stood an electric fire controlled by meter. I seldom used the top light, preferring my reading lamp which had like my electric toaster to be plugged into the metered circuit. Unless fed by an incessant flow of shillings a loud snap, which never ceased to take me by surprise, would plunge the room into darkness, only briefly relieved by the quickly fading glow of the fire's single bar.

I washed and shaved at the basin in the bathroom on the lower half landing in which a brass can of hot water would be placed each morning. The taps ran hot only on bath nights. It was my habit to rise and work for an hour and a half after the seven o'clock cup of tea brought up by Mrs. Mingay and then listen to *Housewives' Choice* on the Light Programme during breakfast.

Almost at once we were given keys. This was unauthorised and offered welcome freedom because after the Air Force some aspects of Cambridge, particularly the lock-up times, seemed almost like school. Mrs Mingay never questioned late returns or even the occasional night out, although she must have supplied some notional account to the College because my bills contained a modest figure for gate fines.

I end this chapter with what amounts to an essay on being an undergraduate up at Cambridge twenty-five years ago. Tom Morrison (Magdalene) 1969-70, sent me this from the extreme north of Canada and although it is only tangentially about lodgings, I think it is worth reproducing entire:

35 Thompson's Lane had a reputation for the wildness of its lodgers. We were the last and possibly the wildest. The lease expired at the end of the 1969–70 academic year, so we had to leave. The lodgings were run by Mr and Mrs Shinn.

A group of five of us got together at the end of our first year — with the intention of lodging together at 35 Thompson's Lane. At the time we were living in various parts of college.

My room in First Court was bitterly cold. In the winter I used to go to bed with cold feet and wake up with cold feet, with my underwear under the blankets to keep it warm. I assume there was a bathroom on the staircase but I do not remember. Heat was provided by a square gas stove with a white firebrick web on the front and a meter beside it. The gas would burn back into the jets, making a honking noise; that could be cured by throwing water at it which had destructive effects on the firebrick web because of the sudden cooling. Then the meter started making strange noises, so I stamped on it, whereupon it stopped working altogether and the room started smelling of gas.

A friend of mine tested for leaks with a lighted match, whereupon a ring of blue flame appeared around the meter glass which we blew out promptly. I think the college maintenance people fixed it after that, or the weather turned warmer so that it no longer mattered. I remember trying to use a typewriter while wearing a greatcoat and gloves.

At the corner of Magdalene Street, 35 Thompson's Lane must have been several buildings joined together because there were floors at odd levels joined by flights of three stairs. Each of the 5 pairs of rooms consisted of a small bedroom and a reasonably large sitting room/study.

Mr and Mrs Shinn lived in a part of the building that fronted onto Thompson's Lane. There was a sixth pair of rooms in their part of the building, separate from the other five, occupied by a fellow called Charlie Knighton. I had a small bedroom and sitting room at the top of a flight of stairs, the only rooms on that top floor.

The only one of the washing facilities that I do remember was the one we used the least — the bathroom. It was unheated and floored with lead. The bath was one of those Imperial-model enamelled cast-iron monsters with lion's feet, in which you will not get lost as long as you have a good astrolabe. The source of hot water was a small gas Geyser which lit up with an impressive 'Barrumph.', but which discharged a stream of hot water about as thick as a pencil. In an unheated room in winter this water gave up its heat at once to the metal of the bath. It filled the bath so slowly that, by the time you had six inches of water in the bath, it had all gone cold. Baths were not frequent. Martin and James used the showers at the rowing club. The rest of us probably washed in the sinks that I assume were in each bedroom.

Magdalene served breakfast, lunch, and dinner cafeteria-style in a room on the south side of the main college buildings; I acquired a lasting taste for tinned tomatoes. Dinner was also served in the college hall with tables and benches, waiter service and candlelight, and was attended by the Master and Fellows who sat at high table. Gowns were obligatory. I remember the food as being good and the beer ('audit ale' which was put on your bill) as being very good. Meals in college were available for all undergraduates, whether they lived in college or not. I think you were charged for them whether you ate them or not.

A bar was opened in the Magdalene Junior Common Room in the 1969-70 academic year after heated debate. I made ample use of the OTC Mess which was in Quayside on the third floor of a decrepit firetrap of a building long since destroyed and replaced. It had an automatic typewriting office on the second floor which clattered away to itself day and night, and nests of enormous wasps in the roof.

You might well ask about nostalgia. Whenever my friends and I meet we always play 'Do you remember', but that is natural. I have had a much fuller and more interesting existence since leaving Cambridge than ever I had when I was there, so I have happy and amusing memories, but not much in the way of nostalgia. I think the same is true of my friends as well. I went back to Cambridge a few times after leaving, but I felt like a ghost, surrounded by other people getting on with their lives and the statement that 'I used to be here' excited no interest.

I have not been back for years.

14

Facets of Office Life

The setting: an unmodernised lodging-house in the centre of town, owned by one of the richer Colleges and run without much overt change since the 'thirties by Mrs Bryant, who has lately lost her husband. Normally the College of ownership will send in its own second-years every Michaelmas, but the two young women allocated to this house took one long incredulous look at the rudimentary bathroom and fled. So I rejoice to have two very central sets to play with, and I offer them to a couple of young men who've been haunting my office for several weeks in the hope of just such a fluke as this. With delight they install themselves and fix up bells on the doorway, for their visitors, one labelled 'Will', the other 'Max'.

A little later in the term, word comes that Mrs Bryant is seriously ill. I'll call, a walk across the little park and down the street with its elegant new shops will be a treat. A man answers the door, a large untidy man with a wart on his nose and unbuttoned trousers. He's pleased I came to enquire about Mrs Bryant. 'I'm her brother', he says, 'she's a bit better than she was, but there, it ud've broken her heart to go to hospital.'

His name is Jim and he's doing the nursing and running the house for the students. He doesn't think much of the modern undergraduate: 'Used to be gentlemen', he grumbles, 'but this lot, one o' them's not better than a tramp.' I try not to look too pointedly at his stained and frayed yellow cardigan. Long circumstantial complaints follow about how he found the bath full of their washing-up after a party, and how one of them nipped downstairs to the kitchen behind his back and borrowed his shaving-towel to wipe up with.

In a fortnight I visit again and this time the brother admits me to the living-room where Mrs Bryant is dressed and sitting up in a chair by the stifling gas fire. She looks frail, but she likes telling me about her pneumonia. She says she's never got over Mr Bryant's death. He was an engine-driver and a most supportive and methodical man: their rates-bills for decades are all carefully filed away with the receipts. He tells me how the window where she is sitting, that looks out directly on the park, was smashed in by drunken yobs on Saturday night. The College had sent round to repair it quick enough, but the noise, the violence and the shock of it had frightened her badly.

I leave, not to tire her, but he keeps me talking at the front door where a vicious November wind whistles round the corner. When she was first taken ill, he had been about to leave on his first trip abroad. 'Me and my mates — the darts team they are at the Adam and Eve — we was going to Benidorm. I got me suitcase all packed with all new clothes. We'd put away week by week for the tickets. But when I heard about her,' he jerked his thumb at the sitting-room door, 'I atter tell 'em to go without me. I couldn't leave her, could I?' This plain and frumpish man, he's a hero.

Suddenly a greyish figure materialises behind him and calls grumpily: 'You'll catch your death talking there'. Mrs Bryant doesn't want her brother talking out of his turn nor does she like him interfering with the students — that's her province and she's beginning to want to command her ship again.

'Thass nice of you to come, Miz Holgate', he says, hastily shutting the door.

Another ten days and she is dead. The Bursar rings to inform me, and explains his intentions for the house. It will be done up and used as graduate accommodation. It won't be a lodging-house any more, and they want my two young men out. I write my sympathy to poor old Jim, and soon he sends for me, much puzzled to know what to do first. He's sorting out a lifetime's accumulations: 'Seventy pairs of shoes she had if you believe me Miz Holford ma'am'.

We sit down in the cluttered little room again. Where does he sleep, I wonder? Could it be on that sofa? He's still got the yellow cardi on.

'You're the first person I've talked to today' — he says, 'it gets kinda lonely here by myself'. How are the boys, I ask? 'They're a right shower', he answers bitterly. 'They got no respect for nobody; leastwise him on the first floor, he's not too bad, but that one up at the top, 'e's had girls in I know all night, and I've been up at two and three in the morning to tell 'im to shut up his music. An' the

state of 'is room, there's no way I can clean it'. He's so appalled I
suggest we go up and look at it. He leads the way. Max is talking to
someone in his sitting-room so we go on to the top floor, Jim puffing now, his fat haunches straining.

Will's room is unspeakable. I've inspected endless student rooms
but this one takes the biscuit. A white china bedpan holds half a
term's fag-ends, 60 cassettes are tipped in a flood over the carpet,
peanut butter smears the armchair and nowhere can one put foot
without standing on a half-filled mug or discarded sock or little
pools of clothing propped up with a dozen or so bottles of drink. I
can't even face his bedroom after one glimpse of a greyish disaster
area of a bed.

'Just leave it till he's gone', I say, as we clump downstairs again,
rather gloomy. He throws open the room by the front door where
Mrs Bryant used to sleep and no doubt died. Mountains of old
clothes are stacked up. The dark room smells of them and of old
commodes. Do they never open the windows in this house? We settle at the table again. Jim tells me about nursing her, how he got
her Horlicks when she couldn't sleep and she would moan it was
too hot to drink, how he heaved at her backside to get her across
the bed when she was too weak to lift her legs, how the lady doctor
said: 'She's going fast' as they sat by her in the grey dawn at the
end, Jim holding her hand.

'I'm not boring you am I?' he says, rather shy. I reassure him
and he waxes more confidential.

'I'll show you something I found' — he pushes a photograph at
me, a plump wary little boy standing in a doorway. 'That's me,
when I was three about'.

'You're the executor, I suppose?' I ask. 'Didn't the Bryants ever
have any children then?'

He gives me a funny look, hesitates then makes up his mind.
'Well, Miz Braybrook, I may as well tell you now she's gone. She
was me mother. Things were different in the old days, people had
to hush things up. So we allus give out I was her brother. Mr Bryant, he was very good to me, he allus called me 'Boy'.'

I reflect that if the College had known the truth back in the 'thirties, they would never have given Mrs Bryant a lodging-house, nor
could she have held a licence.

In my office drawer is a little locked book, the black book of disciplinary action taken by the Syndicate, with entries continuing well into this century:

> Mr X's licence revoked on account of his getting the
> serving-maid with child.
> Mrs Y no better than she ought to be, and found the worse for
> liquor.
> Mrs M's daughter who lives at home has lost her character:
> licence cancelled.

The innocent undergraduate was not to be corrupted by venial failings in those who served his breakfast and carried his coals. The less than impeccable Mrs Bryant would not have got a look in.

At least those randy young men upstairs must never come to hear this story. Will and Max, one by one, make contact at the office, very cross at being turned out of their handy little pads. I tell Will I've seen his room and gently intimate my shock. 'Oh you must have called the day before my weekly turn-out', he says gallantly and I hoot with laughter. They contemplate fighting it out with the College, taking them to the County Court. I think of earnest Jim, trying to pack up, settle the bills, do his mother justice and get back to Ely and his own pottering life there. How could they stay on, there'd be no furniture, no electricity. I give Will a lift back to his lodging in the rainstorm, it's dark, nearly Christmas, he will have to go home for the vacation. His face is young and troubled in spite of the belligerence.

'Pack up your own stuff and leave it as straight as you can', I advise, 'and I'll do my damnedest to get you somewhere else to live next term'. I stop the car on the roundabout to let him out, impatient men honking behind me. Will rabbits on, arguing about his rights. 'Shut up and get out', I say, shoving him, and he goes laughing into the rain, his long hair curling, the thin black overcoat frayed whiteish at the collar.

My final visit. Jim's rather proud of the way he's organised everything, sent for the Sally Ann to fetch away the things the auctioneers reject. He tells me: 'Max knocked the door and shook me by the hand; 'is father was fetching 'im home in the car. So I said to 'im, 'I've got two good suits here, two of Mr Bryant's suits, one's a dinner suit, and both been cleaned and pressed. Would you like 'em?' So he was that pleased, 'Thank you very much', he said, 'I can make good use of them'. 'E's a big chap, just about 'is size.' What about Will, I ask? 'Oh 'im, says Jim contemptuously, ''e was moving about and packing till four this morning, and 'e went off without never a word'.

'You'll be leaving these curtains', I say unguardedly, looking at the seaweed-coloured shiny stuff hanging dingily at the window. 'Best not leave bare windows with these vandals about'. 'Leave the curtains.' says Jim in horror. 'Why there's six of them and the quality is beautiful'.

'I'd a loved to go on if they'd a let me', he says to change the subject. 'What, with a lodging-house do you mean?' I ask. 'Yeah, if only I were a few years younger, Miz Holford, I'd a been real keen'. Just in time I stop myself saying: 'But you can't stand students'. 'Ah well', I substitute rapidly, 'the College has other plans'. 'Thass right', he says and turns sentimental. 'It's like the end of an era, in't it?'

In the fascinating little street a new antique shop has just opened, with its naming in gold on a fashionable dark green fascia. . . what does it call itself? I read 'My Auntie Had One But She Threw It Away'.

2

A vague, irresolute woman's voice on the telephone asked if I would be interested in a room for an undergraduate on Histon Road. 'I certainly would' I said promptly enough. 'I'll drive round tomorrow and we'll talk about it'.

It was January and cold: most people were safely housed by now but one always had to cater for changeovers and the odd late arrival; this house, I could tell by the number, was very central, down at the town end of Histon Road and ideal for someone at Fitzwilliam for example. I might well make use of it.

I parked and walked across to the house shivering in the East Anglian blast. The paint was peeling and the front window looked dirty but there wasn't time to take in much before the woman opened the front door and motioned me inside with a duck of the head. She was thin and grey and wrapped closely in a thick shabby dark overcoat. We sidled along the hall, our feet clonking on the bare floorboards. 'That's the front room', she said motioning towards a closed door, but making no move to go in there: instead we went through into a large space at the back of the house. 'This is my daughter here,' she added softly. I smiled at the younger woman. She looked lost, hunched against a wall, long fair straggly hair in a pony-tail, peaked face, body tense in a coat like her mother's. She didn't smile back and turned to stare out of the window.

It was so cold in the room. I realised why they were so wrapped up — there was no means of heating. Still more, there was no furniture. An old black gas-stove stood next to an old-fashioned china sink, and had two chipped mugs and a tin kettle on its hob. Behind it a filthy uncurtained window gave on to a scruffy backyard brown with the weeds and husks of winter. Round the walls were ranged perhaps six or seven black plastic dustbin bags stuffed with — old clothes perhaps? A few scraps of newspaper littered the bare floor. One crazy wooden chair with broken slats leaned at an angle. Maybe they took turns to sit, I thought. A box of tea-bags and a half-full milk bottle stood on the draining-board. The older woman looked at me enquiringly. I swallowed. 'Perhaps you haven't been here very long?' I managed to ask. 'Are you just moving in? 'Oh no' said the mother — 'we've been here some time now, quite a few weeks anyway.'

My heart sank and then jumped. A white shape skimmed softly past my head and then another swept in a diagonal across the room with a whir, and as I looked up, a third and fourth fluttered in the far corner making cooing expostulations: they kept a tenuous hold on the picture-rail. 'Oh they're just our doves' the mother said carelessly, much as though everyone kept pigeons in their kitchens. 'What about this student then?' The girl looked round at this, to see what I would say. 'Well' I temporised, 'he'd need a place he could study in, you see. He'd expect a bed and a desk and chair and somewhere warm he could sit and write. And he might want to do a bit of cooking for himself . . . '

I gave a hopeless look at the obsolete gas-stove, and the single cold tap. 'You'd need a bit of time to get the things together, wouldn't you?' I said, going on with this charade that the place was possible. 'Maybe you could ring me again when you're ready. It's so nice of you to think of us'. 'Perooo, perooo,' said the doves, mourn-fully.

I backed towards the door and both women came to see me out, smiling as though we'd all had the cosiest of chats. A week later the same voice on the phone, but stronger, quite accusing the tone this time round. 'Is that the woman what came round here?' 'Yes'. 'What did you report us to the Social Service for?' O God, she's put two and two together, I thought. 'Well, I felt you needed some help, you see. Your daughter looks so sick . . . Can they do any-thing for you? . . . The phone went dead. Was I a ghastly meddler, a do-gooder interfering with broken lives? A busy-body? Next time I drove up the Histon Road the house was boarded-up.

Did they, I wondered sadly, allow people to bring their doves with them when they were taken into Fulbourn?

3

Going to see Mrs Dewing in Park Street was one of the first land-lady visits I ever paid. She lived in a dear little house, with a neat garden in front and a gate to the road. It must all have been much pleasanter before they built the multi-storey car-park opposite, that pollutes the whole area now.

A trim little dark woman answered my knock. I knew from her record that she had been a Trinity bedmaker, was now widowed, and worked at the OTC on Quayside in the mornings. She let a very comfortable set with double glazing and took Queensmen or Trinity until they no longer needed lodgings: after that she ac-cepted Fitzwilliam people, preferred older men and had a reputa-tion for not fussing over visiting friends. A model landlady.

She drew me in to her kitchen-sitting-room at the back, a warm inviting place with a window overlooking the garden, and almost automatically put the kettle on. I sank back on a sofa in a huddle of floral cushions. Suddenly an ingratiating hoarse voice let off in my ear: 'Hallooa,' it said, on three notes. I whipped round, having sup-posed we were alone, and there smirking at me and ducking its beak up and down in greeting, was a smallish dusky, sooty, bird, perched in a cage on the wall.

'Good God,' I said, 'whatever is it?' 'Aoh that's my old mynah bird' said Mrs Dewing. 'A course you haven't met him before, 'ave yer? I'd be lost without him — ever such good company 'e is, my old Jacky, aren't you darling?' Jacky twirled and preened, gratified at the notice.

Then I noticed that the room was spotted with minute specks of white. 'Do you let him out?' I asked apprehensively —his beak and twiggy legs looked rather scratchy.

'Aow, he has his little fly every day, has to, for exercise.' Mrs Dewing was busy at the sink, making coffee for us. 'Hallooa mynah,' screamed the bird, wanting to share in the conversation. Then I realised his voice was a grotesque imitation of Mrs Dewing's. He caught just her emphasis and change of pitch. I nodded and halloed back at him.

Mrs Dewing brought me a cup. ''E was a very naughty boy yesterday,' she said with an admonitory flap at the cage. 'Shall I tell you what 'e did? I was busy making a pudding — apple meringue it was and I was beating up the egg-whites over here. Jacky was flying about and like a fool what does he do but fly into the mixture and get it all over his head and wings. Proper state he was in and egg white all over the room. Damn the bird I said and ran about till I got hold of him and held 'im under the tap to get all the sticky off of 'is feathers. Only I didn't look what I was doing and I 'eld 'im under the 'ot tap by mistake. Gor, to 'ear him squawk and swear — , I don't know where he gets it from, I'm sure. So cross 'e was and gave my finger a great peck and there I was, all running with blood, and both of us all of a muck with meringue. Took me hours to clear up, tacky old stuff'.

Jacky's head was ducking and swelling with pride at having his exploits described: clearly he knew just what we were talking about. He jumped off his perch, the cleverdick, and minced towards me. 'Aoaw,' he suddenly squawked, 'ain't it a *damned* shame?' and did a triumphant jig around his cage. Even as I collapsed in giggles, my mind envisaged all the neighbours, sisters, fellow lodging-house-keepers who, in a succession of calls, had sat there alongside Jacky and told or sobbed their sad stories of oppressive husbands, erring daughters, absconding lodgers. And to each Mrs Dewing had listened and nodded and had made them tea, and had finally said in that throaty warm-hearted, marvellously cockney voice, 'Aoaw, ain't it all a *damned* shame'.

4

It is the Friday I am to be alone in the office: my assistants are
either on leave or yet to be appointed, and you find me, a little
bemused, the slave of the ever-opening door and the ever-ringing
telephone. Yet most of the day has already gone by and though
solitary, I have found entertainment enough in this constant
stream of everchanging personalities.

It is true I am not giving them as good a service as my experienced staff, who handle this information all week long but I flatter
myself I am trying hard. I am at least *accommodating*.

Who's this then, half-way through the afternoon?

A stocky, gnome-like man trots in, fair hair, fair would-be jaunty
beard. He looks at me wistfully almost, lunges into a chair and bur-
sts into fretful speech.

'I'm a victim of persecution. I lodged in Oakington and while I
was away for a few days my landlady changed the locks and
dumped everything I possess in the ditch.'

'Dear dear', I hum sympathetically, 'Whatever had you done?'

'*Done?* Nothing.' said he, falsetto. 'All I did was to empty her waste-paper basket. Yes, I went in her sitting-room and took out the
waste paper basket, while I was cleaning up her tip of a flat, that's
all. Oh, and there was, I admit, a mug of hers I broke'.

He fixed me in the eye.

'Deliberately. It had on it the picture of a woman dictator. Well I
couldn't stand for that could I?'

'No, by no means' I hastily agreed.

'So I picked it up, this mug, and went to the open window and
held it out . . . and my fingers just let go' His lips curled in triumph
as he lived the moment again.

'But all my clothes, everything I possess, all my papers, ruined,'
he squealed.

'You must go and consult the Citizens' Advice Bureau' I said, all
sweet reasonableness.

'But I'm a solicitor' he rejoined, to my stupefaction. He didn't
look like a solicitor.

'Mind you', he tapped a huge filofax wallet stuffed five inches
deep that he had plonked on the desk between us: 'I can pay for
anything. There's £400 in there and another 400 at the end of the

month. I'm staying at the University Arms Hotel.'

'We'd better get you out of there pretty soon or it will all go.' I said. 'What are you doing in Cambridge, tell me?' I felt I had better bring this chat to some definite point. He looked suddenly vague.

'I've had a lot of surgery, my head isn't what it was. I think I might be what they call burnt-out,' he faltered. 'I did have a year at —— college, but whether they'll let me do a Ph.D' his face fell.

He embarked on a long and wandering explanation about his answer-papers and the examiners. It suddenly struck me that his breath fumed with alcohol. Surreptitiously I felt for the panic-button under the desk: what was it you pushed?

I studied his clothes while the protestations gathered speed and squeak. A red tie, a check shirt, different check tweed trousers and a weird sleeveless jerkin of padded creamy cotton, over-printed with small scarlet flowers, rather the sort of garment a woman with arty-weary ethnic tastes might choose. The tale was coming round again to where we'd started off . . . .

'I never laid hands on the woman, that landlady of mine,' he volunteered as if I had accused him.

'I should hope not' I murmur deprecatingly.

'I didn't attack her, or make any sexual proposals to her,' he bridled as he said it: 'though that's what she's going to say I did if I sue her over the damage she's done to my stuff.'

His watery blue eyes focussed harder on me and his voice grew vehement 'I'm quite normal you know. I'm not one of these homosexuals.' Nothing, I indicated, was further from my thoughts. But he'd run out of steam and deflated before my eyes, more like Humpty-Dumpty than ever. He was tired now, what with the drama of the telling and the alcohol taking effect. I gathered my wits to get him out. We pretended to discuss a little where he could stay for a while and I wrote out a few addresses which he pocketed without looking. Rather sheepish he stumbled to his feet, taking up the filofax.

'Goodbye' I said gaily, the relief flooding me. 'So nice to meet you.'

'I'm quite *normal* you know' he went out muttering.

'Yes, yes of course you are'

5

Mrs Connolly's Story

Mrs Day in Jesus Lane was clearing her students' rooms one morning, and in the first one she went to she found the waste-paper tin awash with a strange liquid. She took it downstairs to show her husband:

'What's this then, Ron? It looks like urine to me.'

'Well of course it's urine,' replied Ron with a gesture of disgust. 'What dirty beggar was than then?'

'Him in Number 1,' said Mrs Day 'must have been taken short.'

'I'll give him short,' said Ron. 'That Threadgold.'

Next day Ron was cleaning the brass on the front door in the sunshine. Someone comes jumping down the staircase two at a time.

'Morning Mr Day,' carols the incontinent undergraduate, without a care in the world.

'Good morning Mr Threadgold,' answers Mr Day blandly, blocking his exit. Then his voice hardens, for all the street to hear: 'And who pissed in the bucket then?'

6

Undergraduates are more and more anxious to be independent and will do anything to avoid being allocated a room in a house where there is a resident landlady. For many, the ideal is to acquire a house to share with their friends. So how did a shared student-house look in July 1992?

I am invited to visit the upper flat before the owner Mrs X. clears it up at the end of its occupation by four undergraduates, among them one who has been serving a year as an elected student representative. I've been to this address before, on a similar errand. It is a modern house in a splendid central situation, purpose-built to an architect's specification as a letting speculation. The owners were willing to accept undergraduates because their academic year dates fit in with letting to summer tourist visitors during the Long Vacation. But this neatly dove-tailing policy has now been given up because the students' mis-usage left the place too tatty to offer to holiday makers.

The front door is left ajar for me and Mrs X. is waiting upstairs.

There is no mat in the door-well, instead a litter of uncollected letters, bills, newspapers. I pass the silent door of the ground-floor flat and remember afterwards that I never asked to what use that was put — God help a long-term tenant who has to endure the noise from above.

The soiled walls of the stairway have surely not been repainted since my last visit (? six or more years ago). The steps are covered with thin grubby drugget that does little to cushion the sound. The entry has nice operational spotlights and modernistic black clothes-pegs on the wall. It leads into the main living-room looking out to the open ground and trees at the back, a pleasant view. Such curtains as remain throughout are eggy-yellow and beige with many missing hooks, and they hang in dejected limp sags, but I notice they are lined and were originally good. The carpet on the floor is dark charcoal grey with a small woven pattern — not bad but spoilt by a long diagonal bulge across one corner. I would ascribe it to poor laying, but Mrs. X. has had the carpet-man in, and he excuses it by saying there must have been many spills.

A long '50s-style sideboard fills the wall between the windows, and she points out the ruined top surface. A few wilting plants still stand on it, and obviously they have been over-watered. I gently recommend Tops and she says she's already bought some to do it with. Jaded dried flowers are plonked in jars on the dusty sill. The only furniture is a dreadful sofa with an ill-fitting loose cover dragged over it in the same doggy colours, its springs visible through the holes in the original cover; and two disasters of chairs, one missing a wooden arm and the other with chewed-off rubber paddings along the arms. Mrs X. pulls up the sordid maroon slat-cushion and hurriedly shoves it down again, saying, 'Well, perhaps we won't look at that.' She tends to blush pinkly over her face and throat, especially when I say things such as, 'You can of course pick up perfectly good armchairs to replace these at the Sally Ann in Mill Road.'

'Oh, but that's just what I do,' she rather ingenuously confides.

The walls are badly marked and pocked with nails and drawing-pins, and a few scrawled notes are still pinned up. The kitchen is an L-shape off this living-space, and is not in too bad nick. The handle has come off the grill compartment of the cooker and some 30

magazine-cuttings of popstars and bimbos are pinned or stuck over
the whole upper wall-surface. The 'stainless steel' sink belies its
name. Mrs X. says resignedly that she will scrub everything down
and wash all the cutlery. On the same floor we pass on to a large
front room with the old grey cord carpet that I remember. No-one
has hoovered. A cheap woodchip desk, with a fixed shelf at the
back, staggers against the wall: a few bookcases with collapsed
shelves and raw edges, another broken armchair. But there is also a
comparatively good bed on a sprung base with drawers in, and the
mattress covered with a dingy stained bedspread. It could be so
nice but the furniture is really grotty.

We turn to the stairs: a length of banister trails down the steps, a
wooden bar torn off from the steel wall-fastenings. The builders of
the X's new flats next door will repair this. These stairs are really
nicely carpeted. On the upper floor are three rooms: the first has
just a mattress on the floor. Mrs X. says the base and headboard
have disappeared — they may be up in the loft but she believes
furniture has been swapped between other shared houses; certainly
a fan-heater (electric, for occasional use, this being a gas centrally-
heated house) has disappeared for ever in this way. Another cheap
ply-wood desk, ricketty and not really suitable for serious work. In
one corner is a pile of old belongings, on the top of one bag a pair
of black evening-dress trousers perhaps worn to a May Ball, with
the hems of the trouser-legs turned up with safety-pins.

What, begs Mrs X, is she supposed to do with their possessions? I
ask whether the keys have been handed in. 'All but one,' she
answers. Does someone intend to come back, perhaps with a parent's car, and collect all this junk? Or is she supposed to hire a skip
or a lorry and dispose of it all? Or must she store it safely in case of
eventual reclaim?

In another bedroom a grey mattress has a blood-stained cover
and a torn pillow. Perhaps five plastic bags and bundles huddle for-
lornly, containing some china, a jug, a camera, bedclothes and a
pair of black suede high-heeled boots in good condition. Here the
curtains have been flung in a corner and an odd jumble of hand-
printed white cotton is hung askew across the window, which is so
closed and clouded that I ask the owner if the house is double-
glazed.

'Oh, yes' she says, 'but you can get ventilation if you open this side' and shows me how. It has evidently not often been exercised. She spits on the closed window and rubs it experimentally — the grey fog doesn't change. Without conviction, she murmurs the window may need replacing.

On this floor is a lavatory and a separate bathroom — the light doesn't come on but as far as I can see both are in good condition though in need of cleaning. The bathroom has no window but an air-conditioning system. The third room has a Velux window, a double mattress and a single mattress which, Mrs X. says, don't belong in the house, a fitted cupboard, a hard chair and a crumbling arm-chair. There is no desk or work-top.

Nowhere is anything pretty or graceful or orderly. I wouldn't give 50p for all the furniture in the place. But how am I to judge what the house was like when it was first let to this group? Mrs X. has a theory that one girl's original partners all deserted her because she was impossible to live with. Other people joined up with her and imported stray partners of their own, so that often the house held far more than the four who took out the formal contract. I suspect mismanagement yet Mrs X insists they visited regularly if only to empty the electric coin-meter. She says their remonstrations as to the state of the students' house-keeping had no effect whatever.

I talk about inventories and the need to check them through in the presence of the tenants, both on arrival and departure. But this lot had evidently fled before the stated date to avoid the consequence of an inspection. Is she entitled to withhold a part (or even the whole) of their deposits? She only holds £75 from three of the so-called four tenants, one having defaulted on the last month's rent. I agree that she can charge for laundering mattress covers and bedclothes, (blankets etc.) and for clearcut damage such as arms off armchairs. On the other hand, what is a Sally Ann chair, costing £5 to £10 worth after two years' even tender usage?

Mrs X. expects new tenants on Monday (i.e. in four days time) but they are willing to have the decorators in during their occupation. I promise a visit in September to see the improved state of the house after clean-up, redecoration and re-furnishing. Then, I insist, I would be competent to judge the state of the house on the new

tenants' departure. Is she really prepared to spend the hundreds
of pounds that professional repainting will cost her? Yet the house
is potentially a delightful place to live and undergraduates would
give their eyes to live so centrally. What is one to make of this dreary tip? Can students not be trusted to housekeep in any civilised
sense?

The answer, I conclude, is for some system of oversight on the
part of the University, to protect both landlord and tenant and to
insist on minimum standards of upkeep and hygiene.

7

Joanna looked after the reception office in the mornings, Caroline
took over after lunch. It was a good arrangement, not too long a
stint for either, and each had the half of a day to organise their lives
at home. This particular morning, Joanna's family got in one of
those sour breakfast muddles and made her late. Annoyed, she
heaved her bicycle into the tin shed round the back of the office
and puffed round to open the front door. A man was waiting on
the pavement. 'He would be,', she thought bitterly as she let them
both in.

He was a young hairy man and he looked grumpily at his watch,
wanting her to know that she had kept him waiting. Pompously he
launched into his tale of grievance.

'You'll have to see the Secretary about this,' said Joanna as soon
as she grasped he was an undergraduate. 'She'll be in about ten if
you'll come back then.'

A look of disgust crossed the censorious one's face. 'Soom people
have got work to do,' he grumbled, and shambled himself out, leaving the front door wide open to the chill air of January.

Joanna sighed, slammed it shut and made herself a cup of coffee.
'Trouble,' she said as I arrived. And so I was ready to receive him,
later that morning with an elaborate air of courtesy.

'Well now, what is this you have to tell me?' I asked, taking in the
face opposite. He looked a country boy, a bit hobbledehoy, with an
extraordinary fringe of sparse reddish hair all round his chin and
chops.

It reminded me of the oil painting at home of my great-great
grandfather, gazing with a mild sanctimonious air out of his bony

face, with whiskers the very image of those before me.

He couldn't wait to tell me.

'Ah came home last night, and there sat me landlady in her chair, proper plastered.'

His eyes were popping out with the shock and the sin of it.

'Ah thought she was ill at first or asleep maybe, an Ah went oopstairs quietly, but oh dear, she started up abusing me and shouting and calling oop the stairs.'

'What was she cross with you about?'

'Noothing, I never said noothing. She called me a spoilt brat and a fairy and I don't know what.'

As he spoke, his lips jutted out like a child about to blubber and a bleb of inner lip came down over his lower lip and got stuck on his protruding teeth. He was the picture of misery and I couldn't take my eyes off him. I'd had a hint that Mrs Hancock took a drop too much before, but that had been two years ago or more. I knew that a college had dropped her as a bedmaker but when I phoned to find the reason, they had given her a good character reference apart from this weakness for alcohol.

'What was she drinking?' I asked 'could you see any bottles?'

'Ah went on oop to bed,' he said virtuously. 'She shoot oop about woon in the morning and I got to sleep. But she was still there when Ah came down to get ma breakfast and the light was on all night. On her face was a great brown bruise, all over her chin. It gave me a turn, I can tell you.'

'O Lord, poor old soul' I said. 'She must have fallen and bumped herself.'

'That's as maybe but I wasn't going to get the blame — it was noothing to do with me, so I went off and got a neighbour to come in and clean her oop and bit and Ah called a policeman' . . .

I gasped. 'Whatever for?'

'Well, Ah had to have a witness didn't Ah?'

I remembered how private Mrs Hancock was, how she hated to have the street know her business. A picture came into my mind: myself ringing at the door, no-one answering, but two houses away down the street, another door opening quietly and a crafty face peeping round it to know who was calling.

'I daresay there's a sad story of loneliness and unhappiness

behind all this.' I said to the young man, trying to move him out of
his priggish self-satisfaction.

'That's not my problem' said the boy.

'It's a problem for all of us in so far as we're human beings.' I re-
torted, disgusted with him.

'Now look here' he began, almost intimidating, 'Ah came here
for you to find me soomwhere else to live, pretty quick, Ah don't
approve of living with droonken women.'

'I'm not to be bullied young man. That's not quite the tone to
take if you want help from me.'

I could be stern and formally cold when I chose but I was also acutely aware that my predecessors would have been preoccupied
with concern for the young 'in moral danger' in a case like this. It
was my job, true enough, to rehouse him and notions of fair notice
could fly out of the window, so I turned to my list of available lodgings and wrote him out the addresses of three or four. About one I
had a doubt — 'You don't smoke do you?' I asked.

He swelled smugly. 'Ah'm a non-smoker and Ah'm a non-
drinker too' he said, emphasising each word, loud with virtue.

I sighed. What a prematurely-old little man he was. Off he went
with a mulish air to choose a niche to his liking.

'Oh dear, who's fifty years young?' grinned Joanna. She was
good at catching a man's character.

I let two or three days elapse in decency, to give the bruise a
chance to fade. Then as I was driving round town one afternoon,
ostensibly in the opposite direction, I forced myself to turn the car
towards Mrs Hancock's street.

'No good dodging it' I whispered to myself fiercely, but even so I
hoped the woman would be out. To call but in vain, leaving a com-
pliments slip through the letterbox would salve my conscience
comfortably.

The street was in that part of Cambridge that looks most like a
colliery village or a Midlands railway town. Rows of rather mean
grey-bricked houses, the windows prim with net, fronting straight
onto the pavement, no trees, no gardens except the arid yards at
the back. It made one's heart sink with its air of frigid respectability. And yet each door would be neat-painted and numbered and
the knocker polished. I knocked. She was in.

She ducked backwards, beckoning me in. The reek of stale urine rose to my nostrils. We looked at one another, two smallish women, probably much of an age. There were brownish bags under Mrs Hancock's eyes but otherwise she looked as usual with no mark of injury. I was in no mood to dissemble, the whole point of coming was to have the truth in the open between us.

'Has he gone?' I began.

'Gone yes, went this very day. His mother came for him and moved him out. I never saw such a mother's boy. Why do you know, she would come over here every fortnight to change his bed-linen. Great ninny.'

'Yes, but how are you?' I said. 'It's you I'm worried about. Is it lonely for you, is that why you do it? There's help you know, you could see your doctor. You could join a club. You don't have to bear it all by yourself.'

'Who told you?' demanded Mrs Hancock, quickly on the defensive.

'Well the boy of course,' I answered. 'But I'd had a hint before, frankly. You must see I can't put an undergraduate here ever again: they're too young, too vulnerable. It wouldn't be right to land them with the responsibility. But that's not what I've come about.'

Mrs Hancock relaxed a bit. 'I thought you'd come to tick me off.'

'No, no, I want you to know that I know, that's all, so that we don't have to pretend. We must think what you're to do.'

The landlady sat back in her chair arranging a rug over her thin knees and looked around her familiar sitting-room, rather pleasant and warm if it hadn't been for the pervasive smell. She thought a while. It was a novel situation for her to be talking the truth instead of euphemisms. All her life she'd been buttoned up, trying to be 'proper' and avoid comment.

'It's my son mostly. His marriage broke up and he was sleeping here on a camp-bed and it just worried me to death, having him around moping. Then he set up with this new girl, Valerie, and I hoped he'd be happy again. But last weekend they had this terrible row, and he came back here, said it was all over, she wouldn't have him.' Her face puckered 'Well I couldn't stand it, it was like his dad all over again, shouting and that, before he went off and left me . . .

I hadn't you know, I hadn't touched alcohol for eight months.'

'Poor old you' I said tenderly, 'that's very brave.'

Mrs Hancock picked up some handsome knitting she'd nearly finished, then went on,

'It's all right again though. They said last night they're definitely taking that house together . . . .and they're that loving to me. I'm making this for Valerie' She shook out the jumper. 'I can't quite get the sleeves set in right.'

I got up to go and made the conventional remarks about how she was to phone if she wanted help.

'I've tried those Alcoholics Anonymous' said Mrs Hancock, 'they wasn't much good.'

But our eyes met and we smiled at one another in a long silent exchange.

'It's nice to have a friend,' she said and I kissed her lightly and left.

Idly reading the evening paper, towards the end of that academic year, I came upon a report of a court hearing that caught my attention.

A former Cambridge student who carried out 'revenge' thefts from other undergraduates has been ordered to pay back £725 in compensation by City magistrates . . . he had admitted two charges of theft, four of deception and asked for sixty four other matters to be taken into consideration, including cycle thefts . . .

The former student had had a desire to carry out 'revenge' against other people. He took post from pigeon holes at —— College and spent hundreds of pounds with stolen credit cards . . .

Mentally I called up the whiskered one, stood him in front of my desk and addressed him thus: 'You doan't smoak, you doan't drink, you joost thieve.'

8

'Mr Walters was on the phone, wants you to ring him back.' That was the message.

Oh, no, not Mr Walters, my bachelor landlord, the apple of his mother's eye, not more in the saga of the Churchill undergraduate who's booked to go there next October and keeps fussing now in March about how he's going to hang up his net curtains in the sitting-room so as not to be distracted? I thought we'd already set-

tled, in some half-hours of earnest debate, that he could safely
suspend them from the pelmet by invisible screw-in hooks so as not
to risk dropping some heavier tool against the costly double-glaz-
ing or spoil the genuine mahogany window-frames with vulgar
little screw holes.

But it's not that: it's the present incumbent, Mr Jeffries, a young
aspiring theologian I'd established there two terms ago, thinking
he wouldn't be likely to cause much trouble.

Mr Walters' voice is hushed. Evidently it's something really serious. Could I call round for a chat? I certainly could.

He lives in the neatest of bungalows, set back inside a low His-
pano-concrete wall. In summer two flowerbeds either side the path
flame with a vibrant march of salvia, each scarlet plant three inches
to the side of a honeyed rosette of alyssum. All day he works in his
garden; I'm enjoined never to phone him before four when, exhausted, he goes indoors.

At the back a very plaisance meets the eye, where a plastic heron
broods over a little pool of fish, and gums and specimen trees break
up the geometric regularity of a city suburban plot. It is truly
charming. And so is its owner, now retired but once the head
buyer of soft furnishings and household linens for a main city department store.

Mr Walters has such an even, soft voice. You can hear him taking
Madam's esteemed order for loose covers. When I asked him if
he'd let his student lodger use his kitchen he hesitated briefly then
purred away . . . . 'Oh I don't know about that quite . . . I'm rather
like a woman with a new cooker, I don't really want anyone else
using it . . . ' Well, thou sayest . . .

But now there is this immediate crisis. I call, the garden is bare
this end of winter day, and my poor Mr Walters' face is full of
trouble. He draws me in, the bungalow is warm, soft to the foot and
so comfortable.

'Mr Jeffries is leaving me,' he comes to the point, 'but it's all quite
amicable. We thought it best after our little disagreements.' Mr
Walters looks pensive.

'What were they about then?' I prompt.

Mr Walters plunges into the story.

'Well, the first thing was, I liked to go in his bedroom in the

morning and just open the window for half an hour. You know
how fuggy bedrooms get, and his is just a small room. So I went in
as usual and threw up the frame, this particular day, and I noticed
he went back in five minutes after and closed it again. I asked him
why should he do that and he said, he didn't like me to do it
because it made the room cold when he went to bed. Well, that's
just nonsense, Mrs Holbrook, because the central heating comes on
at three and it's as warm as toast by evening. Anyway, next day I
thought I'd wait till he'd gone off to college and open the window
then, but when I went in his room, lo and behold he'd taken the
keys of the window with him. That evening I challenged him about
it and he said he'd taken the keys to stop me ventilating the room. I
didn't like that and I told him so.'

'Oh dear,' I said, just to keep the conversation flowing, and I
make sympathetic movements with my mouth. Mr Walters' eyes
grew liquid and mournful. His voice goes down a few notes. 'Next
thing is the question of his young lady.' He sighs and I lean towards
him to learn more.

'She usually came about late afternoon and they would stay in his
sitting-room till six perhaps and then go off to Hall together for
supper. They made a lot of noise always but I didn't take too much
notice of that.'

I nod encouragingly; that sounds a liberal attitude, given that he
was a lonely bachelor.

'But then he started coming in late at night, sometimes one and
two in the morning. Most nights I get up' he stumbled a little, self
disparagingly, 'to go to the bathroom, and I'd notice his bedroom
door was still open so I knew he wasn't home. And after that I
couldn't get back to sleep for thinking about the safety catch not
on, on the front door.'

'Well,' I began, 'they're adult young men you know, and entitled
to come in when they see fit as long as they don't disturb you . . .'
but my voice trailed away rather, seeing him lying there, sleepless,
as agitated and vulnerable as any of my widowed or spinster landladies, feeling a prey to the night, to the possible marauder.

He digested this and left it hanging. His thought returned to the
girl.

'Did I ever tell you, Mrs Holbrook, about his teddy-bears?'

'Why no,' I reply, startled.

'Oh he has at least ten or twelve teddies, they perch around his sitting-room on all the chairs. I thought it a bit funny at first but then I said to myself, they keep him company perhaps. But one night when Mr Jeffries and his girl went off to college, I went in to see if his curtains were drawn . . . '

Maybe he was always popping in after every exit, to catch up on the state of play, I thought rather cynically . . . . Mr Walters was eyeing me now with an admonitory stare. Was the denouement at hand?

'They'd evidently gone off in a hurry and left the room in such a state. What they'd been doing I can't imagine . . . ' He paused for dramatic effect. My mind raced rapidly through all the possible perversions I could imagine involving teddies . . . surely not? . . .

His outrage gathered force. 'Mrs Holbrook, I think they'd been throwing those teddies at one another.' he brought out. 'And my velvet cushions too, they looked all concertina'ed and screwed up as though they'd been chucked all over the shop' His voice spluttered as he remembered the decent dralons and ruchings and exhibitory smoothings of the soft furnishings department.

List of Secretaries

May 1876
The Syndicate recommend the appointment of a responsible officer to inspect Lodging houses annually, report to the Syndicate and generally assist. He must be a resident Member of the Senate. To be appointed by an absolute majority for a period not exceeding three years, and to receive a stipend not exceeding £150 per annum.

The Rev. F.G. Howard, M.A. of Trinity: appointed May 1877 (for 1 year only) re-elected for two years from Midsummer 1878 re-elected unanimously for three years from Midsummer 1880; February 1883 his health did not permit him to offer himself for re-election.

MrT, F.C. Huddleston, M.A. of King's, from Midsummer 1883 for three years; re-appointed for three years from Midsummer 1886; re-appointed for three years from Midsummer 1889

Mr H.G. Fuller, M.A. of Peterhouse, for three years from Midsummer 1892

May 1895 Mr Dodds appointed to act as temporary Secretary during Mr Fuller's absence through illness.

Mr W. Chawner, M.A. of Emmanuel, elected for three years from June 1895 but in October said he wished to resign the office at an early date and in November 1895 Mr W.W. Buckland, M.A. Fellow of Gonville & Caius was elected Secretary till June 1898.

Mr Huddleston was appointed a member of the Lodging House Syndicate for four years from 1 January 1894.

Mr Chawner had sat on the Syndicate for several years before being appointed Secretary. Signing Minutes as Master of Emmanuel and Vice-Chancellor's deputy as Chairman since December '96 with Mr. Huddleston still a Syndic. Mr Chawner signing, as Chairman, in May 1898 the advertisement for a Secretary but resigned from the Lodging House Syndicate in June 1899.

Mr W.W. Buckland re-appointed for three years from June 1898

April 1901: Mr J H. Gray, M.A. of Queens', appointed for the term in place of Mr Buckland who is absent from Cambridge. He went to the Cape of South Africa on health grounds.

The Rev. C.A.E. Pollock, M.A. Corpus Christi elected Secretary June 1901 for 3 years; re-elected June 1904, June 1907, June 1910, and June 1913 for three years in each instance.

November 1913: The Rev. C.A.E. Pollock resigns. He is a Syndic in January 1916.

December 1913: Mr F.M. Rushmore, M.A. of St Catharine's, appointed Secretary for three years (The stipend is still £150 p.a.); re-appointed for one Year from December 1916 and for two years from December 1917

April 1919: Mr Rushmore resigns.

Mr T.A. Walker of Peterhouse appointed June 1919 for three years.

Mr Pollock in January 1920 raised the question of the Secretary's stipend in view of hugely increased workload, The Chairman wrote to the Secretary of the Financial Board who replied that the Syndicate should recommend an increase of stipend to the Council of the Senate. Increase to £250 a year approved from March 1920–June 1922.

Captain J.T. Baines, M.A. of Trinity appointed in June 1922 for three years, Dr Walker not offering himself for re-election. The stipend to be continued at £250; re-appointed June 1925 and June 1928 for three years in each instance. The question of an increase of stipend was discussed.

January 1929: Leave of absence granted to Secretary for three months from the middle of June to visit S. Africa.

October 1929: Mr Balnes reported ill and in hospital in the Transvaal. Mr P. Brodby, M.A. of Downing, engaged as temporary Secretary, but Mr Baines back for meeting of 12 November 1929.

January 1930: An honorarium of £50 paid to Mr P. Brodby 'for his services as Acting Secretary during the illness of the Secretary', with a note of special thanks.

Baines re-appointed Secretary for three years from 25 June 1931. Letter from Mr Baines read at May meeting 1933 asking to be allowed to resign. Mr van Grutten, a Syndic, acted as Secretary.

The Chairman to consult the Vice-Chancellor on 3 alternatives:
a) to appoint a male Secretary
b) to make an appointment of a male Secretary at a lower salary with additional appointment of a woman to assist in inspection
c) to appoint a woman Secretary

The Council of the Senate agreed to the appointment of a woman and the post was advertised 19 June 1933 for two years at £250.

Miss M.CD. Kennett appointed. May 1935: Miss Kennet re-appointed Secretary for three years from Midsummer.

Michaelmas 1957: Mrs S.M. Storr appointed (died April 1963).

September 1963: Mrs Rita M. Phipps appointed for three years.

1972: Mrs D.M. Ker appointed for three years from 1 October; resigned November 1973

1973: Mrs F.M. Holbrook appointed for two years from 1 December 1973, ;re-appointed and served until her retirement on 30 September 1992.

Obituary

'Sadie' Barnet

15 August 1991

Courtesy of the *Daily Telegraph*

"SADIE" BARNETT, a Cambridge legend, who has died aged 80, was one of the last of the great Dickensian landladies — and certainly the sole surviving private landlady in King's Parade.

She presided over the most splendid digs in the University at No 9 King's Parade, overlooking King's College Chapel and the Gibbs Building.

Mrs Barnett's social expectations of her lodgers were as traditional as the ambience of her rooms — and in this respect she was perhaps more of a Trollopian than a Dickensian figure.

She would frequently ask Gonville and Caius College, from which she held the leasehold, to supply her with "proper young gentlemen". When Caius undergraduates became too *bourgeois* for her liking, she turned to Magdalene and Pembroke.

She greeted the representative of one noble family with the words: "The last time we had a lord here, he hanged himself in room four."

To another, upon receipt of his Coutts' cheque at the end of his first term, she declared: "You're very modest, aren't you? You didn't say you was no *Hon.*"

In later years. Mrs Barnett took in undergraduates from less exalted backgrounds, but she took a dim view of their career prospects when compared with their landed co-evals'.

"*Nah*, he's labour," she would say dismissively — though it was unclear whether by this she meant that he was destined for manual labour or was merely perceived as a supporter of the Labour party.

Mrs Barnett never entertained doubts about the rectitude of her grander residents.

"He was such a gent," she once said. "When he was sick he was always sick out of the window."

One recent resident, Simon Sebag-Montefiore, set much of his fictional university memoir *King's Parade* (1991) at her house; but the publishers are said to have found the character based on Mrs Barnett beyond belief, and she was duly excised.

Mrs Barnett was always very proud of the achievements of her "boys", who latterly had included the historians Andrew Roberts and Michael Bloch. She regularly corresponded with her *alumni* all over the world, and would sometimes stay with them on her travels.

She was born Sarah Wolfschaut on Jan 3 1911 at Stepney, east London, the daughter of a Jewish fruit and vegetable trader in Aldgate.

Young Sadie was the seventh of 10 children and began life in the rag trade, as a dressmaker. At the age of 15 she met a waiter, Michael Barnett, whom she married in 1932.

They moved to Cambridge where Mrs Barnett began her career as a landlady. They separated during the Second World War but their childless union was never dissolved.

From the late 1940s Mrs Barnett enjoyed the leasehold at King's Parade. Although *kosher* herself, she cooked breakfast of eggs and bacon for her lodgers, and had strict rules about women and hours of residence.

She regretted the passing of the more deferential undergraduates and after the upheavals of the 1960s felt sorely tried by her more high-spirited lodgers, who preferred an unsupervised existence.

Some claimed that Mrs Bar-

Queen of King's Parade

nett was an unconscious exemplar of enlightened despotism, but in reality she was a maternal neo-feudalist who exercised great care over her wards. She could display an almost Plantagenet "*ira et malevolentia*", which concealed a fundamentally good heart.

This fierce protectiveness manifested itself when the constabulary arrived to arrest one tenant after some undergraduate excess: "You leave him alone, he's not a burglar. He's not a murderer. He's one of my nice young men."

On another occasion, when some anti-field sports campaigners, enraged by the sight of a brace of pheasants hung out of her window by one of her lodgers, sought to gain entry to the house, she gave them short shrift. "He can kill what he likes," she told them. "He's a *sportsman*, you know."

Attired in a quilted dressing-gown, Mrs Barnett would sit in her room for much of the day watching the trade test transmission card on BBC. "I am waiting for the Royals to come on...I know they will be on soon — Ascot and all that," she would say, whatever the season.

When some undergraduates tried to disseminate the "free Mandela" message to her lodgers, she showed them the door with the parting shot: "Who is this *Nelson Piquet* anyway?"

Mrs Barnett could always detect the tread of women's feet on the stairs and would display remarkable swiftness in bounding after them in order, prematurely, to enforce the official curfew.

She was intolerant of the ways of the Modern Girl and when introduced to two of the species at a tea party declared: "'*Pickle*' and '*Pooh*'? What sort of names are those? Get out of here, you brazen hussies! You're here for one thing — and for one thing only."

On one occasion she was found on her hands and knees outside the door, eavesdropping. Within, a lodger had a "punk" girl friend with dyed green hair, whom he hid under a blanket when Mrs Barnett suddenly demanded entry.

Mrs Barnett poked the bedding with a broomhandle, thereby revealing the naked punk. She threw out the tenant, observing: "I wouldn't have minded if it was only the hair on her head that was green."

Sadie Barnett was an efficient landlady who was capable of great kindnesses to those in need — particularly foreign students, who for years afterwards would write her grateful letters.

But not for nothing did the university newspaper describe her as "King's Parade's Boadicean landlady".

Contributors

Index

Bibliography

Cambridge Antiquarian Society, Octavo Publications, 1924.

Cambridge University, *An Episodical History*, (Cambridge, 1926).

Cambridge University Review, 124, March 1859. University Archives

Hastings Rashdall, *The Universities of Europe in the Middle Ages*, (OUP, 1894); new edition, ed. Powicke, F.M. & Ernden, A.B. (OUP, 1936)

Fowler & Fowler: *Cambridge Commemorated* , (CUP, 1984.)

Gunning, Henry, *Reminiscences of the University Town and County of Cambridge from the year 1780*. (CUP 1932)

Leach, A.F., ed.: *Educational Charters & Documents*, (Cambridge, 1911)

Murphy, Michael J, *Poverty in Cambridgeshire*, (Oleander Press, 1978).

Palmer, W.M., ed., *Cambridge Borough Documents*, vol. 1, (Bowes & Bowes, 1931).

Pantin, W.A., *Oxford Life in Oxford Archives*, (O.U.P., 1972).

Parker, Rowland, *Town and Gown*, (Stephens 1983)

Porter, Enid., 'For Unruly and Stubborn Rogues', *East Anglian Magazine*, vol.18 (Nov.1958-Oct.1959).

Reeve, F.A., *Cambridge*, (Batsford 1976).

Reeve, F.A., *The Cambridge Nobody Knows*, (Oleander Press, 1977).

Venn, J. et al., *Biographical History of Gonville and Caius College 1897-1978*.

Willis, R. and Clark, J.W., *Architectural History of the University of Cambridge* 4 vols., (Cambridge, 1886)

Winstanley, D.A., *Unreformed Cambridge*, (CUP, 1935)

Wordsworth, Christopher, *Scholae Academicae*, 'Some Account of Life at the English Universities in the Eighteenth Century', (Cass & Co. London, 1968).